Family
Caregiving
in Mental
Illness

DATE DUE

FAMILY CAREGIVER APPLICATIONS SERIES

Series Editors
David E. Biegel, *Case Western Reserve University*
Richard Schulz, *University of Pittsburgh*

Advisory Board Members

Volumes in This Series:

Family Caregiver Applications Series
Volume 7

Family Caregiving in Mental Illness

Harriet P. Lefley

Published in cooperation with the
Mandel School of Applied Social Sciences,
Case Western Reserve University

SAGE Publications
International Educational and Professional Publisher
Thousand Oaks   London   New Delhi

This book is for Keith, Jack, and Carla

For information address:

SAGE Publications, Inc.
2455 Teller Road
Thousand Oaks, California 91320
E-mail: order@sagepub.com

SAGE Publications Ltd.
6 Bonhill Street
London EC2A 4PU
United Kingdom

SAGE Publications India Pvt. Ltd.
M-32 Market
Greater Kailash I
New Delhi 110 048 India

Printed in the United States of America

Library of Congress Cataloging-in-Publication Data

Lefley, Harriet P.
  Family caregiving in mental illness / author, Harriet P. Lefley.
    p. cm. — (Family caregiver applications series; v. 7)
  Includes bibliographical references and index.
  ISBN 0-8039-5720-3 (cloth: alk. paper). — ISBN 0-8039-5721-1
(pbk.: alk. paper)
    1. Mentally ill—Home care. 2. Mentally ill—Family
relationships. 3. Caregivers. 4. Mentally ill—Home care—Social
aspects. I. Title. II. Series.
  RC439.5.L44   1996
  362.2′042—dc20   95-41722

This book is printed on acid-free paper.

96 97 98 99 00 10 9 8 7 6 5 4 3 2 1

Sage Production Editor: Diane S. Foster

Contents

Series Editors' Foreword

For many of us the phrase "family caregiving" evokes images of physically disabled or cognitively impaired older persons being cared for by their relatives. The vast literature on caregiving is heavily weighted toward studies of older persons who because of age-related disabilities rely on family members to help them live in the community. In actuality, however, family caregiving is a phenomenon that occurs throughout the life span. Family caregivers may provide care to young children or adults with chronic illnesses, as well as to the elderly. This book deals with family caregiving to one such population. It examines the challenges and impact of caring for young adults with severe and persistent mental illness.

The existence of significant numbers of family caregivers of adults with mental illness is in large part an outgrowth of contemporary deinstitutionalization policy that tries to unite patients with their families as a means of providing community care. As Dr. Lefley notes, this policy "catapults the patients' relatives into a caregiving role for which they are untrained, unprepared, and from which they have been systematically excluded in the past" (Chapter 2). The central theme of this book is that this particular class of caregivers is different from all others, and in the pages that follow she shows us why this is so.

A very valuable feature of this book is the exhaustive treatment of the topic. In order to understand family caregiving for adults with mental illness, it is essential to know something about the illness. One needs to know about the historical and cultural factors that have shaped the definition of mental illness, as well as models of etiology and pathogenesis of mental illness. This background is provided in the opening chapters. They lay the foundation for the heart of the book that examines the experience of mental illness in the family. One of the unique aspects of caregiving for adults with mental illness is that it lends itself and, indeed, demands to be treated from a life-course perspective, and this is exactly what Lefley does. By showing us that caregiving must be viewed from a life cycle perspective of both the person with mental illness as well as of the family, Lefley presents an innovative framework for examining caregiving of all types.

This volume provides the reader with an overview of the nature of caregiver burden as well as an analysis of coping strategies used by families. The volume also includes extensive discussion of a wide range of services that have been developed in recent years to address the needs of family caregivers of persons with mental illness. The literature pertaining to burdens experienced by caregivers of persons with mental illness, though extensive, has paid little attention to how the role of the mental health services system affects caregiver burden. Lefley's analysis rectifies this shortcoming and provides an expanded conceptual framework in which to understand the causes of caregiver distress.

After examining individual and family views on caregiving, Lefley brings us back to the broader societal perspective on this topic. The roles of culture, federal and state governments, and advocacy groups are described in the concluding chapters of the book. She shows us how together these forces will shape the future of family caregiving in mental illness.

Richard Schulz
David E. Biegel

PART I

Introduction and Overview

1

Mental Illness
and Caregiving Needs

An Introduction

This book deals with families who are caregivers of adults with severe and persistent mental illness, an issue of increasing social importance since the onset of deinstitutionalization. The term *mental illness* has been applied to a range of diagnostic categories and conditions. There are numerous people who are diagnosed, and self-identified, as having or having had a mental illness, and some have experienced multiple hospitalizations. But many of these individuals are symptomatic only occasionally. Some persons who suffer from mood or anxiety disorders, for example, are for the most part cognitively and functionally intact. Even some individuals diagnosed with schizophrenia seem able to live independently as productive members of society (Harding, 1988).

Mental disorders are distinguished by differences in diagnosis, length and episodicity of illness, and levels of functional impairment. Their range and heterogeneity are exemplified in the now well-established link between heightened creativity and some forms of mental illness, such as major affective disorders (Jamison, 1993). The roster includes such famous persons as Beethoven, William Blake, Samuel Coleridge, Leonardo da Vinci, Herman Melville, Sylvia Plath, Robert Schumann, Anne Sexton, Virginia Woolf, and Vincent Van Gogh, to name a few. It is apparent, therefore, that a certain percentage of people with major psychiatric disorders not only are capable of being productive but have been superior contributors to society. These types of individuals may need the support of caring persons but they are not representative of the population typically in need of family caregiving.

DEFINING THE POPULATION
IN NEED OF CAREGIVING

When we speak of people who need the help of caregivers, we are specifically referring to a population of functionally impaired adults with periodic needs for crisis stabilization and hospitalization and with ongoing needs for outpatient care and long-term rehabilitation. These are persons who meet the criteria for chronic mental illness in terms of diagnosis, duration, and disability (Bachrach, 1988). The diagnoses typically include, but are not limited to, the schizophrenias, major endogenous depression, bipolar disorder, disabling obsessive compulsive disorder, and psychotic states. Of these, the schizophrenias and major affective disorders comprise 55% of hospital admissions and 65% of inpatients under care. Schizophrenia remains the major diagnostic category for persons requiring periodic psychiatric hospitalization at any given point in time (Center for Mental Health Services, 1993; Manderscheid & Sonnenschein, 1992).

These individuals have been ill for over a year—most have been ill for many years—and they are disabled in major areas of living. They are typically unable to fulfill societal roles normally expected of persons of their age, physical intactness, and intellectual capacity. This is the population most likely to be involved with family caregiving.

In 1989, the National Institute of Mental Health (NIMH) collaborated with the National Center for Health Statistics on a survey of the U.S. population to determine the number of household residents with serious mental illness. Their definition of serious mental illness was based on the criterion of "any psychiatric disorder present during the past year that seriously interfered with one or more aspects of a person's daily life" (Barker et al., 1992, p. 255). There were approximately 3.3 million adults 18 years of age or older in the civilian noninstitutionalized population who had had a serious mental illness in the past 12 months, a rate of 18.2 adults per 1,000 persons. Approximately 2.6 million adults had specific limitations attributed to their mental illness in functional areas such as work, school, personal care, social functioning, concentrating, or coping with day-to-day stress. Of these, more than half were limited in their ability to work. Within the context of the entire adult population, NIMH concluded that the seriously mentally ill population can be conservatively estimated at 4 to 5 million adult Americans, or 2.1% to 2.6% of the adult population. This figure is exclusive of persons who are institutionalized. In addition to the household population, NIMH estimated that 200,000 persons with serious mental illness are homeless on any given day; 1 to 1.1 million are residents in nursing homes; 50,000 to 60,000 are residents in mental hospitals; and approximately 50,000 are inmates of state prisons (Barker et al., 1992). Presumably, a percentage of institutionalized persons will return to their homes, thus increasing the number of potential recipients of home caregiving.

It has been estimated that in the United States, 65% of psychiatric hospital patients are discharged to their families (Goldman, 1982). Residential caregiving varies greatly by ethnicity, but a number of studies suggest that about 35% to 40% of persons with severe and persistent mental illnesses live with their families on an ongoing basis (Lefley, 1987a). In the most recent national scientific survey of 1,401 member families of the National Alliance for the Mentally Ill (NAMI), the known figure (N = 1390) was 41.7% (Skinner, Steinwachs, & Kasper, 1992). Seeman (1988) states that in Canada, approximately two thirds of persons with schizophrenia—about 80,000 Canadians—live at home with their families at any given time.

A recent study of characteristics of patients in New York state who met the Office of Mental Health criteria for severe and persistent mental illness indicated that more than half resided in household settings, the majority (68%) with relatives. It was estimated that from 13,000 to 49,600 adults with severe mental illness lived with one or both parents between 1990 and 1994. Of interest is the fact that among these mentally ill adults living with parents, 84% were 25 years or older; 65% were over 30 years of age, and 12% were over 50 (Grosser & Conley, 1995). This is a category of adult dependents whose caregivers are or will soon be part of the geriatric population.

Research indicates that even when mentally ill relatives live separately, family members give a great deal of themselves in terms of time, money, and social support (Clark & Drake, 1994). Today we are seeing the fruition of predictions made some years ago, when large mental institutions began to empty their hospital beds. Arnoff (1975) predicted severe social consequences for families as deinstitutionalization policy began to return dysfunctional people to their homes. Families with no caregiving skills, no training, and vastly different lives from those of their hospitalized relatives would be facing enormous stress with little or no help from the treatment system. In the early 1950s, sociologists Parsons and Fox (1952) had already stated that the modern American family would be unable to provide adequate assistance and support for its sick members. They maintained that the nuclear family, with its limited adult resources for caregiving, has little margin for shock absorption and for tolerating the dependency of persons with long-term disabilities.

Caregiving of adults with disabilities generally involves discontinuities in the lives of both the recipient and the provider. The disabled person is typically unable to fulfill an age-appropriate role, whereas the caregiver endures a disruption of her or his normative activities at a particular stage in the life cycle. Over the course of a chronic mental illness, caregivers may be relatively young parents of late adolescents or young adults or very elderly parents of disabled offspring in late middle age. They may be wives, siblings, adult children, or other relatives. In almost all societies, the primary responsibilities of caregiving for psychiatrically disabled adults are likely to be performed by females, sometimes interfering with options for alternative roles or careers (Ascher-Svanum & Sobel, 1989).

MENTAL ILLNESS AND
THE CAREGIVING LITERATURE

Despite numerous studies of family burden, the experiences of families of persons with long-term mental illness have rarely been mentioned in the caregiving literature. Perring, Twigg, and Atkin (1990) note that the research and clinical literature on disability have largely ignored this category of caregiver. This may have been due to the episodic nature of psychosis and the variable levels of impairment found even in unremitting, chronic mental illness. But the omission may also have reflected traditional prejudices against families of persons with psychiatric disorders. So much of the literature on mental illness has dealt with families as pathogenic agents that it may be difficult to reconceptualize family members in a nurturing role. Furthermore, the psychiatric and psychological literature on mental illness has concentrated on the well-being of patients, marginalizing or ignoring the well-being of the persons dedicated to their sustenance.

Studies of informal or noninstitutional systems of care have focused on caregivers of people who require personal tending because of physical disability or cognitive incapacity. Caregiving in mental illness does not typically involve nursing duties or tending to physical ailments but it may indeed involve hours devoted to activities of daily living. Caregiving may also involve multiple expenditures of time and energy in trying to obtain timely services from the mental health, welfare, and medical systems, and in interactions with the legal and criminal justice systems. This range and intensity of investments is not usually required in caring for physically or developmentally disabled family members.

The emotional stress involved in dealing with behaviors that may be disruptive, assaultive, self-destructive, socially constraining, and, above all, incomprehensible, has been accompanied by a notable lack of information and help from the treatment system. A small number of books directly addressed to a family readership on how to deal with a mentally ill relative have been initiated by mental health professionals associated with NAMI; examples are Bisbee, 1991; Burland, 1992; Hatfield, 1990; J. Johnson 1994; Torrey, 1988b; Walsh, 1985; Wasow, 1982. Recently, Mueser and Gingerich (1994) developed a comprehensive coping guide for families, largely based on behavioral principles.

A parallel literature, focusing on families of persons with major mental illness, is directed to mental health professionals. Examples are Bernheim and Lehman (1985), Hatfield (1994b), Hatfield and Lefley (1987), Lefley and Johnson (1990), Lefley and Wasow (1994), Marsh (1992), and Vine (1982). Another major source of literature for practitioners derives from the clinical research on psychoeducational interventions with families. These include books by Anderson, Reiss, and Hogarty (1986); Barrowclough and Tarrier (1992); Falloon, Boyd, and McGill (1984); Goldstein, Hand, and Hahlweg (1986); and Kuipers, Leff, and Lam (1992). Mueser, Glynn, and Liberman (1994) and McFarlane (1994) have also contributed greatly to the psychoeducational literature.

In the present book, family caregiving in severe mental illness is viewed within a larger framework. Caregiving responsibilities are obviously related to multiple variables, including family structure and resources, cultural values, and contemporary social policy. In the United States, the family's caregiving role has largely been driven by clinical, ideological, sociocultural, and political developments that have changed the face of mental health service delivery. Historically, the experiences and quality of life of persons with major psychiatric disorders, and their families, have been dominated by forces over which they had little or no control. Today, the major stakeholders are beginning to exercise some control over their destinies. Political action has become a vital part of the caregiving picture.

Part I begins with a historical overview of the family's role in caregiving from preinstitutional times to the current era of deinstitutionalization and community care. Mental disorders have always been less clearly conceptualized than physical or developmental disorders. In Part II, the unique characteristics of mental illness are explored. Various definitions and conceptual models are presented, including an overview of lay, cultural, and scientific definitions. Diagnostic and functional distinctions are discussed, including the critical issue of heterogeneity within as well as between nosological categories.

A number of disputed theories have involved the family in the etiology or precipitation of major psychiatric disorders. This section continues with a discussion of the family's role in psychodynamic, family systems, sociological, anthropological, biological, and biopsychosocial-cultural theoretical schemas, together with empirical research findings on conceptual models and family needs. The implications of these findings for family caregiving are discussed, as well as the effect of unfounded pathogenic theories on families' lives.

Part III deals with the experience of mental illness in the context of the family life cycle and developmental stages of the illness. Dimensions of objective and subjective family burden include the existential aspects of living with mental illness as well as social stigma, treatment barriers, and iatrogenic stress. This section reviews caregiving from the perspective of the life cycle of both the caregiver and the person with mental illness in terms of their discrete kinship and role relationships within the family system. The effects of cyclical patterns of psychotic behavior on young children, siblings, spouses, and aging parents are discussed, as well as the meaning of being mentally ill to the afflicted family member. We discuss the stages of familial response and specific types of family coping strategies, including the reasons for behaviors that may seem maladaptive. Although the research indicates substantial family burden, new studies are showing some positive contributions of the mentally ill member to the family's welfare. We end this section with a discussion of professional and nonclinical services for families. These include psychoeducational and clinical interventions, as well as family support groups and other self-help models.

Part IV deals with family caregiving in social context. Cultural factors affecting family caregiving are discussed in the international context and in terms of ethnic differences within the United States. Included are World Health Organization research findings relevant to family roles. Racial-ethnic differences in the United States involve cultural patterns in service use and residential caregiving as well as cultural appropriateness of services.

In Part IV, the effect of citizen, family, and consumer advocacy movements on caregivers is reviewed. The influence of the family movement, NAMI, is discussed in terms of its functions and national effect, legislative advocacy, spurring of new research, effects on professional attitudes and clinical training, and general family empowerment. The effects of the primary consumer movements are similarly analyzed. Our discussion includes consumer empowerment, the development and therapeutic potential of consumer-operated services, and the positive implications of the consumer movement for family caregiving. Consumer groups, which show great variation in their political attitudes and organizational agendas, are discussed in terms of both the problems and the promise of their activities for persons with mental illness.

Families' relations with the service provider system are reviewed in terms of the effect of hospital closings, deficits in community care, premature discharge policies, and families' problems in finding desperately needed services for their loved ones. An ongoing problem for caregivers of severely mentally ill adults is the tension between treatment needs and legal barriers to care. The issue of forced treatment poses a profound dilemma for family caregivers. The burden of caregiving for a person who periodically rejects medications and decompensates is discussed within the context of mental health law and its effects on patients and families. Legal, ethical, and clinical issues are involved in a discussion of needs versus rights, protection and advocacy, involuntary interventions, the criminalization of illness, and the family's reluctant roles vis-à-vis the courts, police, and the criminal justice system. Alternative approaches to involuntary interventions are discussed.

Changes in family-professional relationships have been accompanied by collaborative roles for families in treatment planning, resource development, support and educational groups, mental health systems planning, agency governance, and professional training. An exploration of future directions in mental health service delivery ends with an analysis of the social policy and therapeutic implications of family caregiving. Confronting the gradual disappearance of the total care environment of the institutional setting, the critical lack of wraparound community services, and caps on inpatient and outpatient services, we reconsider families' roles in an era of managed care. Alternative models to family caregiving and the maintenance and growth of consumer-run services are explored. We end with a discussion of the advocacy efforts that are needed to improve community support systems and to integrate caregiving and rehabilitative resources for persons with mental illness.

2

Historical Overview of Family Caregiving

The designation of madness and negative social attitudes toward persons who today are considered mentally ill have a long tradition in human history. A variety of societal measures have been applied to deal with this generalized condition, dependent on indigenous etiological views and whether the condition was viewed as a negative attribute that required punishment, an aberration that required remediation, or, in extremely rare situations, as a gift of special vision. The latter construction, however, was typically restricted to persons who were classified as seers or shamans; in most cultures, this category of individuals was sharply differentiated from persons considered insane. Anthropological studies show that different cultures seem quite able to distinguish the special knowledge of the spiritual healer, who uses possession and visions to attain insight and power, from the delusions and hallucinations of the person labeled mentally ill (Koss, 1987; Sandoval, 1979). Instead of being dominated or driven by their voices, spiritual healers are empowered by them to bargain with the gods or control nature for the social good. In all societies, the behaviors labeled as mental disorders are consensually perceived as alien to cultural norms (Horwitz, 1982). In contrast, the behaviors of shamans and other visionaries are highly syntonic with cultural norms.

Because the manifestations of mental disorder were often viewed as either the product or the personification of malevolent possession or sorcery, appropriate remedies were typically related to some type of supernatural intervention. Although these symptoms were also considered physiologically based as far back as ancient times (Kagan, 1994), the concept of madness as illness, treatable by psychological or medical means, is a relatively recent development in Western culture.

PREINSTITUTIONAL
FAMILY CAREGIVING

Preceding the idea of treatment was the mandate of social control. The idea that society must restrain such individuals implied that their behavior and destiny would be supervised by others. Reisser and Schorske (1994) note that in precolonial and colonial America, the family was the basis of community life and disruptive behaviors were considered their responsibility. In circumstances where families could not handle the responsibility, however, they could turn to the courts and town officials for help. The authors note a 1676 Massachusetts law cited by Deutsch (1949) that referred to "distracted persons in some tounes that are unruly, whereby not only the families, wherein they are, but others suffer much damage by them" (p. 43). This law ordered that "the selectmen in all tounes where such are hereby impowered and enjoyned to take care of all such persons, that they doe not damnify others" (p. 43). In this management schema, Riesser and Schorske (1994) note that the family might be paid from the community treasury to build a separate secure dwelling for the mentally ill relative or the town might pay other members of the community to provide habitation and management of this person.

According to Grob (1994), during the seventeenth and eighteenth centuries, when society was predominantly rural with small scattered communities, "mental illnesses were perceived to be an individual rather than a social problem, to be handled by the family of the disordered person and not by the state" (p. 5). However, the presence of persons termed "distracted" or "lunatick" was of serious social concern on two counts: Their behavior might be threatening to their own safety or the safety of others, and their inability to work meant that others must assume responsibility for their survival.

> The care of the insane remained a family responsibility; so long as its members could provide the basic necessities of life for afflicted relatives, no other arrangements were required. Yet in many instances, the effects of the illness spilled outside the family and into the community. Sometimes the behavior of "lunatics" or "distracted persons" threatened the safety or security of others. . . . Sometimes afflicted individuals were unable to work and earn enough for sustenance. In other cases the absence of a family required the community to make some provision for care or for guardianship." (Grob, 1994, p. 6)

COMMUNITY SUBSIDIES
FOR FAMILY CAREGIVING

Although the first level of caregiving responsibility began with the family, it was recognized that protracted illness of one of its members could have a disastrous effect on the family as a whole. In that case, the community was required to provide assistance and, if necessary, substitute caregiving. The latter might involve an alternative family setting or, depending on the type and degree of antisocial behavior, a prison, workhouse, or poorhouse. For the most part, however, custodial care for persons deemed insane seems to have been based on humane rather than punitive considerations. Grob (1994) has pointed out that early colonial law was based on the English principle of societal responsibility for the poor and dependent. A statute enacted in 1694 specifically made all insane persons without families the legal responsibility of the community.

In most communities, family caregiving of persons considered insane was a socially acknowledged stressor. It was recognized that the person's aberrant behaviors and dependency caused emotional and economic distress to other family members, and many communities offered subsidies to families to enable them to care for their mentally disordered members at home. Home care was subsidized primarily in the absence of threatening behaviors when the afflicted person was viewed as bizarre but relatively benign and harmless. When mentally ill persons committed an antisocial act or even a murder by reason of insanity, they might be confined to a small locked dwelling maintained by a relative but paid for by the community.

Until modern times, no treatment for symptom reduction was readily available, and family caregiving of persons with severe mental illness was difficult and unrewarding. The difficulties were enhanced by the lack of understanding and misconceptions regarding the symptoms of mental illness, including the still-persisting questions of the person's control over his or her aberrant behaviors. Some families could not tolerate the stress. Some mentally ill persons wandered away from the family homestead and became derelicts or hermits. Many disordered persons who lost or were abandoned by their kinship supports ended up homeless or in such public facilities as jails or almshouses. Some were isolated even with home support. Because of their disruptive behavior and frequently because they were considered "cursed," mentally ill persons who were severely symptomatic were sometimes kept in a locked room away from the family, provided the family had adequate space to afford this separation. In some cases, their very existence was denied to the outside world. Given the strains of living with an untreated severely symptomatic individual, the close living quarters of most colonial and postcolonial homes, and the economic interdependence of most family units, it is rather miraculous that families were able to endure and survive this early caregiving process.

CAREGIVING AND TREATMENT COMBINED

Prior to the nineteenth century, mental disorders were primarily conceptualized in terms of society's need for control rather than the individual's need for treatment. The distinction between mental and physical disorders was ill-defined, and when mental disorders were treated medically, it was typically through the accepted therapeutic interventions of the time—bleeding and purging. Just as today, however, there were numerous explanatory models of the origins and nature of mental disorders —religious, supernatural, and astrological, as well as medical and scientific. The behavioral manifestations of madness were typically invested with religious content. Madness was the wages of moral weakness and sin, and healing required divine intervention. Later, it was postulated that moral and mental weakness of the mind "gave rise to bodily illness, which in turn reacted back upon the mind to weaken the power of reason. Madness thus involved an interaction of moral excesses and physical illnesses" (Grob, 1994, p. 11).

Families' management of their mentally ill relatives was based on the knowledge base of the time. Riesser and Schorske (1994) note that professional guidance typically came from community ministers who advocated a harsh theology oriented toward impulse control. Their therapeutic interventions sometimes involved beatings to rid the patient of satanic or demonic possession. Many families were forced to go beyond their own natural coping techniques to seek external advice or professional interventions for behavioral management. These outside resources were rarely rewarding. The theological strategies involved prayer, restraint, and physical punishment to exorcise demons, whereas the medical strategies involved bloodletting and herbal purgatives.

BEGINNING INSTITUTIONS

As populations grew, there was a commensurate increase in the number of sick, aged, abandoned, orphaned, and otherwise dependent persons.

This led to the growth of almshouses and other institutions that typically merged physically and mentally ill persons with others who were incapable of economic self-sufficiency. Out of a mixed system of public welfare and privately financed facilities arose the modern hospital. Grob (1994) suggests that until the latter part of the nineteenth century, the hospital was more akin to the almshouse than to the modern medical center, serving socially marginal groups and only secondarily functioning as a training facility for aspiring physicians.

During the middle of the eighteenth century, several public hospitals for the mentally ill were founded in the United States—in Williamsburg, Virginia; Philadelphia, Pennsylvania; and later in New York. In Virginia, the legislative act creating the hospital made no distinction between mental illness and mental retardation. Its intent was apparently custodial rather than treatment oriented: "To make provision for the support and maintenance of ideots, lunatics, and other persons of unsound mind" (cited in Grob, 1994, p. 20).

Nevertheless, the notion of illness brought mental disorder into a domain in which "moral treatment" became the curative function of the clinician rather than the theologian. It was the French psychiatrist Philippe Pinel who first began the scientific study of persons with mental illness, observing and analyzing behaviors and maintaining extensive case histories. He recognized that mental illness could be chronic, intermittent, or show long periods of remission. Grob (1994) notes that as an empiricist, Pinel judged therapies in terms of their outcome and found bleeding, punishment, and other traditional therapies ineffective, whereas seclusion and restraints were deemed inhumane.

Pinel's moral treatment—which referred to environmental changes that might affect disordered behaviors—was concomitant with other humanitarian approaches to treatment of the mentally ill that were taking place in Italy, England, and the United States. The stage had been set for the notion of asylum rather than prison or workhouse for persons suffering from disordered minds.

THE RISE OF THE ASYLUMS:
SEPARATION OF PATIENTS AND FAMILIES

Katz (1985) notes that although moral treatment influenced psychiatric thinking, it was practiced in only a few hospitals and did not survive the socioeconomic changes induced by the Industrial Revolution of the

1860s. "Facilities increased in size, support for institutionalization grew, and the treatment of patients and management of staff deteriorated" (p. 1578). The advent of large state institutions was spurred by the crusading work of schoolteacher Dorothea L. Dix (1802-1887), who devoted 30 years to advocacy for the establishment of mental hospitals. She was largely responsible for the creation or expansion of a network of institutions, including St. Elizabeth's Hospital in Washington, DC. Despite the intent of providing humane treatment in institutional settings, the asylums went through cycles of public criticism and corrections for the excessive use of restraints, arbitrary commitment procedures, poor quality of staff, and the political appointment of superintendents. Nevertheless, institutional networks expanded and were considered the correct placement for persons with severe mental illness. Following World War II, Katz (1985) notes that some institutions studied the use of psychoanalytic concepts in treatment and somatic treatments such as insulin shock, pentylenetetrazol, and electroconvulsive therapy became prominent. Large numbers of patients continued to receive only custodial care, however.

According to Rothman (1971), the asylum was also seen as a haven from the stresses of society and from any kind of emotional excitement. For that reason, many institutions immediately cut off contact with the patient's family. Rothman noted that medical superintendents unanimously believed that at the first symptom, the patient must immediately enter a mental hospital and that treatment within the family was doomed to fail. They recognized the apparent illogic of their position. "Since families had traditionally lodged the insane, it might seem a cruel and wanton abdication of responsibility to send a sick member to a public institution filled with other deranged persons" (p. 137). Nevertheless, they felt that isolation among strangers would provide a safe, calm environment, introduce regularity, "and take the place of restlessness, noise, and fitful activity" (p. 138).

To enforce this therapeutic paradigm of a true asylum, the mental hospitals were built at a distance from the centers of population, with ample grounds and a tranquil, rural environment. "Moreover, the asylum was to enforce isolation by banning casual visitors and the patients' families. . . . Correspondence was also to be strictly limited. Even the mails were not to intrude and disrupt the self-contained and insular life" (Rothman, 1971, p. 138).

As Terkelsen (1990) notes, this concept of isolation from the family was not because the family was viewed as toxic—this came later—but because the family lived in the community and was unable to shield the patient from the confusion and pressures of community life. The point was to ensure a quiet, orderly existence with no excitement.

The consequences of these restrictions were self-evident. They distanced the patient from the family and eroded whatever skills the families had developed in dealing with the patient. Moreover, because patients tended to spend long years in the hospital, these policies encouraged psychological separation and abandonment. The emotional effects of this abrupt severance of human bonds were not considered. Perhaps most salient for family caregiving was the loss of relational and behavioral skills. As Terkelsen (1990) observes,

> Prompt removal of the patient brought prompt removal of the conditions under which a family and a community could acquire and maintain skills for living with a mentally ill person. . . . No longer regarded as relevant in an asylum-oriented culture, these skills may have disappeared inside of one generation's lifetime. (p. 9)

Separation of patients and families was of course reinforced by later psychodynamic theories that saw their mission as helping the patients resolve issues of parental pathogenesis. The exclusion of families from any knowledge of diagnosis and treatment and from any contact with primary therapists thus began in the institutional setting.

When family therapy was introduced to the institutional setting in the 1950s and 1960s, it seemed as though the process had finally been reversed. This new approach did bring the family together with patient and therapist but its mission was to pinpoint those "crazymaking" familial interactions that made the patient mentally ill. Like psychodynamic approaches, institution-based family therapy also transmitted a message of familial culpability, gave no scientific information about the illness, and gave no help with behavior management.

> Instead of feeling guilty about not having protected the ill person from external pathogens, the family had to contend with the guilt of having been the pathogen. Instead of losing sight of the patient for long stretches of time behind the walls of the institution, the family had to confront the patient's most disorganized behavior during visits to the hospital, during family therapy sessions, and during the patient's furloughs into the community. (Terkelsen, 1990, p. 11)

SURROGATE FAMILY CAREGIVING

Family care is the term that has been used to refer to foster home placement rather than to home caregiving by relatives. The practice of boarding patients with surrogate families has not been widespread in the United States. Rothman (1980) reported that in the early part of the twentieth century both patients and their relatives objected to family care in foster home or boarding home placements and that patients actually preferred institutional settings. As late as World War II, only eight states had even experimented with this procedure and only 3% of the institutional population were in family care throughout the United States.

Rothman (1980) pointed out that it was not in the best interests of the state hospitals to board patients out in the community. The steadily working inmate was crucial to institutional functioning. Also, the costs for home placements in the community had to come from institutional budgets because state legislatures would not allocate additional funds for family care. Grob (1994) notes that hospital officials were reluctant to assume added supervisory responsibilities. Also, the candidates for home care were typically the more quiet and tractable patients, exactly the kind the hospital wished to retain. Another factor was that many patients suffered from physical impairments and required comprehensive institutional monitoring of their conditions.

Some families readily accepted their relative back from the hospital, but others were reluctant to assume this responsibility. Prior disruptions or long years of separation were barriers to reintegration. Grob (1994) reports on a study at Worcester State Hospital between 1934 and 1938 that found that 23.4% of the patients considered ready for community placement had been rejected by their own families and family circumstances prevented acceptance of an additional 46.7%.

The difficulties in administration and supervision of the mentally ill were formidable, and community resistance to the presence of former patients—particularly in urban areas—remained significant. . . . As the consequences of the boarding-out experiment suggested, it was unrealistic to base any policy on the expectation that families would be able to care for their discharged relations or tolerate others. (pp. 168-169)

THE ERA OF DEINSTITUTIONALIZATION

The impetus toward deinstitutionalization developed with the massive changes taking place during and after World War II. The war saw the growth of a corps of psychologists and psychiatrists in the military service doing diagnostic screening and dealing with war-related psychiatric disorders among combatants. Mental health professionals were now out of the state institutions where they had been largely based. The work of army clinicians was to screen out psychiatrically vulnerable candidates and to effect speedy cures of servicemen with transient combat-related psychiatric disorders. Their mission was to get patients out of the hospital as quickly as possible and return them to their natural settings, the combat zones, where indeed many were able to perform as well as before. The idea began to gain ground that long-term hospitalization might not be necessary or the treatment of choice.

In addition to the postwar social upheavals, the process of deinstitutionalization was primarily spurred by a conjunction of historical events. First was the increasing social criticism of often horrendous conditions at state mental hospitals, which typically had poorly supervised staff and few protections of patients' rights. There was a growing recognition that these so-called places of healing tended to kill rather than cure the human spirit. There was also a growing voice among mental health advocates and social scientists that institutionalization was inappropriate for many patients, that commitment procedures were often arbitrary and inhumane, and that long-term custodial care could result in dependency and increased dysfunction rather than improvement of mental disorder. The advent of psychotropic medications enabled many patients to leave the back wards and ultimately be discharged into the community. Long-needed reforms affirming patients' rights coincided with a search for less costly alternatives. This spurred an unlikely alliance between civil libertarians and fiscal conservatives respectively seeking the least restrictive and least expensive placements in community settings. The move toward closing hospital beds was reinforced by the community mental health centers legislation of 1963, which promised to develop a network of community support systems for deinstitutionalized patients.

Deinstitutionalization has resulted in a two-thirds reduction in institutional beds since the late 1950s as well as the closing of many state hospitals. The sequelae of deinstitutionalization have now been well explored in various studies and books, with a focus on the failure of community systems to replace the total care environment of the hospital and the enormous social problem of the homeless mentally ill (Isaac & Armat, 1990; Lamb, Bachrach, & Kass, 1992; Lewis et al., 1991). We have portrayed the deliberate separation of patients and families in the institutional era, both through administrative policy and psychiatric theory. Today, there are social policies that also generate the separation of highly dysfunctional adults from the caring networks of their families. These policies may directly or indirectly facilitate homelessness (Lefley, Nuehring, & Bestman, 1992) or they may inadvertently promote separation by closing local hospitals and transferring patients to distant facilities.

For the most part, however, contemporary deinstitutionalization policy tries to unite patients with their families as a means of providing community care. This policy catapults the patients' relatives into a caregiving role for which they are untrained and unprepared and from which they have been systematically excluded in the past. In contrast to other types of disability, professionals have had a minimal and often a counterproductive role in the preparation of families for the caregiving role in severe psychiatric impairment. In the following pages, we discuss some of the theoretical paradigms that have distinguished this particular class of caregivers from all others, beginning with basic definitions of the concept of mental illness and the epistemological changes that have brought us to the current era.

PART II

The Unique Background of Mental Illness

3

Defining Mental Illness

Historical and Cultural Influences

Among mental health professionals and medical practitioners in Europe, Great Britain, and most of the rest of the world, definitions of mental disorders are derived from the World Health Organization's (1979) International Classification of Diseases, 9th revision, Clinical Modification (ICD-9-CM). In the United States, they are currently derived from the Diagnostic and Statistical Manual of Mental Disorders, 4th edition, or DSM-IV (American Psychiatric Association, 1994). All codes of the immediately preceding edition of the DSM (DSM-III-R) are in ICD-9; in the forthcoming ICD-10, the coding will be identical in these two major systems. It would seem then that there is no conflict about definitions of mental illness.

Yet there continue to be numerous disagreements about the historical and cultural universality of the diagnostic categories of Western biomedicine. There are arguments about mental illness as a construct and its parameters, intensity, duration, mutability, and social meaning (see Barrett, 1988; Boyle, 1990; Fabrega, 1982; Gaines, 1992; Kleinman & Good, 1985). These arguments are not merely academic. They form the basis for a school of thought in which individuals from many backgrounds—sociology, anthropology, mental health law—a community of former mental patients, and some psychiatrists themselves question that mental illness even exists in any individual outside of its interpersonal context. Some believe the term is purely a social construct, whereas others suggest that if there is such an entity, it cannot be defined in any consensually acceptable way.

This questioning has ramifications that affect the accessibility and organization of services for people who are designated as mentally ill.

Inevitably, these definitions have an effect on the resources available for treating mental illness, on societal perceptions of the need and locus of caregiving, and on appropriate roles for those involved in treatment and care. In at least one country, Italy, a radical social constructivist approach to mental illness has spearheaded the closing of mental hospitals and dramatically revamped the total mental health system. There have been salutary effects from the Italian experiment, most notably in northern Italy, with the emergence of cooperative enterprises run by former patients, with resources on the cutting edge of psychiatric rehabilitation. In many parts of Italy, however, families are greatly burdened by a major caregiving role and inadequate clinical supports to deal with psychotic behavior. In the south, Jones and Poletti (1985) report that community support systems are virtually nonexistent.

WHAT IS MENTAL ILLNESS?

Historical eras and cultural systems have varied widely in their human experience. Yet in every society throughout history, some individuals have been identified as manifesting thoughts and behaviors that deviated from the normative behaviors of their culture. These behaviors were different in kind from purposive antisocial or criminal behaviors, such as theft, arson, battery, homicide, or defiance of religio-cultural rituals—crimes that adversely affected the social unit to which all owed allegiance.

In most societies, certain behaviors were clearly recognized as meriting the rubric of mental disorder and assigned derogatory terms analogous to insanity, lunacy, or madness. The defining criterion was that these behaviors were clearly bizarre and role-inappropriate for that particular time, place, and cultural context. As Horwitz (1982) notes, "Whatever the particular cultural standards of comprehensibility may be, mental illness labels are applied when observers cannot comprehend the meaning of behavior within the typical categories of the culture" (p. 22). Thus whatever form they took, behaviors defined as mentally disordered were consensually perceived as alien to cultural norms.

In many respects, these behaviors were similar to those comprising the positive symptoms of schizophrenia, mania, or psychotic states. They might have involved, for example, self-communications that were outside the boundaries of interpersonal contexts and considered nonnormative. Examples are persistent subvocalization or extra-ritual communication with voices or visions that others could not experience but without the overlay of shamanistic power or spiritual enlightenment. They might have involved obsessions, compulsions, nonsymbolic self-mutilation, and other behaviors indicated today in DSM or ICD classification systems. Extreme agitation, unprovoked aggression, paranoid ideation that exceeded the boundaries of culturally normative suspiciousness, or negative symptoms such as extreme apathy and withdrawal might be viewed as alarming in most social systems.

In some cases, persons considered mentally disordered were viewed as lacking normal cognitive function but endowed with special pockets of knowledge, similar to idiots savants. But this was totally different from the special knowledge of the shaman, who used apparent delusions and hallucinations in the service of attaining spiritual insight and power. Instead of being dominated and driven by their voices, shamans were empowered to use voices and visions to bargain with the gods and to control nature for the social good.

As today, persons characterized as having some form of mental illness suffered socially from two types of opprobrium. One was based on the incomprehensibility of their behaviors, which did not follow the common cultural rules of social intercourse and which often made others uncomfortable, fearful, or angry. Another was based on their dysfunction. In many cases, persons afflicted with this condition could not fulfill their age-appropriate social or productive roles and often became drains on their families and on society. They were usually less well tolerated than persons whose disability was visibly connected to their physical incapacity to perform some productive function.

DIFFERENTIATING PHYSICAL, DEVELOPMENTAL, AND MENTAL DISORDERS

Dualism is a philosophical and theological system going back to Plato and Aristotle, which views mind and matter as distinct and irreducible principles. The French philosopher René Descartes (1596-1650), our most prominent modern dualist, maintained that the physical world is real, mechanistic, and divorced from the mind, with God as the intervening connection between the two entities. It has often been said that Cartesian dualism distinguishes modern and traditional world views as well as professional and folk psychiatry (Gaines, 1992). Most cultures are non-Cartesian; that is, they do not distinguish between body and mind and view all disorders as imbued or interrelated with spiritual content.

In certain respects, modern medicine is a return to a monistic view, as developmental and mental disorders are increasingly perceived as having an organic origin, whether genetic, viral, or through traumatic insult to the brain. Developmental disorder is primarily manifested in mental retardation; this is perceived as a permanent condition of low cognitive capacity, although the learning threshold may certainly be affected by environmental interventions. Other types of developmental disorders, such as autism, seem to bridge an ambiguous never-never land between the neurobiological and psychological nosological systems. Although manifested behaviorally, these types of conditions are perceived as congenital. Their etiology may be related to the antecedent social environment—that is, nutritional or viral stressors may have generated intrauterine insult to the growing organism—but not to the concurrent social environment after the individual is born.

But what of the relationship between physical and mental disorder? Some social scientists seem to assess the dichotomy not in terms of intrinsic characteristics but in terms of social response.

> People are seen as having a physical disease when there is some disturbance in the normal functioning of the body. Because illness is located within the human body, it is viewed as part of the biological world of organic system. . . . In contrast, the mentally ill are those whose problems seem to be located in their *minds equally.* . . . The distinction between mental and physical illnesses is a fundamental one, because different commonsense frameworks are used to interpret each type of illness. The body is viewed as part of the physical world and is therefore subject to the laws of cause and effect. In the physical realm, things "happen" but are not intended. Unlike the body, however, the mind is viewed within a cultural framework of motives, actions, meanings, and responsibilities that are applied to social objects. (Horwitz, 1982)

DEVIANCE, DISEASE, AND ACCOUNTABILITY

The definition of mental illness as deviance rather than disease has long been popular among many social scientists. Social labeling and constructivist approaches, discussed in greater detail in the next chapter, essentially imply that cultural attributions drive the attributes of the disorder.

According to this definition, mental illness is inherent not in the individual but in his or her interactions with society. The essential quality of mental illness is its deviance from normative behaviors. The essential quality that differentiates this type of deviance from other types of deviance, such as criminal behavior, is its incomprehensibility. Observers can differentiate criminal and mental deviance by assessing motivation and assigning accountability. As Horwitz (1982) states,

> In contrast to (criminal) deviants, people who are seen as mentally disturbed are so labelled not when their behavior is seen as morally wrong but rather when it cannot be attributed to a comprehensible reason. . . . In contrast, most deviants violate social rules in such a way that observers can link the deviant act to the motive that is perceived to lead the actions. . . . Because deviants act to obtain some recognizable value, they are held responsible for their behavior. . . . Whereas most deviants strive to obtain some value, the mentally ill do not appear to gain anything from their behavior; it seems pointless and purposeless. Thus the attribution of responsibility to the mentally ill is far more problematic than it is for most other deviants. (pp. 27-28)

If cultures have tended to vary in their boundary definitions of aberrant behaviors, they have also varied in their views of the person's control over these aberrations. Jerome Kagan (1994) suggests that among the ancient Greeks, there was a "supposition that hallucinations, depression, and delusions were signs that the patient had violated a moral standard" (pp. 14-15). In many cultures, although the behaviors might be viewed as nonwillful, their bearer was viewed as a medium of external evil. Thus a mentally ill person who was "possessed" might pay the same price as a criminal, albeit without the onus of criminal intent. More typically, persons exhibiting the behaviors of mental illness were considered objects of ridicule or pity. In either case, the deviance definition would hold that it is social response rather than disease that defines mental illness.

QUALITATIVE AND QUANTITATIVE PROPERTIES OF MENTAL ILLNESS

Although all cultures have some concept of mental illness, they may have different ideas about the temporal, distributional, and differential properties of what is essentially a diffuse global construct. Temporal qualities refer to whether this is considered a brief, reactive or long-term condition. The differential qualities depend on the nosological system. The DSM and ICD classification systems have hundreds of diagnostic categories and subcategories of mental disorders. Some cultures may have very specific diagnostic entities. Although these have been labeled culture-bound syndromes, the debate is still joined as to whether these are actually unique forms of mental disorder or variants of internationally recognized categories, such as hysterical reactions or anxiety disorders, expressed in a cultural idiom (Griffith & Gonzalez, 1994).

An important distinction relates to the heterogeneity within and among diagnostic categories. The term *schizophrenia* covers not only multiple schizophrenias but multiple levels of impairment. Persons with a diagnosis of affective disorder in the main may be more functional and suffer less cognitive impairment than persons with schizophrenia. But a subset of individuals in each category will be more similar to each other in symptoms and functioning than to peers with the same diagnosis.

Another definitional problem relates to the acute-chronic distinction. The World Health Organization's international pilot study of schizophrenia in 10 cultures demonstrated diagnostic uniformity but prognostic disparities, with continuing findings of better outcome in the developing countries than in the industrialized West (Jablensky et al., 1991). Other research had demonstrated that in developing countries, schizophrenic conditions are sometimes briefer, less likely to occur, and less virulent over time (Lin & Kleinman, 1988). There is a body of opinion that holds that chronicity in major psychotic disorders is an artifact of cultural belief systems and expectations regarding etiology, duration, and curability (Lefley, 1990a). If public expectations have a significant effect on prognosis, this would seem to lend some support to the deviance or social labeling position.

The distributional qualities are another aspect of conceptions of mental illness. One model postulates a continuum, another a dichotomy. This is an important distinction because the continuum implies that anyone can become mentally ill given enough stress, whereas the dichotomy postulates that some people have innate propensities for becoming mentally ill, whereas others do not. The distributional model of mental illness also postulates a bell-shaped curve in which the characteristics of normative and deviant behaviors may vary widely according to time and place.

LAY AND SCIENTIFIC DEFINITIONS: HOW DO FAMILIES LEARN ABOUT MENTAL ILLNESS?

Most family caregivers are laypersons, and their history of caregiving usually begins with an attempt to understand what is happening with their loved one as the first psychotic episodes take place. Laypersons tend to eschew the very term *mental illness* and to speak of "a nervous break-down," conceptualized as a transitory acute episode or even a series of acute episodes that will be cured within a foreseeable time frame with appropriate professional care.

The notion of chronic mental illness is extremely threatening to family caregivers on several counts. It implies a lifetime of caregiving and the deterioration or stasis of persons who might have been quite productive and promising in their premorbid state. But chronicity also implies that their loved one will become a socially devalued person, someone stigmatized and diminished by society. Mentally ill persons are associated with dysfunction, disorder, and particularly unpredictable violence. There is a very small subset of patients with histories of violent behavior but the majority of persons with serious mental illness are no more violent than the general population (Torrey, 1994). In many areas, they are less so.

Studies of the public's conceptions of mental illness have primarily been based on the discrepancy between lay definitions and contemporary scientific knowledge (Furnham & Bower, 1992). Among the educated public, lay ideas tend to replicate whatever is current in the scientific literature, filtered down through the popular media. The media in recent years have reflected a possible biological basis for mental illness, both in print and in audiovisual media. Scientific programs on public television and a few fictional television plays and movies have portrayed mental illness as a no-fault disorder requiring public compassion for patients and families. Unfortunately, this is outweighed by the media's continuing to highlight violence among "former mental patients" as well as to associate psychosis with homicidal tendencies in print and on film (Torrey, 1994).

Gantt, Goldstein, and Pinksy (1989) found that families of persons with schizophrenia tended to be ill informed about the disorder, pointing to the need for state-of-the-art education. In their research, nearly two thirds of the families reported that they had to turn to the media to obtain information about what was wrong with their relative. One of the most difficult problems for families is finding an explanatory model about what is happening from the persons who are actually treating their loved ones. A major deterrent, of course, has been the conventions of confidentiality and the boundaries erected against communications that may breach therapeutic trust. There is another salient issue, however, and that is the multiplicity of conceptual models that families may encounter. The medical, psychological, and social science disciplines have all contributed their ideas to scientific notions of mental illness.

Families' major interactions are with the mental health professionals treating their loved ones, but all may have been trained in very different etiological models. It is not unusual for family members to encounter psychiatrists who are primarily interested in psychopharmacologic response and others who are most interested in psychodynamics or family transactions. The psychologists, social workers, counselors, and case managers that families meet may have been trained in psychoanalytic, family systems, behavioral, or cognitive-behavioral theories; in a variety of psychotherapeutic approaches; or in atheoretical rehabilitation modalities. Some may also have been trained in social science disciplines that questioned the validity of the very concept of mental illness. Thus the problem with families finding out the latest in scientific thought is that there are many sciences and many thoughts.

CHANGING DEFINITIONS
THROUGH POLITICAL ACTION

Causal interpretations have varied as a function of cultural belief systems. Clearly, these also include the belief systems of Western social scientists with respect to the nature-nurture debate and the relative contributions of inheritance and cultural conditioning to human behavior. As we shall see in the forthcoming chapter, conceptual models also have derived from the belief systems of social scientists.

But definitions of mental illness are also subject to the political influence of stakeholders as well. Social factors have certainly had an effect on our thinking about developmental disorders—manifested most clearly in the extensive political work of the National Society for Autism to change the conceptual and nosological approach to infantile autism (Park & Shapiro, 1976). This group was powerfully instrumental in changing what was formerly considered a severe emotional disorder of childhood, attributable to "refrigerator parents" and defective childrearing, to a biologically based pervasive developmental disorder. The current work of some members of the National Alliance for the Mentally Ill (NAMI) in changing the designation of specific emotional disturbances of children to neurobiological disorders is another case in point (Peschel, Peschel, Howe, & Howe, 1992). As we will see in a later discussion of mental illness and political action, NAMI has also been working to obtain insurance parity between physical and mental disorders on the grounds that both are based on organic dysfunction. In all of these cases, the arguments have been supported by empirical research. These are all examples of stakeholders trying to force epistemological change through the publicization of contemporary research findings. They reflect an attempt to change thinking in the field through political means.

Political action supported by confirmatory research has also served to depathologize conditions formerly considered evidence of mental or emotional disorder. Homosexuality has only in recent years been omitted from DSM III as a psychopathological condition. Current research findings indicate possible genetic factors for sexual orientation. These suggest a congenital basis for certain types of behaviors that political protagonists hope will be perceived as variance, rather than deviance, from the societal norm.

In all of these cases, whether they refer to "symptom bearers" or to their family members, there is an attempt by social victims to reduce their victimization by using science to change scientific thought. However, these actions take place only after a long and arduous process of self-education.

In sum, the definitions of mental illness range from behavioral deviance from a cultural norm to a no-fault biological condition that results in disordered thinking; from purposive antisocial behavior (badness) to incomprehensible aberration (madness); from psychic functioning alone to mind-body unity; from a condition under personal control and accountability to one of noncontrol and nonaccountability. Persons with mental illness have been differentially viewed and penalized as a function of (a) their difficult behaviors or (b) their nonproductivity and dependency. Psychiatric disorders have been viewed as a violation of social rules, an insult to a moral standard, or a medium of external evil. Mental illness is considered by some the negative end point on a mental health continuum and, by others, a dichotomous condition to which only some will succumb.

Society's definitions affect attitudes and behaviors toward persons who are mentally ill. Cultures vary in whether they consider mental illness a brief, temporary aberration or a long-term condition, and this conceptualization may have some effect on prognosis. Although families learn about mental illness from the media, which presumably reflects current scientific thought, there are often differences in lay and professional definitions. Families may encounter professionals with a particular orientation, whether psychodynamic or psychopharmacologic, or clinicians who espouse theoretical models that are counter to the experiences of family caregivers. In closing this chapter, we have suggested that the family advocacy movement, NAMI, may have a political effect in chang-ing definitions of major mental illnesses in both children and adults from emotional to organic dysfunction. This has practical implications because it affects health care and insurance parity. As we shall see also in the next chapter, these definitional initiatives are not only oriented toward a more precise conceptualization of major mental illness but may have a direct effect on the treatment of clients and their family members.

4

Conceptual Models
of Mental Illness

Family caregivers have been directly affected by various conceptual models of mental illness. All contemporary models implicate family members in the etiology or transmission of severe syndromes, such as schizophrenia or major affective disorders. Biogenic models postulate genetic linkages or maternal exposure to viruses or toxins during pregnancy, resulting in insults to the intrauterine environment. Psychodynamic, family systems, anthropological, and sociological models postulate childrearing practices and intrafamilial transactions that give rise to the disorders. Learning theory similarly assumes an environmental background, with a history of differential reinforcement of the behaviors of mental illness by significant others.

These models differentially affect how families of persons with mental illness are perceived by others. Biological and genetic factors apply to a wide range of medical conditions and appear to be involved in personality characteristics, general giftedness, and special talents as well. Family members are not held culpable for muscular dystrophy or Down's syndrome; these are biogenic conditions considered beyond their control. But in psychogenic and most sociogenic models, the aversive behavior of family members is perceived as having generated or precipitated their relatives' distress.

Conceptual models have informed generations of different treatment strategies and mental health policies. They have had an enormous influence in shaping professional and societal attitudes toward families of the mentally ill. Essentially, these concepts determine the resources and tools available to patients and families to enable them to cope with the demands of mental illness. In this section, we begin with biogenesis, go on to the psychosocial explanatory models, and then return to an integrative model that seems most in accord with contemporary thinking.

BIOGENESIS

The biological model of major mental illness has had a circular history, with roots deep in history and a dramatic revival in the current era. Jerome Kagan (1994) suggests that biogenesis was primary and nurture secondary as far back as the ancient Greeks.

> Although the ancients were open to the suggestion that psychological variation within the normal range could be influenced by childhood experience—even Plato accepted that argument—they regarded the serious mental afflictions of depression, mania, and schizophrenia as physiological in origin. The ancients believed that some environmental factors were potent, including air, diet, exercise, rest, and excretion and retention of fluid, but none was social in nature. (Kagan, 1994, pp. 20-21)

Mental illness historically has also been equated with theories of external causality—primarily witchcraft and other satanic forces throughout the Middle Ages—but the notion of biogenesis has apparently persisted over the years and was widely prevalent in colonial and postcolonial America. According to Rothman (1971), an empirically supported concept of mental illness as brain disease was present in the United States in a book by Isaac Ray as early as 1838, the source cited in the following words:

> Every general practitioner in the pre-Civil War era agreed that insanity was a disease of the brain and that the examination of tissues in an autopsy would reveal organic lesions, clear evidence of physical damage, in every insane person. Isaac Ray, one of the leading medical superintendents of the period, when presenting the consensus of his discipline to the legal profession, confidently declared: "No pathological fact is better established . . . than that deviations from the healthy structure are generally present in the brains of insane subjects. . . . The progress of pathological anatomy during the present century has established this fact beyond the reach of a reasonable doubt." (Rothman, 1971, p. 110)

These earlier primitive studies are receiving increasing confirmation from contemporary research. Today, theories of biogenesis are largely empirically based. They are derived from a proliferating body of evidence from such diverse areas as epidemiology, neuroradiology, neuropathology, neurochem-istry, hematology, pharmacology, and genetics indicating that biological parameters are involved in major mental illnesses, such as the schizo-phrenias, major endogenous depression, bipolar disorder, obsessive-compulsive disorder, and others as well.

From the multiple studies of high-risk children of persons with a major mental illness, adoption studies, twin studies, and the like, the evidence of heritability is profound and seemingly incontrovertible. In the major psychotic disorders, the closer the genetic relationship to an affected proband, the more likely the probability of a similar diagnosis. For example, in schizophrenia, the general population prevalence is 1.0%. The probability of schizophrenia in someone with a schizophrenic relative rises as follows: non-twin sibling, 8%; dizygotic twin, 12%; child with one schizophrenic parent, 12%; child of two schizophrenic parents, 40%; monozygotic twin, 47% (Kaplan & Sadock, 1991).

In bipolar disorder, 50% of probands have at least one parent with a mood disorder. If one parent has bipolar disorder, the chance of any child having a mood disorder is 27%. If both parents have a mood disorder, the probability that a child will be similarly diagnosed rises to 50% to 75%. Adoption studies show similar prevalence of mood disorder in the bio-logical parents of both adopted and nonadopted mood-disordered chil-dren, whereas adoptive parents have the same baseline rates as the general population. Twin studies of bipolar disorder show a concordance rate of .67 for monozygotic and .20 for dizygotic twins (Kaplan & Sadock, 1991). A recent study of identical and fraternal female twins reported 70% heritability of lifetime major depression, with an environmental compo-nent of 30% or less (Kendler et al., 1993). Thus genetic linkages seem quite clear in both unipolar and bipolar disorder.

The current debate on biological etiology revolves around genetic contributions and factors relating to fetal development and birth trauma, particularly in schizophrenia. We know that even identical twins are not entirely concordant, but the environmental factors seem to be primarily in utero rather than in rearing. Recent studies have indicated that when one identical twin is schizophrenic and the other is not, their fingertip dermal ridges are different (Bracha, Torrey, Gottesman, Bigelow, & Cunniff, 1992). Dermal ridges are formed during the second prenatal trimester when there is a massive migration of neural cells to the cortex.

Intrauterine stressors during the second trimester seem to be especially important in reinforcing genetic vulnerability to schizophrenia. In 1957, a virulent Type A influenza epidemic spread through European countries.

Studies in Helsinki, Finland, showed that during the height of the epidemic, when women in the second trimester of pregnancy were exposed to the virus, their offspring were significantly more likely to develop schizophrenia than individuals born any other time that year or during the same time period in other years. Confirmatory replications of this finding were reported in separate studies from England and Wales, Ireland, Tokyo, and later from Scotland, Australia, and all of Finland (Mednick, Huttunen, & Machon, 1994).

Mednick and his associates believe the second trimester is a particularly vulnerable time because critical cortical brain structures, whose inappropriate development may produce a specific predisposition for schizophrenia, are formed at that time by the migration of young neurons from the ventricular zone to the neocortex. It is thought that individuals will be at increased risk for schizophrenia if they experience a viral infection during the critical period and also have a genetic predisposition for defective generation, migration of young neurons of the schizophrenia-critical structures, or both. Bracha et al. (1992) have called this the "two-strike" theory of the etiology of schizophrenia: a genetic diathesis together with a second-trimester environmental stressor.

PSYCHODYNAMIC MODELS

The psychoanalytic-psychodynamic model of major mental illness is based on the Freudian structural model of id, ego, and superego. Freud theorized that these structures develop during infancy and are totally in place by the end of the oedipal period, or ages 3 to 5, at which point there is presumably a stable integrated ego. In the Freudian model, all psychopathology arises from conflict among the three basic structures, and the differences among schizophrenia, bipolar disorder, and less damaging neurotic conditions are essentially a function of the timing of maturational arrest.

Willick (1990) has summarized the basic psychoanalytic model of etiology. Profound developmental failures in the first few months of life may result in autistic or symbiotic psychoses. Failures to achieve differentiation between self and object representations up through the first year of life will result in schizophrenia. If profound developmental problems occur after such differentiation, from the end of the first year through the second year of life, possible outcomes are manic-depressive disorder, psychotic depression, and borderline conditions. If the first two to three years have been successfully mastered and object constancy has been achieved, oedipal conflicts may result in neurotic conditions. The major psychotic disorders are generated prior to the oedipal stage, before the development of the integrated ego.

McGlashan (1989) explains the psychodynamic model for schizophrenia.

> The difference between schizophrenia and the neuroses is purely quantitative, not qualitative. Schizophrenic conflict is more intense and requires the use of very primitive (i.e., developmentally earlier) defenses such as denial and projection, which frequently involve a break with reality. The ego functioning of the schizophrenic patient regresses to developmentally earlier stages or levels of organization, the exact level being determined (or fixated) by one or more psychological traumas. (p. 746)

Later psychoanalysts disagreed with the Freudian model primarily in terms of the schizophrenic person's capacity for transference and the role of the ego in schizophrenic development.

All psychoanalytic theory implicated the mother in the arrested development that would later lead to psychosis. In the view of Harry Stack Sullivan, the pathogenesis of schizophrenia

> begins with a mother who is more anxious than normal and who imparts this tension to her child as excessive not-me experiences. The child's self-system, developing around the time of speech acquisition, overcompensates with excessive dissociation and warps its own further development. (McGlashan, 1989, p. 748)

Later, the overwhelming sexual needs of the adolescent assault this inadequate self-system, the defensive structure shatters, and the disorganizing not-me anxiety returns with attendant terror. The adolescent ego fragments into primitive states of mind, and there is a collapse of the integrated self-systems. Other psychodynamic theoreticians, including object-relations theorists, similarly postulate relationship failures as etiological precursors of schizophrenia. McGlashan (1989) notes the following:

> Virtually all psychoanalytic theorists postulate an experiential disharmony between the mother and her preschizophrenic infant. Whether this derives from genetic or constitutional factors in the parent is secondary, as the purported central pathogenic elements are dysphoric experiences which

become internalized as aberrant psychological structures. Explicitly or implicitly, the psychogenic models of schizophrenia regard these experiences as sufficient to explain most, if not all, cases of the syndrome. (p. 751)

McGlashan points out that psychoanalytic theories of etiology seem to lack credibility and are discordant with research findings on infant development and the observation that schizophrenia often develops in basically healthy families. Nevertheless, he finds that psychodynamic models are often useful in clinical exploration.

FAMILY SYSTEMS THEORIES

Systems theory must be understood from two vantage points: the value of a systemic approach to understanding the experiences of family caregiving, and the negative effect of older family systems theories of psychopathology. As Marsh (1992) notes, a systemic-ecological approach is essential for understanding the family's experience of mental illness and for developing effective methods of helping caregivers deal with their roles, tasks, and subjective reactions. A cybernetic model that views the family as an integrated entity with interdependent elements, continuously interacting with multiple other units in the social environment, is essential for understanding family caregiving in mental illness.

A systemic model considers not only the person with mental illness but also the effects of the illness on others and how this condition mediates changes in the family system. In addition, the family as a microsystem within a macrosystem is affected by policies, barriers, and helping resources in the larger environment in which the illness is experienced. This type of systemic model is extremely helpful for understanding the continuing processes of coping and adaptation.

On the other side of this issue is the negative effect of theories that have essentially attributed major psychiatric disorders to the family's need for these disorders. The mentally ill person is seen as the manifestation and bearer of the family madness (Shaw, 1987). Family systems theories have also explained major psychopathologies in terms of the family's transmission of aberrant modes of thinking and interaction to a member who is designated as the "identified patient." The symptoms are presumed to be necessary to maintain a spurious homeostasis, with the assumption that they will diminish or disappear when they are no longer functional in the family economy. Family systems theories specifically eschew the question of etiology, considering "causality" circular and recursive rather than linear. Nevertheless, the family therapy literature abounds with parental trait definitions or descriptions of family characteristics that seem etiologically related to specific diagnoses. Thus affective disorders are related to "parental overinvestment in the achievement of children, especially parents' social prestige aspirations," as well as a history of harsh discipline. Psychopathy "is associated with family pathology where children have been found to carry out overt or covert needs or wishes of a parent" (Fleck, 1985, p. 291).

Family therapy as a discipline evolved from the study of families of persons with schizophrenia, with an attendant body of theories that were essentially etiological in their descriptions of family transactions. There were a number of major explanatory models, mostly based on deviant modes of behavior and communication. The double-bind hypothesis of Bateson, Jackson, Haley, and Weakland (1956) postulated a history of incompatible mutually contradictory directives from parent to child, generating emotional paralysis. Lidz, Fleck, and Cornelison (1965) postulated skewed and schismatic families. In the skewed family, power was unequally distributed between the parents with the power centered in the mother; this family was more likely to have a male schizophrenic child. The mother was described as powerful and domineering, the father, withdrawn, passive, and compliant. In the schismatic family, there was no consensus about the distribution of power. This was more characteristic of female schizophrenic offspring.

The communication deviance model of Lyman Wynne and his associates (Wynne, Singer, Bartko, & Toohey, 1977) was based on the notion of ambiguous, confusing modes of intrafamilial communication and inability to maintain a shared focus of attention. Wynne also noted pseudomutuality, a false expression of solidarity, within the families of people with schizophrenia. In recent years, Wynne (1988) seems to have modified his position on the salience of communication deviance and has attested to the biological etiology of schizophrenia.

THE PERSPECTIVES OF SOCIAL SCIENCE

In defining mental illness, social science theories typically have not distinguished between what were formerly called neuroses and psychoses, between endogenous and reactive disorders, or between chronic and acute conditions. Some comparative studies have indeed focused on a particular syndrome, such as schizophrenia or depression. But for the most part, social scientists have used a global definition of mental disorder, conceptualizing a continuum ranging from socially adaptive, personally satisfying behavior (mental health) to grave psychological impairment (mental illness). Using both psychodynamic and behavioral theories as an implicit if diffuse background, social science theories generally look to sociocultural factors and correlative childrearing practices as the basis for mental disorder. Defective parenting and familial interactions are presumed to encapsulate the stressors of the larger environment and to perpetuate maladaptive behavior.

ANTHROPOLOGICAL MODELS

Anthropological theory has primarily focused on the universality of Western concepts and categories of mental illness. Cross-cultural epidemiology, culture-bound syndromes, folk beliefs, and indigenous healing practices are ongoing targets of research. Culture change and acculturation, presumed to be stressors, have been studied as etiological factors in mental disorder.

Although psychological anthropology began with the study of the universality of Freudian theories, Favazza (1985) claims that today psychoanalytic concerns are not at all central to either modern anthropology or cultural psychiatry. He states the following: "The psychic unit of mankind *may* be a valid concept but it does not necessarily follow that the psychoanalytic notions of mind and mental processes are applicable or meaningful when applied to non-western groups" (p. 249). From the exploration of universal instincts and drives, anthropologists have gone on to investigate the relationships between cultural childrearing practices and adult personality, the validity of the construct of national character or modal personality, and the concept of mental disorder as deviance from a cultural norm. The latter makes the concept of mental illness flexible and malleable, an artifact of social context rather than an attribute of the individual. The concept of mental disorder as deviance is central to social labeling theory in the field of sociology.

The work of contemporary anthropologists has added exceptionally rich insights to our knowledge of the experiential aspects of mental illness. Ethnographers such as Sue Estroff (1981) and Nancy Scheper-Hughes (1987) have studied the community lives of deinstitutionalized patients. Athena McLean (1990) has analyzed the functions of the family organization, NAMI, in the production of knowledge about mental illness. Of special relevance to our central topic is the work of anthropologists Janis Jenkins (Jenkins & Karno, 1992) and Peter Guarnaccia and his associates (Guarnaccia, Parra, Deschamps, Milstein, & Argiles, 1992; Milstein, Guarnaccia, & Midlarsky, 1994), who have studied families and mental illness in cross-cultural contexts within the United States. Their work is elaborated on further in Chapter 11 in the section on cross-ethnic differences in family caregiving.

Today, many anthropologists specializing in cultural psychiatry have a cultural constructivist approach; that is, all human behavior is viewed in fluid interaction with the environment, affecting and affected by ever-moving historical-cultural currents. The key assumptions of cultural constructivism are that all medical systems are ethnomedicines, specifically including modern biomedical psychiatry. Ethnomedicines are constituents and expressions of their respective cultures and ever in flux. Cultural constructivists feel that adherence to the beliefs of professional biomedicine poses many problems. They note that psychiatric knowledge and practice are highly heterogeneous and that medical systems are always unfinished products of cultural history (Gaines, 1992). In this sense, mental illness can be conceptualized and studied only as an interactive, constantly changing process within and among patients, families, healers, and other critical figures in the social environment. Cultural constructivism is similar to sociology's symbolic interactionism, focusing on microencounters and their meanings to the individual rather than the influence of macrosystems on individual behavior.

SOCIOLOGICAL MODELS

Sociological theories have generally focused on macrosystems, proposing hypotheses in several major domains. These have included socioeconomic status (SES) and social disintegration as etiological factors in mental illness, interrelated childrearing practices of lower SES families, social selection versus social stress theories, disastrous life events as a factor in mental disorder, and social labeling theory.

The notion that poverty environments generate mental disorder was derived from massive epidemiological studies in the United States that showed highly significant correlations between various mental disorders and lower SES (Dohrenwend et al., 1980). A significant association between serious mental illness and poverty continues to be confirmed in contemporary national household surveys (Barker et al., 1992). Prior review of international research had similarly shown significantly higher rates for psychopathology in lower SES groups around the world (Segal, 1975). In the Stirling County studies in Canada, Alexander Leighton and his associates (Leighton, Clausen, & Wilson, 1957) had demonstrated that social disintegration, rather than social class, was the major factor associated with mental disorder. My own research with two American Indian tribes who were blood-related and members of the same ethnolinguistic group found that greater social disintegration in one tribe affected child-rearing practices and was significantly related to poorer mental health in both mothers and children when compared with the other tribe (Lefley, 1976, 1982).

The highest rates for mental disorders in children have been found in poor urban communities. Here, family structure seems the most influential variable. Epidemiological data have indicated that mother-father families have the lowest risk, families headed by mother and another adult have varying risk, and loosely organized multichild families with a single head of household, typically the mother, have the highest risk (Kellam, Ensminger, & Turner, 1977).

Again it is evident that "mental disorder" covers a wide range of syndromes so that in assessing children's rates, conduct disorder may be given the same weight as childhood schizophrenia. Because our interest is in family caregiving of severely mentally ill adults, sociological research focusing on schizophrenia may give a clearer picture. Myers and Roberts (1959) studied family and class dynamics in mental illness and found significant social class differences in childrearing practices and in general psychopathology. Among lower SES families of persons with schizophrenia, they found disorganized homes; lack of parental affection, guidance, and control; isolation of the father from the family; heavy responsibility of the mother; and greater childrearing responsibilities for siblings. The authors admitted these characteristics were true of lower SES neurotics as well, that they did not have a normal control group to determine if these family patterns were actually modal in lower SES life, and that these variables could not explain the negative symptoms of schizophrenia. They also cautioned that their findings "should not be interpreted to mean that we believe they are the *cause* of mental illness. . . . Other social as well as organic, constitutional, and intrapsychic factors are correlated with the development of psychiatric illness" (p. 91).

These types of descriptions of family background abound in the psychiatric literature as well, but because they apply to all SES groups and to most types of mental disorder, one must question their specificity to social class and to the rationales given. What is clear is that the culture of poverty poses certain stressors for survival; that lack of jobs and decent housing, overcrowding, and general financial insecurity have a negative effect on family relationships; and that life may be more threatening and disruptive than in more affluent areas. These pressures will affect the entire population of a given area but they may have an even more stressful effect on people with the vulnerabilities of major mental illnesses.

A major issue in the sociology of schizophrenia relates to the *social stress* versus *social selection* hypotheses. The social stress hypothesis has two variants. Cockerham (1985) notes that some sociologists suggest that lower SES life is constricted and that these families transmit a rigid concept of reality to their offspring that impairs their ability to cope with stressful complex situations. An opposing opinion suggests that lower SES families are not at all rigid but highly flexible; they have to cope with more adverse circumstances and have fewer resources to do so.

The social selection hypothesis also has two variants. The *social drift* hypothesis postulates more mental disorder in lower SES groups because persons with mental illness tend to drift downward in society. Others suggest this is an epidemiologic artifact because more mentally ill people congregate and are counted in the poor inner city. The *residue* hypothesis suggests that persons who have good mental health tend to be upwardly mobile, leaving behind a residue of mentally ill individuals. Cockerham (1985) states that current research supports the drift rather than the residue hypothesis but feels that social selection is an inadequate explanation. He suggests that it is more likely that the stress of lower SES life contributes to mental disorder rather than mental disorder bringing about social class position. As with many other sociologists, however, Cockerham's analysis suggests that genetic and constitutional factors may be the primary landscape on which social factors are played out.

The social stress hypothesis has also been related to rural versus urban residence (country life presumably being less stressful). Traumatic life events such as wars and natural disasters have been implicated in the development of mental disorders. Certainly war and refugee experiences are dramatically related to post-traumatic stress disorder (PTSD). More recently, it has been suggested that multiple personality disorders may be a variant of PTSD related to extraordinarily abusive childhood experiences. Again, we have no firm data on why these antecedent events had a differential effect on those who lived through them, incapacitating some individuals but not others. What does seem evident is the relationship between stressful life events and decompensation in diagnosed cases of severe mental disorder. International research by the World Health Organization indicates a significant number and variety of stressful life events during the 3-week period preceding a psychotic episode (Day et al., 1987).

Labeling Theory

The prior body of sociological theory accepted the validity of mental illness as a demonstrable attribute of the individual: The researchers simply investigated sociological variables involved in its occurrence. Much of social labeling theory essentially disputes the validity of mental illness as an attribute of the individual. Analogous in some respects to cultural constructivism, social labeling theory was proposed as an explanatory model that locates mental illness in social interaction rather than in the organism itself. Barrett (1988) goes even further. He rejects any definition of schizophrenia as "an ontological entity residing in patients" and instead conceptualizes the condition as "a category of discourse that has emerged in relation to psychiatric institutions and practices" (pp. 372-373).

Of all sociological theories, this has probably had the greatest effect on families because labeling theory has been used by the antipsychiatry school to protest and restrict access to services that families consider essential. Labeling theories and sociological studies of the asylum (Goffman, 1961) have had a distinct influence on accelerating the closing of state hospitals. Conceptualizing mental illness as deviance rather than disease is allied with rejection of psychotropic medications and other somatic therapies as well as opposition to involuntary commitment for crisis stabilization and hospitalization during acute psychotic episodes.

Yet labeling theory indeed has value in studying the effects of social stigma, internalized stigmatization and self-concept, and the possible effects of social labeling in inducing chronicity (Lefley, 1990b). A review of labeling theory research by Link and Cullen (1990) concludes that the person's perception of labeling has negative consequences on psychological and social functioning but these consequences have not yet been definitively linked to the persistence of psychiatric symptoms.

LEARNING THEORIES

Learning theories provide explanatory models for the expression of symptomatic behavior but are inadequate as conceptual models of etiology. People may certainly learn maladaptive behaviors in early childhood as a function of differential reinforcement. Also, pathological dissociative states have sometimes been linked with childhood abuse or excessive punishment. But the premise that certain infants or children are differentially reinforced for behaviors that subsequently lead to adult psychosis has rarely been postulated or studied.

Yet the basic building blocks of learning theories are extremely relevant to the observed behaviors of serious mental illness. Classical conditioning processes, such as stimulus generalization and discrimination, are certainly involved. Operant conditioning principles may explain the circular interactions of internally stimulus-driven behaviors, reactive environmental response, and the reinforcement of particular patterns of social behavior. Aversive control, escape learning, avoidance learning, and particularly learned helplessness in institutional settings may explain some of the avoidant behaviors, amotivation, depression, or apathy of long-term patients. Social learning theory is extremely relevant to the behavior of persons whose major interactions are with other mentally ill persons. Role modeling and identification have largely been negative in institutional settings. Infantilizing treatment by staff and internalization of societal stigma have reduced self-efficacy and the capacity for modeling socially adaptive behavior. Conditioning theory has been instrumental in developing systematic desensitization of phobic and other anxiety responses. Social learning theory is the basis of many contemporary psychosocial interventions with long-term patients, such as the social skills training of Liberman (1987) and his associates.

Mednick and Schulsinger (1968) incorporated learning theory in a conceptual model of schizophrenia. They postulated that increased autonomic arousal, an increased tendency toward stimulus generalization, and an abnormal recovery rate predisposed an individual to rapid avoidance learning and ultimately to schizophrenic decompensation. In a longitudinal study begun in the early sixties in which "high-risk" children of schizophrenic mothers were compared with control children from so-called normal families, they found more birth complications, greater emotional sensitivity as reported by the children's teachers, and poorer cognitive performance among the high-risk children. These children apparently had more labile autonomic nervous systems and reacted with abnormal latency and amplitude to stress stimuli. As Howells and Guirguis (1985) note, however,

> The twenty high-risk subjects who eventually came to the notice of psychiatric services were not all schizophrenics but were a mixed bag of criminals, alcoholics, and people with personality disorders as well. . . . Moreover, the peculiarities described in the school children in this study by their teachers are not specific to schizophrenia, since similar peculiarities are often seen in emotionally disturbed school children. (p. 272)

THE INTEGRATIVE
BIOPSYCHOSOCIAL-CULTURAL MODEL

Mednick and Schulsinger's (1968) work was based on a diathesis-stress model of mental illness that presupposes biological, and typically genetic, predisposition. Most psychogenic and sociogenic theorists will give an initial bow to biology as a necessary but not sufficient cause and then go on to the essential psychosocial precipitants (see Cockerham, 1985). Some biological theoreticians think that diathesis is paramount and do not accept the proposition that stress is an essential precipitant. They point out that all human experience is accompanied by some type of stress. Most severe mental illnesses have their onset in late adolescence. Yet all people of this age experience the combined stressors of physiological-hormonal growth factors and the transition from dependency roles to self-sufficiency and adult life.

Why do some individuals find these life cycle developments excessively stressful and others do not? Kessler (1989), writing on sociology and psychiatry, notes that

> Early work on schizophrenia demonstrated a "triggering" effect of undesirable events, that negative events can precipitate a psychotic breakdown for schizophrenic patients. However, no evidence was obtained to suggest that stressful events play a more fundamental role in determining who becomes schizophrenic. (p. 299)

Indeed, the most recent comprehensive review of the research on the role of life events reaches a similar conclusion, not only about etiological stress but about factors in relapse. Hirsch, Cramer, and Bowen (1992) ask,

> If discrete stress in the form of life events acts to trigger the onset of illness, over what time-period does it operate? Overall, the evidence existing at present does not give strong support for a triggering effect of life events in schizophrenic relapse up to a time period of six months before onset of illness. (p. 86)

The authors further pose the essential directional question: whether life events had an independent causal relationship to the illness or were in fact brought about by the patient because of the illness. They call for prospective studies that are able to cluster events over time and also address the objective severity of threat of these presumed triggers of illness.

This seems to be our present state of knowledge. Even in studies that demonstrate that stressful life events within a prior 3-week period may precede relapse, the particular stressors seem to be quite idiosyncratic (Day et al., 1987). Apparently, there is no firm evidence that specific stressors in the social environment are involved in etiology, and as Hirsch, Cramer, and Bowen (1992) note, even very mild events may be perceived as threatening by vulnerable individuals. These events would be very difficult to identify and evaluate in any kind of preventive model. Regardless of whether or not stress is a necessary factor, almost everyone seems to agree on diathesis as a first cause. Recent National Institute of Mental Health research on neonatal cortical lesions in rats who mature at different rates of development indicates that (a) it is only as the cortex matures that it becomes vulnerable to stress and (b) brain dopamine systems grow into abnormalities only after puberty. This research yields a model of differential genetic sensitivity with a neurodevelopmental cortical defect that has a delayed effect and thus begins to yield some clues as to why schizophrenic symptoms develop at puberty and not before (Weinberger, 1994).

A biopsychosocial-cultural model does not dwell on the origins of mental illness but on how it is expressed and experienced. Here, sociological and anthropological insights are highly germane. Whether the most perfect rearing environment will produce a mentally ill adult is still problematic. The research of Tienari (1991) and his associates in Finland confirms heritability (the adopted-away children of schizophrenic mothers are significantly more likely to become schizophrenic than control adoptees) but the family environment also seems to be a significant correlate (disturbed families are significantly more likely to have schizophrenic members). Although Tienari refers to a "rearing environment," this is not prospective longitudinal research and we still have no way of knowing whether the childrearing practices of the disturbed families produced schizophrenia or the schizophrenia produced family disturbance.

There is no doubt, however, that mental illness is experienced in a social context and that family, community, and culture can affect the coping and adaptive strategies of the predisposed individual. Some of the research cited in the next chapter will indicate the effect of environment on how mental illness is experienced by patients and families.

5

Research on
Family Theories

Research on families of persons with mental illness is multifaceted, and in this chapter, only the highlights can be covered. We begin with investigations of models of causal relations and some of the implications for family caregiving. The etiological literature is important because, if valid, it would caution a priori against a caregiving policy that might place psychologically vulnerable individuals in unhealthy environments. Analysis of the research on expressed emotion gives a clearer picture of the dimensions and prevalence of so-called pathogenic families and suggests modalities in which families can be helped.

LEARNING THEORY

Learning theory suggests that individuals with severe mental illness may have been reinforced for aversive behaviors or may have learned maladaptive ways of responding to stress. Etiological hypotheses derived from learning theory must be distinguished from therapeutic interventions based on learning theory. We have little research relevant to the former. We have a substantial body of research that shows that both operant and social learning theories are valuable for the development of demonstrably successful therapeutic interventions with patients (Liberman, 1987; Liberman, Cardin, McGill, Falloon, & Evans, 1987; Paul & Lentz, 1977) and with families (Lam, 1991; Mari & Streiner, 1994).

Etiologically, the behaviors of severe mental illness do not seem based on modeling or social learning. For example, abusive behavior toward others in adulthood is not related to physical mistreatment or abuse during childhood. On the contrary, among hospitalized psychiatric patients,

Estroff et al. (1994) found an inverse relationship between childhood trauma and adult violence. "Those who were threatened and attacked in childhood were less likely to threaten or act with violence toward others as adults" (p. 677). Although Estroff et al. suggest that these patients' subsequent reactions may have been internalized rather than expressed as extrapunitive rage, their findings tend to confirm that people do not develop psychotic conditions such as schizophrenia or bipolar disorder because of abusive childhood. There may be an important biological distinction between these diagnoses and certain types of dissociative states, such as multiple personality disorder, that do seem correlated in some cases with severely abusive childhood.

The notion of learned behavior is implicit, however, in theories of family deviance that suggest that individuals with affective or thought disorders may have learned certain modes of response from close family members. This seems to be an implicit assumption in theories of family pathogenesis, in which all members are assumed to participate in a shared pathology.

FAMILY PATHOGENESIS AND COMMUNICATION DEVIANCE RESEARCH

Much of the research has focused on schizophrenia, presumably because this is the major diagnosis among hospitalized patients. Early research based on the notion of "schizophrenic families" was extremely flawed and methodologically untenable. The studies of Lidz, Fleck, and Cornelison (1965) were a case in point: They had no control group, and findings were based on nonblind clinical observations by persons seeking to confirm specific hypotheses. Their writings were based on a sample of 17 middle- and upper-middle-class families of persons with schizophrenia. The categorically negative statements that emerged from books of this nature had a profound effect on the thinking of a generation of clinicians and on the fortunes of the families who interacted with them. Lidz's group concluded, for example, that schizophrenic patients almost always grow up in homes marked by serious parental strife or eccentricity, although they were observing hospitalized patients cross-sectionally. Schuman (1983), describing Bowenian theory and attendant clinical observations, divided families of hospitalized schizophrenic patients into just two categories: the "schizophrenic family," in which all members function at a very low level, and "the family with a schizophrenic member," in which "there may be high levels of social or vocational achievement; on an emotional level, however, significant members possess low levels of self. They function with what Bowen has described as a 'pseudoself' rather than solid self" (Schuman, 1983, p. 43).

The following is an even more comprehensive generalization that encompasses all members of families of persons with schizophrenia:

> In addition to genetic factors there seem to be at least five characteristics attributable to schizophrenic families: 1) excessively closed family systems; 2) shared family myths or delusions; 3) paralogic modes of thinking in all family members; 4) lack of individuation and self-identity of members from the family "ego mass;" . . . 5) intensive pathological symbiotic attachments of the child to parents and of parents to grandparents. (Reynolds & Farberow, 1981, p. 126)

The validity of these types of categorical, all-inclusive statements is immediately counteracted by the preponderance of unexplained variance in the vast body of family research on schizophrenia. In an overview of the literature, Liem (1980) has pointed out that treatment of family characteristics has been analogous to a trait theory perspective, prompting the unwarranted generalization of relationships that may characterize a small subgroup to all families of persons with schizophrenia.

At least 40 interaction studies in the literature have attempted to confirm some of the family systems theories by comparing families of persons with schizophrenia with normal control families (Eaton, 1986). The research typically focused on some group task in which interactions were recorded and coded on various dimensions. Some studies found that parents communicated in the same way with siblings of the person with schizophrenia, whereas others did not. Some crossover studies found that parents of schizophrenic offspring communicated normally with normal offspring of control families, whereas control parents of normal offspring communicated poorly with schizophrenic members of the experimental families. In the entire literature, Eaton (1986) found only four studies that met basic methodological criteria. The results of the best-designed study were contradicted by the findings of a rigorously controlled British replication (Hirsch & Leff, 1975). After an exhaustive consideration of theoretical models and correlative research on familial behaviors, Hirsch and Leff (1975) concluded that "the evidence to date indicates that these ways of behaving are by no means confined to parents of schizophrenics, but are also shown by parents of neurotics, personality disordered patients, and normal people" (p. 109). Other reviews of the literature similarly concluded that there is no empirical support for family causation of schizophrenia (e.g., Eaton, 1986; Goldstein, 1986; Howells & Guirguis, 1985; Liem, 1980; McFarlane & Beels, 1983; and many others). Fisher, Benson, and Tessler (1990) have cited other critical reviews of early family theories and research and stated that these have typically been unfavorable.

Howells and Guirguis (1985) did a very careful methodological analysis of studies testing the theoretical paradigms of Murray Bowen, Lyman Wynne, Don Jackson, Theodore Lidz, R.D. Laing, and others concerning family pathogenesis of schizophrenia. Like Eaton, they found severe methodological shortcomings and questioned the inferences derived from the findings. These authors specified that to establish a causal link, five criteria must be met, as follows:

> *Time sequence.* It should be established that the family psychopathology predates rather than postdates the onset of the schizophrenia.
>
> *Consistency of replication.* The work should be capable of easy replication by others.
>
> *Strength of association.* There should be a direct and strong association between family psychopathology and schizophrenia in one family member. It should be possible to explain why other family members have escaped schizophrenia.
>
> *Specificity of association.* The psychopathology should be unique to the families of the schizophrenics.
>
> *Coherence of explanation.* The research should explain the known features of schizophrenia, such as its onset in adolescence and its clinical course. (Howells & Guirguis, 1985, p. 330)

In conclusion, these authors point out that if the research findings produce a coherent etiological explanation, it should be possible to frame and test interventions that are capable of preventing or eliminating schizophrenic symptoms in the affected family members. To date that has not occurred.

Of all the various early theories, the parental communication deviance (CD) model of Wynne, Singer, Bartko, and Toohey (1977) is still being investigated as an antecedent variable in schizophrenia. CD was a set of factors derived from verbal interactions that suggested that parents of persons with schizophrenia were more likely than others to have language anomalies, contradictory or disrupted sequences in reasoning, fragmented or amorphous speech patterns, and difficulties in maintaining a shared focus of attention. The investigators considered CD a risk factor but also suggested a similarity with the patients' thought disorder that might imply shared heritability of a defect in information processing. Hirsch and Leff (1975), in a carefully controlled study of families of persons with schizophrenia in England, produced findings that they claimed were incompatible with Wynne's transactional hypothesis of transmission of deviant communication styles. Their main finding was that fathers (not mothers) of schizophrenic patients were significantly more verbose than fathers of neurotics; they differed in number of words, not in paralogic or ambiguous communication styles.

The University of California, Los Angeles (UCLA) High-Risk Project (Goldstein, 1985) was a prospective study that followed 54 moderately disturbed adolescents from intact families for more than 15 years, past the main years of risk for onset of schizophrenia. The subjects were recruited from a pool of 16-year-olds presenting for treatment at a psychiatric clinic with typical behavioral disorders of adolescence, excluding all psychosis. Parents and index adolescents were coded for CD and affective style (AS), a measure of the family's emotional interaction. Parents were also coded for expressed emotion (EE). EE, discussed shortly in greater detail, was a measure of familial attitudes toward the patient expressed in his or her absence. In the final follow-up sample for which all three parental measures were available ($N = 45$), schizophrenia-spectrum disorders were associated with the combined parental patterns of high CD, negative AS, and high EE. When data for siblings were included, the predictive value of CD was even greater. Goldstein (1985) concluded that "disturbed patterns of intrafamilial communication and affect expression antedate the onset of schizophrenia-spectrum disorders and are not reactions to psychotic behaviors in already schizophrenic offspring" (p. 7).

Although CD has a logical connection to schizophrenic thought disorder, its specificity to schizophrenia appears to be questionable. The same group of UCLA researchers studied CD in schizophrenia and mania and found that odd word usage was actually higher in parents of manic patients (Miklowitz et al., 1991).

Despite the UCLA findings, there is still considerable debate about the prevalence of thought disorder in family members and the question of directionality when thought disorder is found. Sacuzzo, Callahan, and Madsen (1988) analyzed numerous studies of thought disorder and associative dysfunction in the first-degree relatives of schizophrenic probands and concluded "the evidence for thought disorder in the families of schizophrenics is weak and inconclusive" (p. 371). Romney (1990) did a meta-analysis on a subset of studies and decided that "there is a definite association between being related to a schizophrenic and manifesting (subclinical) thought disorder" (p. 481). He had pointed out previously that "future research should also consider the question of directionality, i.e., *do relatives transmit thought disorder to the patients, or vice versa?*" (p. 481, original emphasis). Yet the question of transmission versus parallel vulnerability was not actually resolved in the UCLA findings and, in fact, the latter remains the most parsimonious interpretation of the data. In all of these studies, there is so much unexplained variance among families of persons with schizophrenia that no cause and effect inferences can be made. Interactional variables in thought disorder remain critical issues for future research (McFarlane & Lukens, 1994).

RESEARCH ON FAMILY
PROCESS AND DEPRESSION

The issue of directionality leads us to the effect of the patient's behavior and mental illness on family functioning in general. This issue will be discussed in greater detail in the sections on family burden and the life cycle. As Keitner, Miller, Epstein, and Bishop (1990) point out, "family therapists have tended to assume that a noxious family environment is in some way responsible for the patient's symptomatology. However, it is becoming recognized that a patient's illness has a major impact on other family members" (p. 5).

Although most of the research has linked family functioning with schizophrenia, a series of studies reported by Keitner et al. (1990) indicate that depressive illness is associated with a greater degree of family strain and impairment than in schizophrenia and other psychiatric conditions. Moreover, cognitive and emotional deficits in family process are in no way specific to schizophrenia. Family members of persons with depression showed significantly greater problems in communications and problem-solving than did relatives of normal controls. They had problems showing love and affection for each other, tended to be emotionally underinvolved or overinvolved, and had difficulty modulating an appropriate affective distance within the family (Keitner et al., 1990). The effect of the illness on family functioning was evident during the acute phase and during remission. The authors emphasize the interactive nature of antecedent family environment and the undue strain of depressive illness, an interaction further demonstrated in the research on expressed emotion.

THE EXPRESSED EMOTION RESEARCH

In the whole body of research on family factors, the only consistent findings are that familial attitudes toward the patient may affect the course rather than the source of illness. Expressed emotion (EE), an empirical construct derived from the early work of George Brown and his associates in London (Brown, Birley, & Wing, 1972), is essentially a test score that discriminates types of familial response that are associated with differential prognoses of patients. These scores are primarily derived from three scales on the Camberwell Family Interview: Critical comments indicating unambiguous dislike or disapproval, hostility expressed toward the person rather than the behavior, and emotional overinvolvement, which is exaggerated self-sacrificing or overprotective concern. A cutoff point categorizes families as high or low EE. Generally, a relative is defined as high EE if he or she makes six or more critical comments, expresses any hostility, or is rated three or above on the overinvolvement scale. Numerous studies throughout the world have indicated an association between high EE and patient relapse, whereas low EE seems to be a protective variable for patients with presumably the same level of psychopathology (Leff & Vaughn, 1985). Differential responses to high and low EE relatives have even been demonstrated physiologically. Research by Tarrier et al. (1988) showed that patients reacted with high skin-conductance levels in the presence of high-EE relatives, whereas the levels decreased significantly with the entry of low-EE relatives, who appeared to exert a calming effect.

Depression and EE

The majority of studies target schizophrenia as the diagnosis and parents as the caregivers. However, the work of Leff and Vaughn (1985) found high EE in relatives of depressed patients as well as of those with schizophrenia, with substantial representation of spouses in both family comparison groups. Hooley (1990) aimed to replicate and extend their findings in a longitudinal study of psychiatric patients and their spouses at three psychiatric hospitals near Oxford, England. Hooley's goals were to (a) examine the predictive validity of EE in another sample of patients with clinical depression and (b) examine the interactional correlates of high and low EE levels in patient-spouse dyads. Over a 9-month follow-up period, 59% of patients with high-EE spouses relapsed, in contrast to no relapse of patients living with low-EE spouses. Moreover, depressed patients tended to relapse at lower rates of criticism than did patients with schizophrenia. Observations during a 10-minute face-to-face interaction indicated that high-EE spouses were more negative both verbally and nonverbally than low-EE spouses. Depressed patients with high-EE spouses were less expressive, less open, and more passive than patients with low-EE spouses. Hooley (1990) suggests that, although EE is a reliable predictor of relapse, the findings "will have little value unless they are couched within broader efforts to gain a process-level understanding of psychiatric relapse" (p. 79).

Understanding the EE-Relapse Linkage

Overviews of the EE research have concluded that relatives' high EE indeed seems to be a robust predictor of relapse but there may be diminishing predictive power over time. For example, Parker and Hadzi-Pavlovic (1990) reported that the aggregated data of 908 subjects in 12 major studies established a likelihood of relapse three to seven times higher for patients from high-EE families. They noted, however, that the predictive strength of EE diminished over the 26-year interval in which the studies were published (1962-1988) and that negative findings were not explained. Questions regarding the stability and consistency of EE and quite a few studies with negative or contradictory findings have led some investigators to question a predictive relationship and to suggest rather that a poor illness course may elicit high EE in relatives. Investigators are still conflicted about the direction of effect and the weighting of relatives' EE and patients' psychopathology in predicting relapse.

Despite the tendency of some clinicians and family theorists to focus on the toxicity of high EE, the international literature has revealed that the majority of families of persons with schizophrenia throughout the world manifest low EE (Lefley, 1992a). These families are described as calm, empathic, accepting, and respectful by EE investigators, who also reject any implication of family pathogenesis in their findings. The EE research is concerned with the course, not the etiology, of schizophrenia and other major mental disorders. It deals with family interactions that may be protective as well as toxic and that may minimize as well as exacerbate symptomatology in patients. The research focuses on specific behaviors rather than global characteristics of families. These behaviors are empirically derived rather than theory based. EE studies are rigorously designed, and the findings have been validated in numerous replications. In all these respects, the EE research is substantively different from the categorical paradigms and the flawed studies of the earlier schools of thought.

Brown (1985) himself had been concerned about misinterpretations of the concept and components of EE. Jenkins and Karno (1992) point out that, in contrast to the prior emphasis in the literature on the etiological aspects of putative psychopathology in families, Brown was interested in whether everyday aspects of family life could be important to the course and outcome of schizophrenia. He specifically disavowed any equation of high EE with schizophrenogenesis, and in fact doubted openly that families were a causal factor in the development of schizophrenia.

> I was skeptical about the published discussion of the role of family relation-ships in the etiology of schizophrenia. These dealt only with parents and emphasized enduring, deeply disturbed relationships. . . . But such families were in fact uncommon, and it seemed most unlikely that they would provide a general explanation for what we were observing. . . . It seemed important that the occasional presence of deeply disturbed or unusual relationships between parents and patients should not be allowed to dominate our thinking. If I had any hunch about what was going on, it was that it often involved something a good deal less fundamental, indeed, commonplace. (Brown, 1985, pp. 21-22)

Criticism, hostile remarks, and emotional overinvolvement are not unusual in families. They are recalled in the childhood memories and adult productions of numerous individuals with no known mental disorder. As Jenkins and Karno (1992) have noted, these behaviors are found in families throughout the world. The primary researchers on EE have emphasized not that schizophrenia is caused by disturbed families, but rather that feelings and emotions found in ordinary families may be extraordinarily stressful to persons with schizophrenia.

Leff and Vaughn (1985), pioneers of EE research, also concluded that disturbed behavior in families is likely to be reactive rather than causal and probably developed over a period of many years. They stated that "evidence is accumulating that from birth onward the preschizophrenic child often manifests minor developmental abnormalities, which may well provoke parental anxiety and overprotection" (p. 218). Although the UCLA High-Risk Project seems to show antecedent high EE as well as communication deviance and impaired affective style in parents, it does not answer the question raised here: that is, whether subtle precursors of later pathology, probably untestable with our current technology, evoke these patterned reactions over time. According to a current review by McFarlane and Lukens (1994), the direction of effect is still highly problematic.

NATURE, NURTURE, AND DIRECTIONALITY

The question of directionality is paramount in all cross-sectional studies, particularly those in which inferences are made about a prior rearing environment. The Finnish Adoptive Family Study of Schizophrenia is a case in point (Tienari, 1991). In this research, a nationwide Finnish sample of index offspring given up for adoption by schizophrenic women between 1922 and 1929 was compared blindly with matched controls of adopted-away offspring of nonschizophrenic biological parents. The adoptive families were investigated by joint and individual interviews and psychological tests. Biological parents were also interviewed and tested. The psychological health of families was rated as follows: healthy, mildly disturbed, "neurotic," rigid-syntonic, and severely disturbed.

Among the 144 index and 178 control offspring, the percentages of psychoses and other severe diagnoses such as borderline syndrome and severe personality disorder were significantly higher in the index adoptees than in the matched control adoptees. Of the 15 psychotic adoptees in the total sample to date, 13 are offspring of schizophrenic biological mothers and 2 are control offspring.

Both global clinical ratings and test data for the adoptive parents also correlate with the symptomatic status of the adoptees. It was found that nearly all seriously disturbed offspring were reared in severely disturbed adoptive families.

The Finnish research is one of the most ambitious and comprehensive investigations of the interaction of genetic vulnerability and family environment. The finding of a 13:2 ratio, with 87% of the mentally ill adoptees the biological offspring of schizophrenic mothers, is one of the most powerful indicators to date of the salience of genetic diathesis. The research also demonstrates that family environment may be a correlative factor. The specificity of family disturbance as an antecedent of schizophrenia, however, is open to some doubt. The data had indicated that with character or borderline disorders, adoptive parents were more disturbed than families of offspring with psychosis. This suggests that the behavior of the offspring may be an important variable because persons manifesting character disorders or borderline syndromes are likely to be extremely disruptive to family equanimity and even more difficult to tolerate than persons with symptoms of schizophrenia.

Another interesting study that shows very different patterns of nature-nurture interaction is the Israeli High Risk Study in collaboration with the U.S. National Institute of Mental Health (NIMH) (Mirsky et al., 1985). This rigorously controlled research began in 1965 and focused on 100 children with an average age of 11 years. The samples were 50 high-risk children with schizophrenic parents and 50 matched controls with non-schizophrenic parents. Within each group were 25 children raised by parents in home environments and 25 raised on a commune, an Israeli kibbutz. At that time, kibbutz children lived communally with their peers in a children's home. They were raised by a professional caregiver and spent relatively little time, most of it quality time, with their parents. It was hypothesized that schizophrenic symptoms found in a kibbutz child would more likely be attributable to genetic factors than to the environment produced by the schizophrenic parent. From large quantities of data, blind analysis revealed two discernible groups. The index children of schizophrenic parents, no matter where raised, showed more pathological symptoms related to mood, social withdrawal, and antisocial and obsessive compulsive behavior and more soft neurological signs than did control children. The main finding in all ratings by clinicians, parents, and teachers was significant global impairment of index children as compared with control children regardless of kibbutz or town rearing.

In 1981, when the children were in their middle to late 20s, the findings were completely opposite to what had been expected. The hypotheses had been, first, that limited contact with a schizophrenic parent might prevent development of the disorder in the at-risk child and, second, that the kibbutz with its supportive atmosphere and enlightened childrearing by professional caregivers would produce more stable individuals. Indeed, kibbutz-reared children were considered among the most psychologically well-adjusted and productive individuals in Israel. Reports on the current study, however, indicated that the most psychopathology was found in the kibbutz-reared sample. Among the index children of schizophrenic parents, 70% of the kibbutz-reared children and 29% of the home-reared children showed signs of mental illness; of the controls, none had schizophrenia and only one raised on a kibbutz had an affective disorder.

Kety (1985) has suggested that it is precisely the lack of a close and protective mother-child relationship as opposed to the "evenhanded benevolence" of the kibbutz caregiver that might damage a vulnerable child. Breznitz (1985) speculated that within a cultural setting in which the peer group rather than the family is the source of authority, constraints, and standards, the vulnerable child will not be able to respond appropriately to this high-demand situation and may escape into loneliness and marginality.

IMPLICATIONS FOR FAMILY CAREGIVING

Aside from supporting the salience of heritability, the research discussed here raises important questions about the caregiving environment. The Israeli study suggests that normative environmental expectations and demands may impose stressors that are difficult to tolerate by someone with existing vulnerability and that this process has little to do with parental characteristics or communication deviance.

But because most individuals are reared by parents or parent surrogates in a family setting, the question raised earlier about directionality is all-important. Does the family create disturbance in the offspring, or does the presence of a schizophrenic member create disturbance in the family system? Tienari (1991) states that a prospective longitudinal study of adoptees at risk is being undertaken to explore the direction of effects between adoptees and adoptive parents. They now have baseline data for a prospective study of index and control adoptees who have not yet passed the age of risk for schizophrenia. Nevertheless, the best way to resolve this issue is a prospective study from the time of adoption of high-risk children whose mothers have already manifested schizophrenia. The families should be followed and evaluated on the healthy-to-disturbed continuum at adoption and then on a time series basis so that correlates of incipient pathology may be observed in subtle adaptations of the family system. Another question that is essential is whether the severely disturbed families have other nonindex children, adopted or biological, who also demonstrate psychopathology. Essentially, it is only this type of difficult, time-consuming longitudinal research that can disentangle the direction of effect.

QUESTIONS RAISED BY THE RESEARCH

After reviewing the communication deviance (CD) and expressed emotion (EE) findings, particularly in relation to the UCLA High-Risk Project, McFarlane and Lukens (1994) concluded the following: "It seems highly unlikely that (1) family dysfunction is widespread among those with schizophrenia, (2) that more circumscribed aspects of family interaction, expressed emotion and communication deviance are unique and ubiquitous, and that (3) these factors cause schizophrenia" (p. 97). What they infer from the data, however, is that the influence of CD and EE on the course and outcome of schizophrenia should be examined within a systems paradigm in which familial responses may be determined by biological, societal, or social network factors at least as much as patients' responses are determined by family interactions. Like other researchers, they suggest that in some families CD may arise from a common and heritable disorder of attention and information processing so that vulnerable offspring are at risk from both biological and social influences during development and on an ongoing basis after the onset of the manifest disorder. Similarly, they suggest that family burden, stigma, and isolation may influence the EE and coping capacities of family members as well as the behavioral difficulties imposed by the illness.

These issues are extremely important for caregiving policy. If even a small subset of the rearing parents of schizophrenic offspring are indeed suffering from subclinical manifestations of the disorder, as has also been suggested by Eaton (1986) and Romney (1990), then social policies that subject them to caregiving stress are obviously ill advised both for themselves and for other children in the family. If the presence of a schizophrenic family member creates high levels of disturbance among parents and siblings, this finding also militates against family caregiving. In the former case, the burdens of caregiving are likely to do further harm to already fragile individuals. Even with planned professional assistance, it may be unrealistic to expect psychoeducational family interventions to significantly improve communication skills in that small group of parents who are also cognitively impaired. In the latter case, there seem to be clear mandates for family education and support as standard mental health practices but with caregiving provided through other resources in the mental health system.

As McFarlane and Lukens (1994) caution, however, these issues are still in a developmental stage of research and it is premature to draw final conclusions from the existing body of findings. These authors allude to family burdens, stigma, and isolation, suggesting these variables may have some influence in generating or exacerbating CD and EE. Yet to date, there has been no attempt to integrate the quantitative dimensions and intensity of family stressors with their effects on the emotions, attentional states, and overall cognitive and motivational functioning of family caregivers. Perhaps our ensuing discussion of the experiential aspects of mental illness throughout the life cycle and the extraordinary dimensions of family burden may provide some insight into these systemic issues.

PART III

Experiencing Mental Illness in the Family

6

Caregiver Stress and
Dimensions of Family Burden

Hatfield (1987) has pointed out that the effect of mental illness on the family is affected by three major variables:

> (1) where the ill person lives and who is charged for responsibility for his or her care; (2) the meaning of the illness to the family and especially the way in which that meaning is influenced by prevailing theories of etiology; and (3) the degree of understanding, compassion, and support given to affected families and the skill and appropriateness of help offered by the community. (p. 3)

In this chapter, we deal with the multiple sources of stress for family caregivers. To date, the effect of mental illness on caregivers has primarily been viewed in terms of a narrow definition of family burden. This concept has typically been restricted to interactions with the mentally ill relative. As Figure 6.1 indicates, however, there are multiple sources of stress that create a burden for the caregivers of mentally ill individuals—situational, societal, and iatrogenic. Caregiver burden derives not only from the experiential aspects of living with severe mental illness in the family but also from the caregiver's interactions and frustrations with the treatment system, the welfare and legal systems, and an indifferent or stigmatizing society. Conversely, burden can be mitigated, as Hatfield (1987) suggests, by understanding and appropriate help offered by the treatment system and the community at large.

We begin with a discussion of the conceptualization and measurement of family burden as it applies in the case of mental illness. The original distinction between objective and subjective family burden referred respectively to the reality demands of the illness and to the caregivers' distress in reacting to or fulfilling these specific demands. Many re-

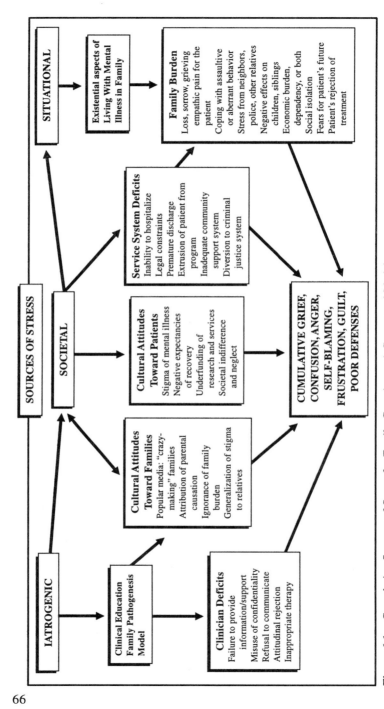

Figure 6.1. Cumulative Sources of Stress for Family Caregivers: A Conceptual Model

SOURCE: Adapted from Lefley (1990c).

searchers, however, consider global emotional distress, whether evidenced somatically or psychologically, as indicative of subjective burden. Emotional distress is manifest as we discuss the experiential aspects of living with someone with severe mental illness, especially within the same household. Various clinical indicators and effects on physical health are discussed and two extremes of the caregiving experience are presented. On the one hand is empirical research on violence in the household, with suggested precipitants and some possible remedies. At the other extreme are a few studies suggesting that some caregivers experience gratifications in this role and the relation of gratification to the clients' behaviors as well as to cultural differences in perceptions of burden. The data presented suggest that psychodynamic aspects of burden seem related to (a) perception of caregiving as normative, (b) the caregivers' mastery of the task, and (c) the level of dysfunction of the mentally ill relative.

As Figure 6.1 indicates, attitudes of the larger society, treatment by mental health professionals, and deficits in the service delivery system can be discrete sources of stress for caregivers. We end this chapter with a current empirically based assessment of caregiver needs before going on to explore the current array of services for families.

CONCEPTUALIZING AND MEASURING FAMILY OR CAREGIVER BURDEN

Schene, Tessler, and Gamache (in press) identified 21 instruments developed to measure caregiver burden in severe mental illness. Almost all researchers made a theoretical distinction between objective and subjective burden. In developing instruments, objective burden has typically been viewed as the number and type of tasks involved in caregiving, with subjective burden the perceived difficulty or distress connected with each task. Some investigators consider symptoms and dysfunction as objective and assess the caregiver's subjective burden in relation to each particular problem associated with the illness. Other researchers also include general measures of subjective burden, such as anger, depression, embarrassment, worrying, and tension, that are not necessarily anchored to measures of objective caregiving.

The analysis by Schene et al. (in press) found that some dimensions are included in almost all instruments. Worrying, the effect of the patient's disorder on family routine, and effects on leisure, distress, and financial consequences are typical. Other dimensions include cognitive preoccupation, feeling threatened, having to change personal plans, and feelings of loss and grief.

Numerous studies have indicated high levels of psychological distress among caregivers of persons with major mental illnesses. Some well-designed studies show figures as high as 75% suffering adverse emotional reactions (Scottish Schizophrenia Research Group, 1985). Research on a clinic sample of caregivers in England indicated that both objective and subjective burden measures on a family burden scale were significantly correlated with anxiety, insomnia, and depression scores on clinical scales (Oldridge & Hughes, 1992). Cook (1988) found a high level of emotional distress among both mothers and fathers residing with a mentally ill adult child, with mothers manifesting significantly higher degrees of anxiety, depression, fear, and emotional drain. In an Australian study, Winefield and Harvey (1993) found that caregiver psychological distress was high compared with norms on various standardized measures of adjustment. The level of behavioral disturbance of the mentally ill relative predicted caregiver distress after controlling for the caregiver's age, sex, and social supports. An unexpected finding was that caregivers of female relatives reported greater distress than those caring for male relatives.

Grieving and loss are an often unacknowledged feature of caregiver burden. Miller, Dworkin, Ward, and Barone (1990) found that families of the mentally ill experience a syndrome of grief and mourning very similar to that experienced by others suffering from real or psychic loss. Atkinson (1994) studied grief among parents who had adult children with schizophrenia, parents who had lost an adult child through death, and parents whose child had sustained a head injury that resulted in organic personality disorder. Mean age at first episode or death in all three groups was 21 to 22 years. The research found significant differences in grieving reactions and substance abuse: Parents of schizophrenic adults had more ongoing grieving, whereas parents of adults with head injuries had more substance abuse.

The authors found an inverse grieving pattern for parents of schizophrenic children vis à vis the other parents. The latter had a greater initial grief reaction—because the child either died or was expected to die through head injury. In both cases, the grieving diminished over time. In contrast, parents of schizophrenic children had low initial levels of grieving that rose over time. The researchers found that most of these parents were not told the diagnosis and prognosis but learned it piecemeal over a period of years. The authors concluded that once learned, parental loss of a child through schizophrenia leads to a pattern of chronic grief. They also suggest that the characteristic pattern of exacerbations and remissions in schizophrenia may play a unique role in shaping the parents' reactions.

FAMILIES' EXPERIENCE OF
LIVING WITH MENTAL ILLNESS

It is evident that objective burden refers to the reality demands of coping with mental illness and subjective burden to family members' personal suffering as a result of the disorder. Yet years of experience in working with families of mentally ill persons suggest that the existing instruments often fail to capture the extent and psychological effect of either of these dimensions. Examples of objective burden go far beyond mere caregiving responsibilities. They include (a) the mentally ill person's economic dependency and inability to fulfill expected role functions, (b) disruption of household routines, (c) caregivers' investments of time and energy in help-seeking and negotiating the mental health system, (d) confusing and often humiliating interactions with service providers, (e) financial costs of the illness, (f) deprivation of needs of other family members, (g) curtailment of social activities, (h) impaired relations with the outside world, and (i) inability to find appropriate alternatives to hospitalization or facilities for residential placement outside the home.

Subjective burden includes mourning for the premorbid personality, perhaps once bright with promise. In many cases, there is a feeling of dual loss—loss of the person who was and of the person who might have been. There are stressful effects on one's own mental and physical health, feelings of stigmatization, inability to make or fulfill personal plans, empathic suffering for the pain of a loved one, and worries of aging parents about the future of a disabled child who will surely outlive them.

Economic strain, real and attributed stigma, isolation, burnout, and need for respite are widely prevalent aspects of the burden of mental illness in the family. Negative effect on other family members, particularly the young, is an ongoing concern and may result in a need for ancillary interventions and a new generation of psychotherapists' bills.

Behavior management issues are ongoing tensions between mentally ill persons and their family members. Caregivers frequently have to contend with abusive or assaultive behaviors; mood swings and unpredictability; socially offensive or embarrassing situations; negative symptoms of amotivation, apathy, or anhedonia; and conflicts over money likely to be ill managed, squandered, or lost.

Conflicts often arise regarding behaviors disturbing to household living. These include poor personal hygiene and offensive odors in the home, excessive smoking and fire hazards, indifference or actual damage to household property, and sleep reversal patterns that may result in pacing or loud music at odd hours of the night. Relatives' refusal to take their medications is a common area of contention, particularly when there is a known pattern of relapse.

Passive withdrawal and excessive inactivity may be as burdensome to families as acting-out behaviors. A study by Cook (1988) of families of severely mentally ill adults enrolled in a psychosocial rehabilitation agency found chronic worrying among mothers. She states the following:

> A look at their offspring's situations leads to the conclusion that these worries were well-founded. These were mothers whose children had histories of medication noncompliance and recurrent psychotic episodes accompanied by repeated hospitalizations. They were mothers whose children led socially impoverished lives, spending large amounts of time alone in their rooms sleeping, being depressed, or living in a fantasy world. (p. 46)

Attentional and information-processing deficits, such as the prolonged silences and delayed reactions of schizophrenia, are frustrating and may be perceived as a lack of human relatedness by family members. Although they may recognize that these are not purposive distancing mechanisms, this interference with normal communication tends to further deprive caregivers of the rewards of human interaction and reciprocity that most people expect from those they love.

Perhaps the most devastating stressor for caregivers of persons with mental illness is learning how to cope with their relative's own suffering over an impoverished life. Persons with long-term mental illness are often acutely aware of their lack of skills, impaired productivity, and poor future prospects. They can see that others of their own age are married, starting families, and finalizing career plans. Typically, they both desire and fear the demands of these roles. For persons who were previously hospitalized, community reintegration poses the threatening need to acquire or relearn vocational or psychosocial coping skills in a competitive environment. Mentally ill persons' own mourning for lost developmental stages of learning, failed aspirations, and restricted lives can be uniquely stressful for those who love them and can feel their pain.

Feelings of helplessness to make things better for their children generate acute suffering in parents of long-term patients. The suffering is compounded by guilt if sympathy alternates with frustration and rage at aversive behavior. Guilt is a theme that often arises in family support groups. With changes in views of psychogenesis, many families have finally learned that they do not have to feel guilty for having caused these devastating disorders in a loved one. Yet there is frequent speculation over whether they are doing the right thing, making the right treatment decisions, or behaving in ways that are most likely to be helpful for their relative, regardless of its cost to themselves.

There is an analogue of survivor guilt among families of the mentally ill—the guilt of normal living. There are frequent expressions of remorse about living in decent surroundings when the patient does not and about enjoying family gatherings or milestones such as graduations, weddings, births, or holiday gatherings in which the mentally ill relative cannot participate because of his or her situation or condition. The relatives may even be exempted from family rituals, sometimes because their presence is too difficult or potentially disruptive, and sometimes because they themselves reject the stimulation. Yet their absence is an accusation and a deprivation, and the family wishes they could be there.

Among caregivers, there is almost ubiquitous guilt about hospitalizing a mentally ill relative, even under conditions of assault, florid symptomatology, or flagrant self-neglect. And indeed, when patients recover, there is a strong likelihood of anger and recrimination toward caregivers for having done that which was necessary and even potentially lifesaving at the time. Caregivers also suffer impossible dilemmas when they must choose between keeping a highly disruptive dependent offspring at home and risk the cause of psychological damage to other siblings or children (Backlar, 1994; Deveson, 1991).

Caregivers must learn to deal both with the patient's behaviors and with their own reactions, to distinguish between volitional and nonvolitional behavior, to recognize and deal with manipulation, and to know how and when to set limits. In controlling their own behavior, they must learn to effect a balance between the criticalness and overinvolvement of high expressed emotion and the dangers of affect-suppression, withdrawal, helplessness, and susceptibility to exploitation that sometimes are associated with low expressed emotion (see Hatfield, Spaniol, & Zipple, 1987). They must deal with their own legitimate anger and unjustified guilt. They must also learn to tolerate the suffering of people they love, avoid being overwhelmed by empathic pain, and come to terms with their own rescue fantasies.

PHYSICAL HEALTH OF CAREGIVERS

Family burden may also affect the caregivers' physical health. In a study of mental illness in families of mental health professionals, Lefley (1987c) found that 38% of the sample reported an effect on the physical health of caregivers, with mothers and siblings being most affected. Research on maternal caregivers by Greenberg, Greenley, McKee, Brown, and Griffin-Francell (1993) reported that subjective burdens related to stigma and worry were significant predictors of negative health status after controlling for multiple variables that might affect these relationships. These included mother's age, education, and marital status; adult child's gender, residence, and psychiatric symptoms; other life stressors; and objective burdens of care. The authors note that family members may seek treatment for health problems exacerbated by the stress of caregiving. They suggest that primary health care professionals should be encouraged to maintain fact sheets on mental illness in their waiting rooms. This may be a mechanism for enabling families to talk to their health provider about their caregiving stress and about coping with a mentally ill family member.

VIOLENCE IN THE HOUSEHOLD

The research indicates that a small group of patients living in the household may pose a serious risk of bodily harm to caregivers. Torrey's (1994) analysis of recent studies and media accounts of violent behavior by persons with serious mental illness led him to conclude that (a) the vast majority of mentally ill persons are not more dangerous than others in the general population but (b) a small subgroup of patients may indeed be more dangerous. This subgroup undermines the efforts of advocates to reduce stigma by denying an association between serious mental illness and violence. Rigorous studies in the United States (Link, Andrews, & Cullen, 1992) and in the United Kingdom (Wesseley et al., in press) have found an association of violent behavior not with mental illness per se but with psychotic symptoms; the sicker the patient, the more prone he or she is to violence.

The implications for family caregiving are profound. In a study by Tulane researchers Swan and Lavitt (1986) of 1,156 members of the National Alliance for the Mentally Ill (NAMI), 38% of the sample reported that their ill relative was assaultive or destructive in the home either sometimes or frequently. The strategy most commonly used by family members to prevent violence was to restrict their own behavior. Parents described patterns of avoiding confrontation, criticism, or even disagreement as "walking on eggshells." Their most adaptive way of dealing with violence was by calming and soothing the patient rather than asserting limits. Parents who were able to separate themselves emotionally from the violent activity and view the patient as ill showed the highest level of positive adjustment. Yet these families paid a heavy price. Their social and recreational activities were restricted, and friends and relatives no longer visited the home.

Personal in-depth home interviews by Gubman and Tessler (1987) with a sample of 30 Alliance for the Mentally Ill (AMI) families indicated that nearly 50% had to cope with violent behavior one or more times and 33% reported having to call the police. A later study of a stratified sample of 1401 NAMI families by a Johns Hopkins team (Skinner, Steinwachs, & Kasper, 1992) found lower percentages: 20% of the relatives with a serious mental illness had threatened to harm and 11% had physically harmed another person. Torrey (1994) notes considerably higher percentages in studies of hospital admissions. Among patients admitted to psychiatric hospitals who had physically attacked someone within the past 2 weeks, Straznickas, McNiel, and Binder (1993) found that family members had been the target 56% of the time, and a similar study by Tardiff (1984) reported that families had been the object 65% of the time.

Estroff et al. (1994), studying a comparable sample of seriously mentally ill inpatients, reported that more than half the targets of violence were relatives, particularly mothers living with a respondent. This pattern of directing violence toward mothers, the primary and often the only caregiver, was found in all of the cited studies. A number of maternal deaths through violence have also been reported anecdotally in NAMI circles as well as in print (Richardson, 1990).

The research team of Estroff et al. (1994) found significant differences in the characteristics of the social networks of persons with various diagnoses. In Estroff et al.'s research, which distinguished between threats and acts, respondents with a diagnosis of schizophrenia were more likely than persons with other diagnoses to commit violent acts but not more likely to threaten violence. Financial dependence on family was associated with more violent threats and acts. Confused thinking was not associated with violence, but denial and perhaps delusional thinking seemed to be operative. Respondents who were violent perceived their significant others as threatening but did not perceive themselves as being threatening in return. "The respondents who were violent felt malice and danger from significant others and perceived and experienced hostility in their interpersonal networks" (p. 677). The authors concluded that the interpersonal and social contexts of mentally ill persons and their perceptions of these contexts are important considerations in assessing the risk for violence.

In the study by Straznickas et al. (1993), patients who attacked parents, children, and siblings were most likely to live with their victims in the same household. Similar proportions of patients who attacked family members and of those who attacked nonrelatives lived with other people rather than alone. Compared with other assaultive patients, those who attacked parents were significantly younger (33.4 + 11 years) and those who attacked their children were significantly older (65.3 + 19 years). This suggests two types of bi-generational living arrangements: In one case, aging parents were caring for younger, assaultive mentally ill adult children and, in the other, "sandwich generation" adults were caring for aging mentally ill parents. Married patients were significantly more likely to attack their spouses. Patients who attacked their parents or nonrelatives were likely to be single. These researchers make the following points:

> Why might the primary caregiver be the family member at most risk? This finding may be due partly to the fact that family members who live with aggressive patients are more frequently in contact with the patients. Therefore, they are more readily available as potential targets when the patients become assaultive. In addition, our results suggest that attempts by caretakers to place limits on patients often precede assaults. Also, psychotic symptoms such as paranoid delusions involving the family caregiver are common in patient assaults on family members, as is concurrent drug or alcohol abuse by the patient. (Straznickas et al., 1993, p. 387)

Suggested solutions are referrals to peer support groups to help families learn how to react to aggressive escalation. Straznickas et al. also suggest that family therapy may be helpful in cases in which a patient's violence is related to difficulties with communication, problem-solving, and conflict resolution. Mentally ill family members with substance abuse problems should be referred to relevant treatment programs and support groups. They make a final suggestion that involvement of the criminal justice system is a viable option for managing violence.

ONGOING ISSUES
IN ASSESSING BURDEN

Cultural Perceptions of Burden

Guarnaccia et al. (in press) have pointed out that there are cultural differences in perceptions of burden and that the more family members see caregiving as part of what one ordinarily does for an ill member of the family (or for an adult child still living at home), the less likely they are to provide accurate information on caregiving tasks and burdens. Phenomenologically, these are not viewed as extraordinary responsibilities.

This finding highlights the need to distinguish respondents' perceptions of both objective and subjective indicators of burden. Distress may be manifested in multiple ways, physiological as well as psychological (Greenberg et al., 1993), and caregiving stress is likely to be a function of individual response styles as well as cultural norms. Thus some caregivers who consider it part of their role to care for chronically ill adults may report no subjective burden, unaware, for example, that their tiredness, dysthymia, and susceptibility to colds are related manifestations of distress. Yet as Noh and Turner (1987) have demonstrated, the family's perception of mastery and control of the situation seems to result in minimal subjective burden. When caregiving is viewed as a natural function and there is no perception of inordinate stress, mastery may be an implicit component of the caregiver's task.

Gratifications in Caregiving

Recent reports in the literature suggest that family caregiving is not invariably burdensome and that there are certain gratifications and rewards in caregiving, both practical and psychological. Elderly adults may suffer from the burdens of taking care of dependent adult children (Lefley, 1987a), but these adult children may also be supports to older parents who benefit from their companionship and physical help in running their households (Bulger, Wandersman, & Goldman, 1993).

In a study of 725 clients with serious mental illness in rural Wisconsin, Greenberg, Greenley, and Benedict (1994) found that 24% of the clients lived with their families and these clients tended to provide substantial help. Of this number, between 50% and 80% helped by doing household chores, shopping, listening to problems, providing companionship, and sharing news about family and friends. For the total sample, family respondents reported that 59% of the clients provided companionship. The researchers point out that recognition of clients' contributions could help reduce stigma and expand community opportunities for persons with serious mental illness. They also caution, however, that not all clients can make contributions to their families. Indeed, they note that in some instances, the help a client provides may be an additional source of family burden because of the poor quality of performance or the effort needed to structure the client's activity.

Relation of Gratification and
Burden to Relatives' Dysfunction

Caregiving gratification does not necessarily translate into acceptance of the caregiving role. In a study of Australian family caregivers by Winefield and Harvey (1994), caregiving gratification was contingent on whether and when the patient was symptomatic or relatively well. Almost one third of the caregivers reported no gratifications at all and this figure rose to 96% when the patient was ill. When caregivers could describe some positive aspects, 64% of their comments referred to enjoying the patient as a person and 27% to the practical advantages of their presence, such as sharing the housework. Another 9% felt that caregiving satisfied the sense of obligation inherent in their role. Despite these expressions of gratification, 78% of the sample preferred that the patient live outside the home.

D. Johnson (1994) analyzed the family burden literature, including the findings of 9 surveys and 12 intervention studies, to determine whether and in what ways burden can be relieved. in examining the research, he concluded that (a) there were no differences between affective disorders and schizophrenia in the amount of burden experienced and (b) there was one common feature that transcended diagnostic categories. The extent and degree of family burden appeared to be related to the level of dysfunction of the mentally ill relative. Johnson felt that although there was some evidence that interventions could be helpful, the evidence was sparse and the research too variable in quality. He suggested a number of program components that had demonstrated success in easing family burden and urged incorporation of these components in prevention programs. This, of course, revives the issue of the willingness of mental health systems to provide education and help to family caregivers.

SOCIETAL AND IATROGENIC STRESS

Societal stress derives from cultural attitudes that tend to stigmatize both mentally ill persons and their families. As noted in Figure 6.1, cultural attitudes devalue persons with psychiatric disorders, with concordant neglect of their needs. The massive underfunding of services and research and negative expectations of recovery clearly affect the resources available to caregivers.

Cultural attitudes toward families often reflect older myths of parental causation. The popular media still talk about "crazymaking" families, and a substantial number of clinicians and media talk show hosts still perpetuate these ideas. For families of persons with mental illness, there is both the shame of attribution and shame by association. In his foreword to the book *Hidden Victims,* which deals with the healing process of families of the mentally ill, E. F. Torrey describes some of these societal pressures:

> Imagine what it would be like to have a member of your family afflicted with a condition whose sufferers, whenever the condition is depicted on television, are portrayed as violent 73 percent of the time. . . . Imagine what it would be like to have your neighbors afraid to come to your house, and your children ashamed to bring their closest friends home to visit. Imagine having your relatives obliquely talking about your ill family member, unmistakably implying that your side of the family is guilty of something akin to original sin. No wonder Eugene O'Neill in *Strange Interlude* had the family hide their mentally ill aunt in the attic so that the family will not be disgraced. (Torrey, 1988a, pp. xi-xii)

Fortunately, mentally ill people are no longer hidden in the attic, but generalization of stigma persists. Objective burdens of stigma may include caregivers being held responsible for not being able to control the patient's aberrant behavior, reluctance of acquaintances to come to the house, or social ostracism of individual family members. Children with a parent or sibling who is mentally ill may be teased, maligned, or rejected by peers. In many cases, mental illness in the family jeopardizes relationships with friends, neighbors, and other relatives (Lefley, 1992b).

THE MENTAL HEALTH SYSTEM AS STRESSOR

Major sources of stress reported by families include (a) reluctant, ambiguous, and contradictory communications from professionals; (b) failure of the provider system to offer training or involvement in treatment planning to caregivers; (c) increasing financial drain, with inability of families to predict cost-benefit ratios of investments in treatment, often at considerable sacrifice to other family members; (d) difficulty in finding legitimate alternatives to hospitalization or adequate services in the community support system; and (e) stressors in dealing with the legal and criminal justice systems. These last are particularly acute when police are poorly trained in recognizing and dealing with psychotic disorders. Legal constraints on crisis intervention or involuntary hospitalization of persons showing florid symptoms but unproven dangerousness are extraordinarily stressful for the families who have to live with these individuals. In the current era of managed care, a further stress on families is generated by fiscal policies of limited inpatient treatment. This often results in premature discharge, with patients returning home still in a psychotic state.

IATROGENIC BURDEN

Many of today's caregivers have endured 15 to 30 years of major mental illness. During this period in history, experiences with professionals frequently have been frustrating and double-binding. For the most part, inconsistent and often contradictory patterns of help and information have persisted throughout the course of the illness. Many of these conditions are still reported today, particularly by families with members who have had multiple exposures to various parts of the service delivery system. In one type of situation, there is tacit rejection of communication with the family, save as respondents to questions on the patient's history. If caregivers attempt to learn more, they encounter deflection of questions, reluctance to provide diagnosis on the grounds of labeling, protestations of confidentiality, and sometimes implications that the family's concern is pathological or self-serving.

In some situations, family members have been catapulted into family therapy regardless of their desires, with the implicit or explicit message that the patient's illness is symptomatic of a family problem. But caregivers' requests for information and education continue to be ignored. There are reports of families who deeply resent what is perceived as enforced family therapy, particularly when they, as reluctant participants, are exposed to the observations of multiple therapists and students. But they are afraid the mentally ill person will suffer or be denied other needed treatment if they reject treatment for themselves. The validity of informed consent under these conditions, the ethics of denying necessary information to caregivers, and parameters of the confidentiality issue are discussed by McElroy and McElroy (1994).

A main problem seems to arise from residual negative attitudes and from professionals' attributions that somehow the patients' symptomatic behaviors must reflect something wrong going on in their families. Cook (1988), who has done considerable research on family burden, is particularly disturbed by persistent clinical attitudes toward mothers, as noted in the following passage.

> Clinicians should be aware of the degree to which the disciplines of psychology and psychiatry have engaged in documented scapegoating of mothers in explaining the origins of pathological behavior in their children. More importantly, they should both acknowledge and attempt to correct for the *effects upon their own clinical understanding* of being taught and socialized in this professional context of maternal scapegoating. (Cook, 1988, p. 48, original emphasis)

MENTAL HEALTH SYSTEM DEFICITS

A related source of family burden derives from deficits in the mental health system. Research indicates that families suffer both because of inadequate services for clients and because an almost total lack of services for themselves. In a scientific survey of 1401 NAMI members (Skinner et al., 1992), respondents indicated a strong concern with finding adequate community programs for their relatives. The respondents reported that 45% of the ill relatives had no productive activity at all. Less than one-half of the clients were involved in rehabilitative activities, such as employment, volunteer work, school, or day treatment programs.

Caregivers' problems stem both from a lack of services and from being ignored by the mental health professionals with whom they come in contact. A focus group study of caregivers found the following:

> Families experienced profound burdens as a result of their interactions with the mental health care system, particularly in negotiating crisis situations; acting as patient advocates and case managers; obtaining adequate community resources, continuity of care, and information; dealing with legal barriers; and communicating with mental health professionals. (Francell, Conn, & Gray, 1988, p. 1296)

More current research indicates that a substantial number of families continue to be dissatisfied with their contacts with mental health professionals (Biegel, Li-yu, & Milligan, 1995).

Despite some progress, in many areas there have been few substantive changes since a decade ago when Holden and Lewine (1982) reported on families' frustrations about lack of employment and adequate living arrangements for their ill members and professionals' failure to direct them to community resources. Hanson and Rapp (1992), studying family members' perceptions of how well community mental health programs and services met their needs, found that few facilities offered families any information about the illness or practical advice on how to cope. There was little in the way of emotional support or communication on the client's treatment and progress. Family members also reported that less than one-third of the programs offered the client follow-up contact after hospitalization, preparation for independent living, or case management outside the office.

The latter is an extremely important point because a study by Grella and Grusky (1989), which similarly found widespread dissatisfaction with services, nevertheless found that family members' satisfaction with specific services seemed to depend on their contact with a case manager.

> The role played by case managers in providing information and support to families even surpassed the impact of overall system coverage and quality in determining family satisfaction. In particular, case managers' role in increasing family members' support of their mentally ill relative was crucial to families. This finding is consistent with the assertions of advocates for the families of seriously mentally ill clients, who stress the need to increase services for families in the form of supportive interactions with system representatives. (p. 835)

This conclusion was strengthened in a study of families' concerns regarding community placement of their relative following hospitalization. Solomon and Marcenko (1992b) found a pronounced need for case managers to be trained in social skills, behavioral techniques, coping strategies for families, and problem-solving techniques. These families indicated they were more satisfied with services for their relatives than for themselves. They indicated a need for family education about medications and about how to motivate their mentally ill relatives. As we shall see, these educational needs form the basis of most of the new interventions described in the chapter on services for families.

7

Caregiving During the Family Life Cycle

The Life Cycle of the Person With Mental Illness

The experience of mental illness differs according to the characteristics of the setting in which it is lived out. Cultural attitudes and belief systems regarding mental illness and familial obligations, economic sustenance needs, psychological ambience, and the extent of competing responsibilities all affect the caregiving experience. Family composition and structure as well as size and density of households are important factors; these in turn are influenced by socioeconomic status and by cultural norms for household living arrangements. Interacting with these multiple variables at any given point, the caregiving experience follows a trajectory of age and time.

Severe psychiatric disorders generally have their onset during late adolescence or early adulthood. The peak age of onset for schizophrenia is between ages 15 and 25 for men and between 25 and 35 for women. The average age of onset for affective disorders is 30 years for bipolar disorder and 40 years for unipolar depression (Kaplan & Sadock, 1991). These are mean ages that take into account later life depression, but modally, the major disorders are likely to become manifest at a much earlier age.

Men with schizophrenia tend to remain single, whereas women are more likely to marry. Persons with affective disorders are far more likely to be married than people with schizophrenia. The individual life cycle of the person with mental illness is experienced within the life cycle of a particular family. The illness may be experienced as a married person within the conjugal family but more typically as a single person within one's family of origin. Regardless of whether or not the person continues living at home, the course of illness affects and is affected by the particular developmental level, needs, and coping capacities of the family unit.

THE FAMILY LIFE CYCLE

Although adults with major mental illnesses may have suffered from diagnosed or undiagnosed disorders in childhood or endured the gradual onset of mental illness through puberty and early adolescence, in most cases the observable symptoms that brought clinical attention were not manifested until late adolescence or early adulthood. This period coincides with what Carter and McGoldrick (1989) view as the beginning of the *family life cycle.* These authors suggest that the family life cycle begins not with marriage, coupling, and the begetting of children but rather when young adults leave the family home and begin the transition into adulthood.

> Considering the family to be the operative emotional unit from the cradle to the grave, we see a new family life cycle beginning at the stage of "young adults," whose completion of the primary task of coming to terms with their family of origin most profoundly influences whom, when, how, and whether they will marry and how they will carry out all succeeding stages of the family life cycle. (p. 13)

These authors then describe six basic stages in the family life cycle as they occur in middle-class U.S. families and presumably throughout the Western world. The stages are indicated here, each with its own emotional process of transition.

(1) Single young adults leaving home; accepting emotional and financial responsibility for the self.

(2) The joining of families through marriage; the new couple, with commitment to a new system.

(3) Families with young children: accepting new members into the system.

(4) Families with adolescents: increasing flexibility of family boundaries to include children's independence and grandparents' frailties.

(5) Launching children and moving on: accepting a multitude of exits from and entries into the family system.

(6) Families in later life: accepting the shifting of generational roles. (Carter & McGoldrick, 1988, p. 15)

These transitions are based on the model of the nuclear family in the Western world. Other cultures may differ significantly in childrearing patterns, generational relationships, flexibility of boundaries, and kinship roles, but most of the developmental stages in the family life cycle are essentially pan-human.

In other cultures, the initial launching process of the young adult may entail such adult responsibilities as work or advanced education but not physical separation. Unmarried children are able to establish adult identity while continuing to live in the parental home. Family structure may require continuity of residence for married children as well so that a son or daughter will bring a spouse back to the family of origin. Nevertheless, the marriage itself will constitute the launching process, the developmental milestone that separates the adult child from the adult spousal role. In most cases, moreover, the new couple will have separate living quarters within the family compound and discrete childrearing responsibilities. As in the Western world, children will be expected to grow up and relieve their parents of further obligations for their welfare. In most cultures, the roles are reversed in old age and adult children are expected to ensure adequate care for their aging parents.

All families may be affected by what Carter and McGoldrick (1989) refer to as vertical and horizontal stressors. Vertical or longitudinal stressors include maladaptive patterns of behavior and relating that are transmitted through the generations. These include family myths, secrets, taboos, expectations, and attitudes that are the individual's heritage at birth. Horizontal stressors include both developmental events, or life cycle transitions, and unpredictable events, such as accidents, untimely death, chronic illness, or the birth of a handicapped child. "Given enough stress on the horizontal axis, any family will appear extremely dysfunctional. Even a small horizontal stress on a family in which the vertical access is full of intense stress will create great disruption in the system" (p. 8).

The authors also noted the importance of the social, economic, and political context as the family moves through different phases of the life cycle. The loss of employment and other grave threats to the socioeconomic health of the family, such as war, political strife, or famine, are horizontal stressors that can strain already vulnerable families to the breaking point. They may also generate the need for migration as part of the separation process for young adults. The need for migration to seek refuge or employment may also result in parents leaving young children behind to be raised by other caregivers.

In contemporary life, we are also seeing the emergence of new child-rearing patterns in which grandparents rather than parents are the major rearing agents. In this process, as with migrating mothers, there has been a disruption at some point in early child development. The young child has experienced abandonment by the mother with delivery to another adult for caregiving. In psychoanalytic schemas, this abandonment may be a precursor of later mental illness, although there are few empirical data to support this hypothesis. Nevertheless, any disruptions of the developmental cycle may be considered stressors; for vulnerable individuals, the stress may indeed be a pathogenic factor.

EXPERIENCING MENTAL ILLNESS DURING
THE LIFE CYCLE OF AN INDIVIDUAL ADULT

Harding (1988), one of the few researchers to investigate the course of severe mental illness longitudinally, has emphasized the need to study individuals in terms of their illness trajectory. This means that the point in time of the developmental path of the illness must be taken into account in studying an individual's progress or the effects of a specific intervention. In addition to cyclical acute phases or episodic exacerbations and remissions of symptoms during the course of the disorder, the illness may involve periods of greater and lesser functioning. Its trajectory may lead to a symptomatic plateau or even full remission in later life.

The life experience of adults with mental illness varies greatly as a function of the specific diagnosis and the age of onset. As we indicated in the introductory chapter of this book, numerous individuals with a known mental illness are found in the pages of history and the arts. For the most part, these have been people with affective disorders (Jamison, 1993). Their disorders may have been evident in mild form from a relatively early age, for example, as depressed moods, irritability, or social withdrawal. But these were not pronounced enough to interfere with the person's ability to develop and grow. Frequently, such individuals were quite able to complete their education, marry, raise children, and fulfill their basic talents or competencies despite periodic bouts of depression, agitation, or even psychosis. Some individuals have been able to use their hypomanic periods in the service of greater creativity and productivity. Nevertheless, they may suffer profound depressive episodes generating suicidal ideation and even suicidal attempts. According to personal accounts, medications and hospitalization may have a profound effect in changing the depressive cycles (Styron, 1990). Similarly, people with episodic bouts of panic disorder or even obsessive compulsive disorders may be able to live productive lives, fulfill careers, and raise families, particularly with appropriate treatment regimens tailored to their disorders (Jenike, 1993).

In many cases, however, unipolar or bipolar mood disorders that emerge in late adolescence are similar in trajectory to profound thought disorders, such as the schizophrenias. Age of onset is actually a more critical predictor than diagnosis because this determines the likelihood of a person's having completed the necessary developmental stages to adulthood. An individual's educational and skill levels and social competencies are highly relevant to her or his capacity for independent living. Some persons decompensate while in college or during the years they are in military service and remain incapable thereafter of pursuing an ordinary productive life pattern.

Several major variables interfere with normal life cycle development among persons with severe mental illness—and again we are speaking of adults who are so severely impaired that they require some degree of caregiving from others. First, there are the strains and vicissitudes engendered by the illness itself. In addition to the terrors of psychosis or profound clinical depression, there are periods of severe disability and inconsistency in one's capacity for fulfilling ordinary work and social roles. Second is the dependency incurred and the internal emotional conflicts associated with one's reliance on others for survival. Among individuals who have been able to fulfill social roles at particular times in the life cycle, as for example, spouses or parents, there are strains incurred in fulfilling associated tasks and responsibilities as well as losses incurred if these roles later become unavailable to them. Last, there is the totality of strain associated with societal stigma. This is manifested in multiple ways, ranging from loss of old friends to open discrimination in employment, housing, and insurance (Campbell, 1989). Both self-reports and empirical research indicate that the effects of stigma on self-concept and functioning are profoundly negative and often create a self-fulfilling prophecy of incapacity (Hatfield & Lefley, 1993; Link & Cullen, 1990).

Despite these pressures, longitudinal research has demonstrated that in later years many mentally ill people do better than expected and in fact are able to lead more normal lives than in their youth. Schizophrenia is arguably the most debilitating disorder; indeed, follow-up research indicates that even after comprehensive treatment, the outcome is generally poorer than for the affective disorders (McGlashan, 1988). Nevertheless, the old prognosis of progressive deterioration has clearly been disproved. Harding (1988) reported long-term outcomes of treated patients in three major studies. Percentages showing recovery or mild impairment were as follows: Ciompi (Italy), 50%; Harding (Vermont), 62%; Bleuler (Switzerland), 66%. A meta-analysis of outcome in schizophrenia of 51,800 patients in 368 cohorts around the world indicated improvement rates of 46.5% using broad criteria (Hegarty, Baldessarini, Tohen, Waternaux, & Oepen, 1994). In the developing countries, approximately 58% of narrow criteria (gradual onset) cases show moderate to good outcome (Jablensky et al., 1991). The longitudinal studies, which typically follow patients at least 25 years after their last hospitalization, give us the clearest picture of what happens to people with severe mental illness after they enter middle to late adulthood. Many of them are able to live relatively normal and productive lives in the community, despite early years of psychosis severe enough to have warranted lengthy hospitalizations (Harding, 1988).

Despite this salutary picture, most of the persons in these studies have not been able to fulfill the family life cycle roles outlined by Carter and McGoldrick (1989). They have not been able successfully to consummate adulthood responsibilities, engage in enduring marital relationships, raise families, and switch generational roles. At various points in the life cycle of their illness, they may have had specific types of relationships with their caregivers or other family members related to their age and kinship roles.

FAMILY ROLE RELATIONSHIPS OF
THE PERSON WITH MENTAL ILLNESS

Mentally Ill Adult Children

Mentally ill persons who cannot fulfill age-appropriate roles in society frequently are still locked into the dependency-independence conflicts of adolescence with parental figures. Frustrations about their diminished social status and poor prospects may be incorporated in their delusional system and projected onto caregivers. As the family burden literature indicates, displaced rage and unreasonable demands may even generate violence, often directed at the major nurturing figure (Estroff et al., 1994). Dependency may still be a major dynamic in the relations of former patients in their 40s and 50s with elderly parents in their 70s and 80s (Lefley, 1987a). A recent study found predictably that parental perceptions of a sample of adult psychiatric patients were more negative than those of matched nonpsychiatric controls. But the researchers also found that the patients described both parents at a more primitive conceptual level and expressed significantly greater ambivalence than did normal subjects. The patients focused "mainly on gratification or frustration provided to the subject by the parent, with little recognition of the parents as complex, integrated individuals having changing internal qualities, feelings, and motivations" (Bornstein & O'Neill, 1992, p. 481).

Need gratification and ambivalence seem to be the keystones of many patients' relations with caregiving authority figures. Seeman (1988) has stated that psychiatric patients frequently accuse both their therapists and their parents of neglect and malevolence. She cites a case of a 30-year-old patient, Allan, who told his doctor that he suffered repeated humiliations at his father's hands. Allan said this so many times and so insistently that the doctor finally arranged to move Allan from his parents' home to a supervised boarding home. To the doctor's surprise, Allan refused to move. Later, the doctor was even more surprised to witness a warm, affectionate interchange between Allan and his father at a family meeting.

> This example illustrates the tendency of both parents and doctors to take too literally the patient's statements. The more attached a patient is to relatives or therapists, the more viciously the patient may attack them for disappointing him or her by not being perfect. (Seeman, 1988, p. 98)

Perceptions of imperfections of the major protectors, of the inability of the once all-powerful parents to make life better, can generate terror and rage in the fragile personality with crumbling ego boundaries. This appears to be a consistent dynamic of mentally ill offspring and may indeed be at the root of family violence.

The Sibling with Mental Illness

Very few persons with mental illness have written about their roles as siblings, and there is virtually no research specifically focusing on that experience. Personal accounts and empirical studies have dealt with the reactions of well siblings rather than the phenomenology of mental illness from a sibling perspective (see Brodoff, 1988; Hatfield & Lefley, 1993; Judge, 1994; Marsh, Appleby, Dickens, Owens, & Young, 1993; Marsh, Dickens, et al., 1993; Moorman, 1992; Saylor, 1994). Yet as Judge (1994) has noted, the sibling relationship is the most enduring of human connections during the life cycle. Siblings are major sources of social support during preadolescence and adolescent development. They are also the supports in later life after parents have died (Moorman, 1992).

Much of what we know about the reactions of the mentally ill sibling must be inferred from studies and recollections of the well sibling. The dynamics may involve denial of disability, rejection of medication, and resentment that a sister or brother is involved in advocacy for the mentally ill (Saylor, 1994). The negative emotions and fears of the well sibling, so amply demonstrated in the literature, are undoubtedly felt and resented by the ill sibling. Major psychiatric disabilities are often accompanied by heightened sensitivity to negative nuance and the unspoken feelings of others. The ill sibling may well feel guilty for being the source of the family's malaise.

The common themes of anger, resentment, fear, or anxiety reported by well siblings may evoke in the mentally ill sibling corresponding emotions. Inevitably, there are defensive reactions to the perceived negativity related to oneself. These defenses may be manifested in oppositional or bizarre behavior or in heightened disruptive activity. Brodoff (1988) describes an effort commonly attempted by siblings, usually at the urgent request of parents: that is, to involve the ill brother or sister in one of their own social activities. Family accounts suggest that these almost invariably end in disaster (Backlar, 1994; Deveson, 1991). The ill siblings cannot tolerate the demands of ordinary social interaction, which may be psychophysiologically as well as emotionally threatening. They recognize their own inadequacy and social ineptitude in comparison with their peers. They feel different, like pariahs, brought along at the charitable behest of the well sibling but essentially unequal and unaccepted by persons their own age. They may respond with withdrawal, abandoning the field, or with acting-out behavior. Their illness may generate an explosive response or they may achieve secondary gains from attention-provoking disruptive behavior.

In fact, the literature on the agony of well siblings gives important clues to the defensive armature erected by the mentally ill brother or sister. The behaviors of mental illness may reflect rage and resentment at being perceived as a source of pain. Denial of illness is one means of rejecting the idea that one is the reason for the family's tribulations. Refusal to take medications reinforces this denial and is a way of repaying family members for their lack of faith in the self-healing capacities of the mentally ill sibling. Defiance is one of the few mechanisms of empowerment available to persons who essentially feel powerless with respect to their well siblings and to the world as a whole (Hatfield & Lefley, 1993).

When siblings become the major caregivers for their mentally ill brothers or sisters, the relationship may evoke in both parties an assortment of psychodynamic reactions relating to their childhood experiences and roles. Old sibling rivalries and jealousies may reemerge, confounded by the new quasi-parental role of the sibling caregiver. Similar dynamics may arise as in parental caregiving, such as unrealistic expectations and demands of the major nurturing figure. Unresolved dependency conflicts may be projected onto the sibling caregiver, combined with furious efforts to disengage and assert independence. When the caregiving siblings are older, they may literally become the maternal or paternal figure remembered from childhood. When the caregiving siblings are younger, jealousy of their greater competence may reinforce the feelings of inadequacy and hopelessness of the sibling who is mentally ill.

But the feelings of mentally ill siblings are not necessarily negative. The behaviors of mental illness may also represent maladaptive attempts to protect loved ones. The disappointment of the well sibling can be justified and validated by acting out. An older sibling's inability to fulfill his or her role may be manifested in behavior that pushes away the younger sibling, forcing him or her to seek mentoring from a more capable source. The ill member may unconsciously exaggerate symptoms to demonstrate how different he or she is from the sibling, who is worried about his or her own genetic vulnerability. The distancing mechanisms symptomatic of a schizophrenic illness may prevent too close contact but they may also deflect the pain of separation and loss of a beloved sibling.

In the self-report literature of former patients, fleeting references to siblings suggest that the writers are well aware of the burden imposed by their illness. There are often references to a "good relationship" or gratitude to siblings for their support and constancy during rough times (Leete, 1993). The literature in fact suggests a great longing for closeness of both well and ill siblings. The new stabilizing medications combined with the new recovery vision may indeed reunite siblings eager to forge new relationships in later years. In fact, accounts by well siblings suggest that, as the life cycle changes, relationships become closer and in some ways more fulfilling, despite the continuing mental illness of the sibling (Moorman, 1992; Saylor, 1994).

The Spouse with Mental Illness

If adult children suffer blows to their self-esteem because of their inability to fulfill age-appropriate social roles, this is even more poignant in the case of mentally ill spouses. These are persons who have been functional enough to engage a mate in a relationship. They have been able to marry or cohabit, and often to produce children, and, accordingly, have some history of fulfilling a socially valued role. In contemporary life, many so-called normal spouses, particularly fathers, leave a marriage because of inability to fulfill these roles. Yet the enforced incapacity of mental illness may be even more demoralizing, particularly to one's self-concept as a person worthy of loving and capable of generating and rearing children (Apfel & Handel, 1993).

Marriage itself is a stressor, and even a single episode of mental illness may begin to erode a vulnerable person's capacity for coping with the multiple demands of the marital relationship. As in the case of dysfunctional adult children, the mentally ill marriage partner may displace rage onto the caregiving spouse. The lack of appreciation and unfounded accusations will exacerbate what is often a mountain of cumulative stress for the overburdened caregiver. In a typical scenario, a mother of young children may have to completely alter her former role: find work, find babysitters, take over full financial and management responsibilities, and monitor her husband's medications and treatment compliance. Contending with the disruptive behaviors of mental illness and with her husband's delusions and displaced rage may simply be too much and may trigger separation and divorce (see Lefley, 1990c). Judge (1994) reports on research indicating that divorce and separation rates for one sample of persons with serious mental illness were 3 to 4 times the rate of the national average.

In a study of spouses of depressed patients, Fadden, Bebbington, and Kuipers (1987) reported that female caregivers experience more burden, particularly if the wife has to become the breadwinner while running the household and fulfilling other family responsibilities. In these cases, the insult to the husband's self-esteem and his resentment at his incapacity may interact with his illness in explosive ways.

Other studies, however, suggest that the long-term disability of a wife-mother has more effect on the family than does a husband's illness, especially when there are young children. Even though a wife may become overburdened and even if she is the breadwinner, the household usually continues to function (Anthony, 1970). On the other hand, when the wife-mother is ill, structural adaptations are usually required to maintain family functioning. In studies of husbands' reactions to the long-term mental illness of their wives, there is a critical point at which expectations and tolerances change (Anthony, 1970; Kreisman & Joy, 1974). Husbands can usually make short-term adjustments to a wife's illness. When there are multiple hospitalizations or long-term disability, however, husbands tend to withdraw from their wives, lower their role expectations, and make other arrangements for continued household functioning.

The provision of a permanent substitute results in a strain on marital ties and tends to isolate the wife-mother as a marginal person in the household. This leaves the mentally ill wife without role or function and adversely affects her feelings of self-worth. Inability to fulfill a valued life role, whether as spouse or parent, adds immeasurable agony to the illness itself.

The Parent with Mental Illness

The low reproductive rate of persons institutionalized for mental illness, a function of their restricted sexual activity, has changed dramatically since deinstitutionalization. Young adult patients now live in the community, mate, have sex, and experience pregnancies. The current rate of births to people with major disorders such as schizophrenia or affective disorders is rising, and there are indications that this birth rate may begin to resemble that of the general population (Judge, 1994). Nicholson and Blanch (1994) report that in the New York State Office of Mental Health Intensive Case Management Program for severely mentally ill adults, 40% of women clients under the age of 35 have children under the age of 18. They cite similar findings from other agencies. The authors point out that these figures apply only to clients needing substantial public support and undoubtedly underestimate the actual frequencies of people with mental illness who are reproducing or caring for children.

When mentally ill persons become parents and are able to keep their children, they become primary rearing agents; but in many cases, their parents or other relatives must assume at least part of the childrearing burden. In some families, a grandmother may be raising the offspring of her mentally ill child who may wax and wane in his or her parenting capabilities. In this scenario, the grandmother fulfills a dual caregiving role. She is both roof and foundation of a shaky house, and as she ages, the edifice may become ever more vulnerable to stress. Yet the three-generational pattern is only one scenario. The mentally ill child may marry, there may be siblings, and the child will grow.

Sexuality and parenting are key elements of existence. They are particularly salient in the lives of people who are deprived of other rewards and who seek meaning and intimacy in life. For many individuals with mental illness, having a child may provide instant identity and a valued social status. They shed the identity of mental patient and assume that of mother or father. They modify their role as dependent adults by nurturing beings more dependent than themselves. Parenting may offer emotional security, purpose in life, and alleviation of loss. Apfel and Handel (1993) note that for men with long-term mental illness, procreation may be a concrete manifestation of male virility. Producing a child may convey a sense of potency and generativity to persons who have suffered great psychological blows to their self-esteem.

Above all, parenting fulfills basic human needs for love and nurturance. Turner (1993), a mentally ill mother, recalls the desire to have a family of her own in exactly those terms. She also points out,

> Having children can provide motivation to recover. Having a family can give one a needed feeling of belonging and an impetus to acquire the skills needed to become functioning in society. Having a mentally ill parent does not preclude a child's having a good and nurturing relationship with that parent. (p. 650)

Nevertheless, parenting also brings demands that are stressful for even the most intact individuals. They may prove overwhelming for persons with the vulnerabilities of a major mental illness. Formerly, state welfare systems were probably too quick to step in and remove infants from the custody of their mentally ill mothers or fathers. Today, with considerable therapeutic resources for stabilization and greater emphasis on patients' rights, many more parents with psychiatric disabilities are able to keep their children with them. Yet there is little evidence that the treatment system offers help with this stressful and most socially important task. Nicholson and Blanch (1994) note that parenting issues are largely ignored in the rehabilitation literature. They also give this caution: "Since people will continue to have children with or without support, lack of attention to these issues may also place numerous children at risk for developmental and psychiatric difficulties" (p. 110).

In a national survey of state mental authorities conducted in 1990, only two states—Nebraska and South Dakota—reported that parenting skills were assessed or included in public sector rehabilitation services for the mentally ill. In the study's second phase, data were collected on 69 programs in 19 states. Only nine of the programs focused specifically on the needs of mentally ill mothers and their children. Of these, only two focused on rehabilitation of the parent with mental illness (Nicholson, Geller, Fisher, & Dion, 1993).

This need is now beginning to be addressed in the literature. Nicholson and Blanch (1994) outlined a model of effective rehabilitation for parental roles. This begins with an assessment of strengths and weaknesses based on legal standards regarding parental competence. Although state statutes vary, most involve a parent's ability to meet the child's minimal needs for food, clothing, shelter, safety, and a stable environment. Each of these criteria can be evaluated. Aspects of how the mother relates emotionally to the baby and how well she is able to learn from instruction and demonstration can also be assessed. The professional in the hospital setting can determine supports that the mother will have available and resources that can be tapped after discharge.

Basic parenting skills are an essential component of rehabilitation of the mentally ill parent. Nicholson and Blanch (1994) point out, however, that parent training skills are not enough because they may be compromised by facets of the illness. In schizophrenia there is a diminished capacity to respond to social cues, especially nonverbal communication. A person with bipolar disorder may have damaging mood swings. Psychotropic medications may affect the parent's expressiveness or spontaneity. Parents must be able to monitor and manage their own symptoms, recognize prodromal signals of decompensation, and have a reliable back-up system to ensure the well-being of the child.

Nicholson and Blanch (1994) point out, too, the need for social relationships and support networks. Interventions should include arrangements for babysitting and child care, both for respite and in the event of rehospitalization. They also emphasize the need to train parents how to explain their mental illness to their children. They note that in contrast to the extensive literature for patients on job-seeking and how to talk to an employer, there is virtually nothing on how to talk to one's own child about parental mental illness. Fortunately, this is beginning to be rectified by the publication of special storybooks targeted specifically to the children of mentally ill parents (e.g., Laskin & Moskowitz, 1991). Yet few clinicians have been taught how to communicate unpleasant realities to children themselves, let alone how to teach such techniques to parents.

Sexuality and reproduction among persons with mental illness are value-laden issues and they can elicit many negative psychodynamics from mental health professionals. Apfel and Handel (1993) point out that persons with mental illness seek to lead as normal a life as possible, and there is often a clash between patients' wishes to be normal and therapists' perspectives of pathology. Treatment staff tend to become angry at patients who become pregnant or who impregnate others and are protective of the unborn baby. Their own negative emotions may exacerbate the patient's already fragile state. Clinicians can be enormously useful if, in addition to their psychotherapeutic role, they are able to present clinical information on medication use during pregnancy, on prenatal and post-partum care, and on parenting techniques.

In this section, we have briefly considered how adults with mental illness experience their life cycle roles in relation to other kin. The literature indicates that in addition to symptoms and functional disabilities, certain types of psychodynamic issues may arise in specific role relationships in terms of the phases of illness. In the following chapter, we discuss these relationships from the other side of the mirror. The responses of caregiving kin are viewed in terms of their role relationship within the life cycle of the family unit and the phases of illness.

8

Caregiving During
the Family Life Cycle

The Life Cycle of the Caregivers

From the perspective of family caregivers, Rolland (1994) suggests a psychosocial typology of illness in terms of onset, course, outcome, and degree of incapacitation. Although he focuses on chronic physical illness, his typology is germane to the major chronic psychiatric disorders. The course of a chronic illness can take three general forms: progressive, constant, or relapsing-episodic. In a progressive disorder, such as Alzheimer's, there is increasing strain on family caregivers caused by exhaustion and by the continual addition of new caregiving tasks over time. A constant-course illness is more stable and predictable. Relapsing or episodic illnesses require a flexibility that can be extremely taxing.

> In a sense, the family is always on call to cope with crises and handle exacerbations of the illness. Both the frequency of transitions between crisis and noncrisis and the ongoing uncertainty of when a crisis will next occur produce strain for the family. Also, the considerable psychological discrepancy between periods of normalcy and periods of illness is a particularly taxing feature unique to relapsing chronic diseases. (Rolland, 1994, p. 27)

Although Rolland was writing about such diseases as spinal disc disorders or multiple sclerosis, the description aptly applies to schizophrenia as well. In this case, the symptoms may involve delusional threats or property destruction. The psychological swing between a cooperative and loving family member and one who is actively disruptive can be extremely disturbing to caregivers. An overview of the research on families

95

and depressive illness similarly shows that family functioning may differ substantially during acute depressive episodes and periods of remission. Coping strengths may be eroded during the acute time phase, however, and problems may continue after remission of depressive symptoms. The duration of the acute episode is also related to impairment in family functioning (Keitner et al., 1990).

Rolland (1994) further discusses the interrelationships of the time phases of illness with *centripetal* versus *centrifugal* periods in the family life cycle. Centripetal periods pertain to family developmental tasks that require intense bonding and cohesion, such as early child rearing. Centrifugal periods, when children are grown, require less cohesion. It is in these periods that members feel free to try out new careers or autonomous roles. Rolland notes that when the onset of an illness coincides with a centrifugal period, it can derail the family.

> A young adult becoming ill may need to return to the family of origin for disease-related care. Each family member's extrafamilial autonomy and individuation are at risk. The young adult's initial life structure away from home is threatened temporarily or permanently. Parents who have recently shifted away from a childrearing focus may have to relinquish new pursuits of their own outside the family. (Rolland, 1994, p. 109)

Because major mental illnesses, such as schizophrenia or affective disorders, typically emerge in late adolescence or early adulthood, their onset inevitably conflicts with a centrifugal period in the family life cycle. However, as Marsh (1992) notes, conflict also arises when a centripetal period in the family life cycle intersects with the centripetal demands of childhood mental illness. In this case, young parents may have little energy for the marital relationship or for other family members. In midlife, the emergence of serious mental illness in a young adult conflicts with the centrifugal needs of parents to pursue their own interests or renegotiate personal and marital issues.

> The main task of family life, which is the launching of children into the adult world, may never be completed. Adult-to-adult relationships with grown children may never be realized. . . . Parents may long for an "empty nest" that never arrives, and for the freedom and independence that are expected to characterize middle and late adulthood. (Marsh, 1992, pp. 68-69)

In late adulthood, the problems of caregivers may be even greater. Increasing numbers of older mentally ill adults, some in their 40s and 50s, are living with their aging parents. Studies done of National Alliance for the Mentally Ill (NAMI) families reveal that 85% or more of the known caregivers were parents, primarily mothers, most in their late 50s to 70s (Lefley, 1987a; Skinner et al., 1992). In the latest study—a stratified national sample of 1,401 NAMI family members—73% of the mentally ill consumers were children of the caregivers, 69% sons and 31% daughters, with a mean age of 37 years. Forty-two percent lived with their families. The modal pattern in these families was of an aging parental caregiver, typically the mother, taking care of a mentally ill son approaching middle age (Skinner et al., 1992). The issue of aging caregivers is discussed in greater detail in the pages that follow.

Psychological distress in caregivers seems to accompany each stage of the relative's illness but the source and nature of the distress seem to vary as a function of the developmental level and stability of treatment. Research demonstrates that the stress of first-episode psychosis can evoke high levels of anxiety and depression in 75% of a sample of caregivers (Scottish Schizophrenia Research Group, 1985). In a sample of caregivers of clinic attendees, the measured psychological distress rate (anxiety, depression, and insomnia) was 36% (Oldridge & Hughes, 1992). The authors point out that this rate is twice as high as the general population norms for the same measures. They suggest, however, that caregivers of recent-onset sufferers are often caused great stress by their relatives' positive symptoms. In the case of long-term clinic patients, the stress is caused by less pernicious negative symptoms to which caregivers may have become accustomed. Oldridge and Hughes (1992) also suggest that a chronic clinic sample may be a selected subgroup, more stable and compliant, and present fewer problems to caregivers than clients who have infrequent contact with services.

Caregivers' reactions to their role and to their mentally ill relative, both positive and negative, are a function of both their kinship relationship and their relative's personal characteristics and illness history. The relatives may represent very different populations. The child of a mentally ill parent relates to an individual who has been intact enough to mate, maintain a marital relationship, and produce offspring. A sibling or parent is likely to remember someone who has decompensated in adolescence. Caregiving burden may be considerably reduced depending on the social supports and resources available in the form of a mate, siblings, or other relatives willing to share in the process. Caregiving stress also varies as a function of physical energy and other role demands concordant with the caregiver's age or a particular stage in his or her life cycle.

AGE OF CAREGIVERS AND FAMILY BURDEN

Parental caregiving for dependent, dysfunctional adult children in later years is clearly a social problem in an era of deinstitutionalization and inadequate community residential services. Many parental caregivers have now reached the period of risk for geriatric illnesses and maladjustment disorders of old age. Lefley (1987a) reported on parameters of family burden and risk factors among aging parents of adult mentally ill children, including the pervasive worry about what would happen when the parents were gone. As indicated previously, other studies show that in some families, caregiving burden may be counteracted by help and companionship from the mentally ill child in the older years.

From a life cycle perspective, the relationship of family burden to the process of aging is an unresolved issue. At least four major studies have found persistence of family burden and elevated levels of psychological distress over time (Lefley, 1987a). However, time is colinear with advancing age of both parents and children, and the cited studies deal with relatively short periods of time during the total course of illness. The literature may be reflecting relatively brief periods of distress that are temporally associated with age rather than lifetime patterns of dealing with mental illness.

The hypothesis that caregiver distress may increase with caregivers' age has been tested in a number of studies. In Gamache's (1989) study of 164 parents of mentally ill adults, there were two major dimensions of burden: care and control. Care involved assisting the mentally ill person with everyday activities of living, whereas control issues involved supervision and management of troublesome behaviors. When Gamache looked at age alone at the bivariate level, she found a significant effect contrary to the hypothesis: the younger the parents, the greater the burden. When the data were controlled for the effects of the ill member's age and sex, the parent's sex, and coresidence, however, there was a change in direction, and parental age did seem to be related to higher levels of burden. Gamache noted that the patient's behavioral problems were significantly related to family burden levels but these problems decreased as mentally ill family members grew older. In another study of parents residing with offspring disabled by severe mental illness, Cook and Pickett (1988) found that parents of offspring who were older, nonminority, and female reported a higher degree of burden than did parents whose children were younger, African American or Hispanic, and male.

Multiple variables confound a simple age-burden relationship. At a minimum, these include length of illness, level of functioning, symptomatology, and behavioral problems of the adult child as well as the psychological capacity of individual parents to deal with stress. Taking these variables into account, we have postulated a number of conflicting but plausible hypotheses about parental age and measures of family burden, as assessed on the Thresholds Family Burden Scale (see Cook, Lefley, Pickett, & Cohler, 1994). This factorially derived measure of burden is described more fully following the hypotheses.

Hypothesis 1. There is a positive linear relationship: Burden increases with age. This is based on the premise of unchanged or deteriorated functioning of the mentally ill relative, decreased capability of caregivers to meet the demands of illness over time, or both.

Hypothesis 2. There is a negative linear relationship: Burden decreases with age. Burden is highest during the early years of the illness. This is a period of acute psychotic episodes, unrealistic parental expectations for speedy recovery, and frustrations in negotiating the mental health system. Families are bewildered, confused, angry, and fearful because of lack of information and guidance and are destabilized by the dramatic change in their lives. Families still remember clearly the premorbid personality and are frantically seeking a cure. After 5 to 10 years of illness, unrealistic expectations diminish. Psychological burden decreases as parents enter the stage designated as "recognition of chronicity" by Tessler, Killian, and Gubman (1987). They begin to accept the situation and revise their career aspirations for their child.

Hypothesis 3. There is a U-shaped curvilinear relationship. As indicated in Hypothesis 2, anxieties about the illness and frustrations with the mental health system may be highest in the early years of illness. With rehabilitative treatment, the mentally ill family member's functional level may improve with a commensurate decrease in behavioral problems. The system may provide alternative residential and treatment programs that will alleviate parental burden. There is a plateau during the parents' middle-aged years as they become resigned to a less-than-ideal but manageable life for their mentally ill offspring. The parents and siblings have learned coping strategies and may enter a stage that Tessler et al. (1987) label "belief in the family's expertise."

Burden begins to rise, however, as siblings disperse and parents enter the older years. From the late 50s on, the caregiver begins to experience growing disability and fears about the patient's future "when I am gone" (Lefley, 1987a). Indeed, "worrying about the future" is the final stage in the nine-stage model of family response developed by Tessler et al. (1987). These elements of burden, elicited by open-ended questions, cannot be measured with instruments that focus only on care and control dimensions as outlined by Gamache (1989). The parents may no longer provide care with everyday activities, nor are behavioral problems likely to be as salient as when the patient was younger. Here we need parental measures of psychological adjustment, specific future concerns, and, if possible, health status. As indicated earlier, both psychological and physical health status are clear issues of concern and they are likely to be even more salient in the case of elderly caregivers.

Hypothesis 4. There is an inverted U-shaped curvilinear relationship. Even though the early years may include acute psychotic episodes and their sequelae, family burden is lower while there is still hope, before the years of dependency and multiple hospitalizations have set in. Burden rises and is most acute during the parents' middle years, when they have to cope with caregiving and with deficits of the mental health system. At the same time, middle-aged parents may have multiple obligations to their other children and perhaps to their own aging parents. Adult siblings may require financial aid for education, buying homes, or sustenance. Divorced offspring may return home to live. Frail elderly parents may require physical or financial aid or nursing home placement.

With time, burden diminishes as other life problems are resolved. Siblings graduate, pursue careers, and may be able to contribute financially. Caregivers' elderly parents die, and former obligations are dissolved. In the caregivers' old age, the mentally ill adult child may be a help and social resource for companionship (Bulger et al., 1993; Greenberg et al., 1994).

Cook, Lefley, Pickett, and Cohler (1994) tested these hypotheses by exploring four possible types of statistical relationships between level of caregiving burden and parental age. In addition to parents' age, the research included the effects of length of illness and functional impairment of the mentally ill offspring and the parents' psychological strength. Demographic characteristics that had been found important in prior studies, such as offspring's gender, parent's gender, educational level, and ethnicity, were used as control variables.

The sample included 222 parents (mean age 55 years) of 134 offspring with severe mental illness. The ethnic distribution included 17% minority families. Offspring had a mean age of 26 years (72% sons and 28% daughters) and an average illness length of 6 years. The Thresholds Parental Burden Scale (Cook, 1988; Cook & Pickett, 1988) was the major burden measure, along with two widely used psychological adjustment scales.

Measures of burden were derived from a factor analysis of the Thresholds Scale. Items were separated into two pools according to whether they assessed emotional involvement (emotional and cognitive strain resulting from ongoing involvement with the ill child) or behavioral conflict related to caregiving responsibilities. Emotional involvement factors included *connection* (feelings of ongoing connection to the mentally ill offspring and to her or his needs), *cognitive* (mental preoccupation and constant worry about the offspring), and *responsible* (perceptions of ongoing and ultimate responsibility for the well-being of the adult child). Analysis of the behavioral conflict items also identified three factors. These were *behavior* (the child's behavior made the parents feel out of control and unable to manage the illness), *disagree* (critical comments and indications of familial discord regarding the mentally ill member), and *future* (concern about whether the illness would recur and about what the future would hold for the mentally ill offspring).

A test of the U-shaped and inverted U-shaped curvilinear hypotheses indicated that age was nonsignificant in each of these models. Linear analysis indicated significant correlations for parents' age and two of the six outcome measures of burden. Older parents scored significantly higher on the responsible measure, and age fell just short of significance in predicting the cognitive factor. Contrary to the aging hypothesis, however, younger parents scored significantly higher on behavior, indicating they were more affected by control and management issues. The parents' psychological adjustment scores and years of education, but not age, were significant predictors of the connection and cognitive factors. In this complex design, other variables, such as offspring's functioning and ethnicity, were also predictive of some emotional involvement factors and may be further studied in the published research (Cook et al., 1994).

The results for the three types of burden representing personal and familial conflict were also interesting. Parents' psychological adjustment and age were significant predictors of conflict, although younger parents were more troubled by their offspring's behavior than were older parents.

Parents' psychological adjustment and ethnicity and offspring's illness length and gender were also significant predictors.

The authors concluded that some aspects of burden are related to the developmental stage of the illness, regardless of the age of the parents. Thus families that have been dealing with the illness longer are at increased risk for burden related to conflict over illness management. Methods of managing disagreements over who will assist relatives in later years are specially needed. They suggest refresher courses in conflict management and problem-solving techniques over the course of illness.

> The results also suggest that specific components of family burden may be related to the developmental stage of the illness in conjunction with the age-defined life-course of the parents. One implication of this finding is that psychoeducational family interventions should be designed for different stages of the illness and different ages of parents. For example, concern over ongoing responsibility was more difficult for older parents and for those whose offspring had been ill for shorter periods of time. Parents who confront the onset of illness later in life may benefit from an intervention approach emphasizing reeducation about mental illness etiology and community treatment, since their knowledge about psychiatric disorders may be outdated. . . . Parents whose offspring become ill in their childhood or teenage years may need interventions targeting substance use and behavioral management, problems characteristic of the young adult cohort of persons with mental illness.
>
> The major implication of these findings is that burden does not increase in a simple linear fashion as parents and their offspring age. Instead, some types of burden appear to abate as parents grow older, while others seem to intensify. [Moreover,] the effects of age and illness length are to some extent independent. Such a finding supports the use of a life-course theoretical perspective on coping with severe mental illness in a relative. (Cook et al., 1994, p. 446)

FAMILIAL ROLE RELATIONS DURING
THE LIFE COURSE OF MENTAL ILLNESS

Parental Caregivers:
Marital and Single Parent Issues

Cook's (1988) research on parental caregivers indicates that mothers show significantly more measurable emotional distress (anxiety, depression, fear, emotional drain) than do fathers, with controls for parents' education, ethnicity, age, and their offspring's length of illness and gender. Applying a feminist perspective, Cook maintains that mothering is a role of central, crucial importance to most women, that women's behaviors and thought are influenced by their primary role as child caretakers, and that societal and clinical attributions lead to greater emotional investments of females in the caregiving role.

Another study, by Cook, Hoffschmidt, Cohler, and Pickett (1992), found that factors influencing marital satisfaction among 131 parents of adult offspring with severe mental illness included the parents' ability to comfort one another, parents' gender, number of offspring, family income, and interpersonal sensitivity. Mothers-wives reported lower level of marital satisfaction than did fathers-husbands. The authors point out that this is the same as in "normal" population samples, although here it could be attributed to the more burdensome maternal role in caregiving. Concordant with normative data also, income level was positively related to marital satisfaction. In contrast to normative research, however, satisfaction increased with the number of other children in the family. The authors suggest that when parents have other offspring on whom they can base their evaluations of themselves as parents, they are able to be more satisfied with themselves and avoid making unrealistic demands on the disabled offspring.

A study of burden of care by Carpentier, Lesage, Goulet, Lalonde, and Renaud (1992) found that single mothers were specially vulnerable to stress, most often lacked resources, were less likely to have the energy to gather information about the illness and about available assistance, and were less able to be a support to the patient.

Parents who shoulder the responsibility alone are more likely to feel depressed and hopeless and to suffer burnout. The special burdens of a single head of household trying to deal with a mentally ill adult child, balance responsibilities to siblings, and maintain economic as well as psychological stability are poignantly described by Backlar (1994), Deveson (1991), and many others. Single parent caregivers have no mate with whom to share the burden and often feel they cannot make demands on their other children. They try to keep the family's life as normal as possible, to integrate the mentally ill child into family life, and to keep a positive relationship going between that child and the other siblings. Often this fails, and in addition to being the sole financial and emotional support of the mentally ill child, they must contend with increasing alienation from their other children as the latter try to distance themselves from a difficult home situation. The single caregiver may also become the target of the anger and frustration of the child with mental illness. Estroff, Zimmer, Lachicotte, and Benoit (1994), citing their own and other research findings, state categorically that "households that include a mother and adult child are at higher risk for violence, especially if there is no other parent present" (p. 677).

The multiple roles that the single parent is forced to play generate both physical and emotional distress. Yet in some cases, the psychological burden of the single parent can be less than that in two-parent families. When families are uneducated about mental illness and unprepared for its many responsibilities, conflict is almost inevitable. Many couples, particularly those who have absorbed naive beliefs from the popular media, are likely to feel that someone in the family caused the illness—usually the other parent. This conviction may even have been reinforced in interactions with mental health professionals. Many couples respond with mutual blaming and recrimination. Separation and divorce are high risks among parents of persons with major mental illnesses. Too many marriages are dissolved because of ignorance about causes, displacement of rage, need to find reasons in human agency, and attrition of energies needed to meet the demands of caregiving.

Spouses as Caregivers

Spouses must cope with mental illness while negotiating their own life cycle responsibilities. They are younger than most parental caregivers but likely to have the role of parent as well as spouse, with competing demands on their time and attention. Meanwhile, they have their own needs for career development and self-actualization as a productive member of society. For women, even under the ideal circumstances of thriving children and a cooperative spouse, personal career fulfillment is often difficult. When a spouse becomes mentally ill, personal goals may become unattainable.

During the family life cycle, a marriage must contend with numerous stressors, but the presence of a supportive mate typically provides a protective shield in negotiating normative life transitions (McCubbin & Figley, 1983) as well as catastrophic events (Figley & McCubbin, 1983). With mental illness in a spouse, there is reversal of source and solution. There is often a loss of companionship and intimacy that might formerly have carried the couple through difficult life situations.

Judge (1994) notes that well spouses of persons with chronic conditions experience many losses. Similar to parents and siblings, spouses may suffer the transformation of the beloved person with attendant feelings of grieving and loss. The cognitive impairments, functional limitations, and displaced rage that often accompany serious mental illness may result in severe behavioral problems that are difficult to deal with and to explain to young children. Research by Gubman, Tessler, and Willis (1987) found no differences between spouses and parents in the most troublesome behaviors eliciting family complaints. These included bizarre or inappropriate behavior, temper tantrums, failure to perform household chores, and failure to socialize with friends. Judge points out that the lack of friends may deprive the caregiver of respite and evoke sadness for the loneliness of the mentally ill spouse. In addition, the couple or the entire family may suffer increasing social isolation because of the behaviors or stigma of mental illness.

Because spouses with severe mental illness are typically unable to work and earn income at their former level of productivity, the family may suffer dramatically altered changes in lifestyle. We have noted previously that contemporary gender roles may differentially affect husbands and wives of mentally ill spouses. Wives may have to become the financial mainstay while continuing to fulfill homemaking and childrearing responsibilities, whereas husbands typically look elsewhere for substitute caregivers to fulfill these roles. Either change will have a psychological effect on the caregiver as well as on the mentally ill spouse.

As Judge (1994) notes, individuals grow with and through their relationship with a spouse or life mate. The erosion of this relationship can mean that the well spouse now has no one to confide in or with whom to share feelings and thoughts. There may also be reluctance to share intimate concerns for fear of upsetting the person with mental illness. Well spouses also tend to hide their dilemmas from family and friends. This creates increasing isolation and erodes the coping strengths of persons with crucial needs for social support.

The burdens of well spouses are increased when there are children in the home. The needs of the ill spouse, rather than those of the children, become the focus of concern (Noh & Avison, 1988). Children's needs for explanations of their parent's illness, for personal support, and for continued stability are difficult to meet when the well spouse is drained of energy, is confused and bewildered by the turn of events, and has received no information or support from the spouse's therapist.

Judge (1994) notes that there is inherent role strain when the roles of parent and spouse conflict. Conflicts inevitably arise because of the eventual imbalance of marital roles. The well spouse is placed in the double bind of trying not to infantilize the ill husband or wife while compensating for his or her limitations. Fadden et al. (1987) found that almost half the spouses of persons with affective disorders came to view their mate as another child in need of supervision. This mutation of the adult role is compounded when sexual problems arise because of side effects of medications or because of loss of libido on the part of either spouse.

Role Relationships and Diagnosis

In working with families of persons with mental illness, support groups of the Depressive and Manic Depressive Association are likely to be composed predominantly of spouses, whereas AMI support groups are more likely to have parents of adult mentally ill children. The commonality of problems shared by persons with a mentally ill spouse is typically more important than diagnosis. Yet with manic depressive disorder, there are very special problems connected with the profligacy and overspending so typical of the manic state. In family support groups, spouses of persons with bipolar disorder have reported cycles of impoverishment and the need to rebuild the financial life of the family. There are cases of a spouse literally giving away the store and the family being forced to recoup losses and replenish their fortunes. Preventive efforts, such as keeping all resources in the name of the well spouse or restricting access to a credit card, make life difficult during periods of remission, and these efforts are sometimes rejected. Marital strife is almost inevitable under these circumstances.

Judge (1994) points out that, in contrast to the advisable separation of mentally ill adults from their parents, maintenance of the spousal relationship means that the individuals must continue to reside together in the same home. The options for spouses are difficult when in-home care exceeds their physical, financial, and emotional resources. Yet separate households are threatening and often not feasible. Fadden et al. (1987) report high separation and divorce rates when a spouse has a serious mental illness. They note that despite the fact that one-third of their own sample of well spouses felt they could not continue the relationship, few had asked for professional help for themselves.

Not too long ago, interactions with professionals were likely to have been as damaging to husbands or wives as to parents. Lefley (1990c) reports the case of an overburdened young wife trying to keep the family together and being informed by her husband that "my shrink thinks you have a need for me to be sick. He thinks you get something out of my symptoms" (p. 133). John Nash, a winner of the 1994 Nobel prize for economics, suffered from schizophrenia and was hospitalized many times during the 30 years following the brilliant dissertation that earned him the prize. After his pioneering work on game theory at age 21, Nash was unable to contribute further to the field. When Nash was hospitalized at a prestigious institution during the heyday of psychoanalysis, his breakdown reportedly was attributed to his wife's pregnancy. Although the pregnancy may indeed have been a stressor, Nash's sister and a friend recalled, "It was the height of the Freudian period—all these things were explained by fetus envy" (Nasar, 1994, pp. 3-8). Nash was expected to improve after the baby's birth but received no help from psychodynamic treatment and instead progressively deteriorated.

Unfortunately, practitioners have been unconcerned with the psychological effect of such theories on the wife, and later, the child. Imagine the feelings of a wife who is seen as the precipitant of her husband's schizophrenia. Consider the distress of being the unwitting source of the destruction of the brilliant career and potential contributions to mankind of a husband-father whose laureate was given for work performed over 40 years in the past. Consider the guilt of the decision to divorce such a man when one can no longer endure living with schizophrenia.

The decision to dissolve a marriage because of mental illness may be agonizing and prolonged, involving tremendous ambivalence. As Judge (1994) points out, such a decision often results in residual guilt and heartache for the well spouse who takes this final step. The following case is rather typical.

A young wife with a 2-year-old baby had endured the severe mental illness of her husband since shortly before the child was born. She felt that her love and support would enable him to get well, and she determined to stand by her husband no matter how long it might take. During a 2-year period, she was able to cope with her spouse's multiple hospitalizations and discharges, with his depressed moods and paranoid delusions. Her husband made no attempt to resume his old job or look for work, did not help around the house, and spent much time in bed. He refused to see old friends. He constantly expressed suicidal ideation and she was always fearful when he took long walks at night.

The husband sometimes had paranoid delusions about the baby, saying she had the evil eye and was penetrating his brain. The wife went to work and was afraid to leave the baby at home. She was unable to obtain day care until the child was older and had to make multiple arrangements for baby-sitting. Money was low. Despite adequate aftercare treatment, her husband was gradually changing in mood from apathy and dysphoria to irritability, anger, and irrational recriminations. He became verbally abusive and threatened physical assault. The wife began to be afraid for herself and the baby. After much soul searching, she finally went ahead with a divorce and sought out a psychotherapist.

Much of her psychotherapy dealt with her sadness about leaving the husband she had once loved. She saw herself as abandoning a man who was sick and helpless. She felt overwhelming guilt. She berated herself for having repudiated her marriage vows of standing by her husband in sickness and health. She felt like a bad person who had committed a crime.

Her self-recriminations began to lift slowly when her therapist reframed the issue. The wife sobbed, "His illness took away his mind and his spirit. Then I took away the two people who were most important to him, his wife and his child. He must have felt so abandoned, so alone."

"Yes," the therapist said, "but perhaps he also felt relieved."

At this writing, this young wife, like many other divorced or separated spouses, still sees her husband and gives him whatever support she can. In this respect, she is similar to the role reported for Alicia Nash, the former wife of Nobel laureate John Nash, who allowed him to live in her home and apparently provided space and caregiving after their divorce, despite continuing hospitalizations (Nasar, 1994). A surprising number of divorced spouses, as well as families of mentally ill relatives who died, still come to family self-help groups and to AMI meetings. This is typically to help others and to show their continuing commitment to the cause of mental illness. Most of those who attended support groups or sought professional help have resolved their guilt but the existential sadness inevitably continues.

Siblings of Persons Who Are Mentally Ill

A study of siblings of persons with schizophrenia found that siblings' reactions to the illness reflected three distinct patterns: collaborative, crisis oriented, and detached (Gerace, Camilleri, & Ayres, 1993). The collaborative approach was characterized by ongoing active involvement with the ill sibling, other family members, and mental health providers. There was an attempt to incorporate the ill sibling into regular routines, with a planned approach to care. The subjects' attitudes were accepting and helpful toward all family members, despite subjective distress over the illness. Crisis-oriented involvement was situation-specific. These well siblings reported involvement only when a difficult situation required their participation. They saw their role as one of problem-solving and "helping to calm the family down" (p. 642). In all of these cases, the subjects saw the ill sibling as wielding too much power and their parents as failing to set appropriate limits. In the detached approach, there was indirect involvement with the ill sibling and attempts to create distance from the situation and sometimes with other family members as well. "These subjects assumed indirect roles while simultaneously attempting to extricate themselves from the sibling's life and problems because of the cost to their own growth and well-being" (pp. 642-643). Indeed, some were working out their separation issues in psychotherapy.

Among siblings, fear, shame, and feelings of loss are common phenomena. There are fears of coinheritance or of being "different," like the ill sibling, and fears of inheriting the problem after the parents are gone (Moorman, 1992). Shame and feelings of stigmatization are evoked by the aversive behaviors of the mentally ill brother or sister. Siblings report objective problems of loss of friends, popularity, and reputation. Among many, there is mourning for a well-loved premorbid personality that is now but a dim memory. There are feelings of loss of the brother or sister they knew, of the person he or she might have become, of deprivation of the mentorship of an older sibling. If the well sibling is older, he or she may feel guilty about not having been able to protect the younger or remorseful about past behaviors. "I wondered if somehow I had caused or aggravated her illness by being the oldest—bossy, tomboyish, teasing and making fun of her" (Saylor, 1994, p. 36).

Siblings report resentment of their parents' focus on the ill sibling and conflicts and guilt about their anger. They recall feelings of isolation within the family and deprivations of their own personal needs. They recall wanting to escape the family and run away from the problem.

They also recall fantasizing about discovering miracle cures or compensating their parents for the loss of the mentally ill sibling. Siblings may assume a parental role over the mentally ill brother or sister and over the grieving parents as well. Marsh, Dickens, et al. (1994) have described the dynamic of "the replacement child syndrome." The term characterizes the striving of some siblings to be perfect children to spare their parents more anguish or to make up for the sibling lost to illness. Many become overachievers in an attempt to provide solace, attaining higher degrees and often entering the mental health professions. A study of mental health professionals with mentally ill family members indicated that a disproportionate number had entered the field because of their relative's illness. Among these, siblings tended to be even more angry than parents at their training in theories of family causation. Having experienced the developmental history of the illness, they felt their parents had been unjustly accused and that theorists had little knowledge or understanding of their pain (Lefley, 1987b).

Feelings of guilt are almost always reported by the well siblings. There is guilt for the divergent developmental paths and relative richness of their lives compared with the impoverished fortunes of siblings who once were close. There is guilt for not doing more to alleviate the burden on parental caregivers. And there is guilt for the distancing that frequently becomes a major adaptive strategy as siblings try to fulfill their own destinies (Brodoff, 1988; Group for the Advancement of Psychiatry, 1986; Moorman, 1992; Saylor, 1994).

Two surveys were conducted through the Siblings and Adult Children Network of NAMI. Respondents who lived with the mental illness of a relative through childhood or adolescence reported a range of adverse consequences for themselves and their families. These included (a) disruption of their own normal development, including difficulties in distinguishing "normal" experiences from those that were not; (b) emotional distress (grief, loss, empathic pain); (c) need to deal with symptomatic behaviors, illness-related crises, and stigmatization; (d) altered roles and relationships; (e) identity issues (fear of developing the illness, impaired sense of self); (f) personal risk factors, including depression and anxiety; (g) familial consequences (family disruption and stress); (h) impaired peer and school relationships; and (i) poor academic performance or superachievement at the expense of a personal life. They also reported a sense of having grown up too quickly.

Personal interviews also indicated objective consequences of the illness for the family as a whole. These included the social withdrawal of the family from extended family and friends, frequently moving because of the ill member's paranoid fears, or unwanted caregiving responsibilities (Marsh, Appleby, et al., 1993). Siblings also reported a legacy of impaired ability to trust others or engage in intimacy, premature marriage to escape the family situation, or unhappily choosing not to have children.

Brodoff (1988) gave a first-person account that incorporated an array of emotional reactions and coping strategies typical of the sibling relationship in mental illness. She described the divergent developmental paths of a brother and sister who were very close as young children. The sister (the writer) enjoyed school, friends, and a wide schedule of activities while the brother's life became increasingly constricted and friendless. She described her conscious efforts as a threatened adolescent to distance herself from a loser who was increasingly depreciated by teachers and peers and the guilt generated by her perceived cruelty. She recalled a thankless attempt to include her brother in social activities and how this turned out to be a fiasco because of his bizarre and disruptive behavior. Resenting the parental attention to her brother, she remembered thinking that the only way to get their attention was for her to become sick also. Yet she recollected her panic that the siblings' identities might become entwined and that she, too, might become schizophrenic. And she spoke about the death-in-life mourning process.

> I've missed my older brother with the persistent ache and longing usually reserved for a loved one lost through death. Although grieving for someone who has died is painful, some sense of peace and acceptance is ultimately possible. However, mourning for a loved one who is alive—in your very presence and yet in vital ways inaccessible to you—has a lonely, unreal quality that is extraordinarily painful. (p. 116)

Children of Mentally Ill Parents

Psychological problems in children of mentally ill parents may stem from two interrelated sources: genetic risk factors and the experiential effect of impaired parenting. Assortative mating is a factor in both variables. In studying the offspring of parents with affective disorders, Merikangas, Weissman, and Prusoff (1990) reported that 41% of the couples consisted of dual matings for psychiatric disorders. Numerous studies have shown higher lifetime rates of diagnosable psychopathology and higher rates of episodes of major depression in the offspring of parents with major affective disorders when compared with children in families without illness (Beardslee, 1990).

Beardslee found that parents' affective disorders caused major disruptions in the youngsters' lives. Suicidal thoughts; persistent feelings of worthlessness, guilt, and self-reproach; social withdrawal; and poor school performance were frequently reported. Drake, Racusin, and Murphy (1990) have reported on suicide among adolescents with mentally ill parents and urged proactive interventions with these youngsters when their parents are being treated. Silverman (1989) points out that risk factors such as ineffective parenting, poor communication patterns, and chaotic environments in households of mentally ill parents may be modified by preventive interventions. These should be targeted to stabilize the family, enable the parent to meet the child's needs, and minimize the pathology to which the child is exposed.

There is evidence from the research and self-report literature that children and adolescents feel embarrassed and stigmatized by the mental illness of a parent. Frequently, older children must assume parenting of younger children, a protective role with the mentally ill parent, or both (Marsh, Dickens, et al., 1993). A comprehensive study of 652 children from 253 families with a seriously mentally ill parent found that the following variables affected children's feelings about themselves: chaotic households, verbal and physical abuse, and the children's need to restrain the mentally ill parent to prevent harm to the parent or to themselves or to protect property. There were also at least two variations of behaviors that suggest identification with the aggressor. One phenomenon involved children joining peers to laugh at the bizarre behavior of their own mentally ill parent—allying with the stigmatizers rather than the stigmatized. The other phenomenon involved symptom modeling, mimicking the paranoid or self-destructive behavior of the mentally ill parent (Rice, Ekdahl, & Miller, 1971).

First-person accounts of children of psychotic parents indicate memories of shame, confusion, anger, fear, and even terror. Frequently reported are memories of a lack of trust because of the parent's inability to keep commitments or maintain consistent control of cognition or affect. These negative feelings often alternated with positive memories of love and kindness, making it difficult to integrate good and bad introjects and perhaps establishing the groundwork for what psychodynamic theorists term *splitting* in a vulnerable child. Feelings of being intrinsically bad, both because of the parent's tirades against the child and because of the child's fear of being like the parent, are also reported (Lanquetot, 1984).

When there are well parents in the household, they may be able to counterbalance psychotic behavior by providing support and healthy role modeling. However, in coping with the demands of the spouse's illness, well parents often underestimate the hardships experienced by the children and may provide little explanation of the ill parent's behavior (Judge, 1994). A study of children of hospitalized patients found that all the children displayed stress symptoms. Older children tended to show poor school performance, younger children to show diminished appetite, crying, and attention-seeking behavior. All reported sleep disturbance and feeling different from peers, and almost all manifested social withdrawal (Shacnow, 1987).

Negative memories in first-person accounts typically suggest that the child has paid a deep psychological price for the mental illness of a parent. These are not uniform, however, because there are positive memories also, and the writers for the most part seem to have evolved into productive, well-functioning adults. There are also striking findings of resiliency in the research literature (Anthony & Cohler, 1987; Garmezy & Rutter, 1983). In these studies, positive interpersonal relationships with other adults were protective for children found to be resilient. Other factors contributing to resiliency were temperament, coping styles, positive self-concept, and feelings of control of surroundings. Beardslee (1990) reported on a study of children of parents with affective disorders who demonstrated a remarkable degree of maturity. A core group of well-functioning youngsters (mean age 19 years at second assessment) demonstrated the following characteristics.

> They were deeply aware of their parents' illnesses, had spent a great deal of time thinking about them, and had developed a considerable understanding. They were very clear that they were not the cause of their parents' disorders and not to blame for them. They believed this understanding was crucial in their coping with the parental disorder. The actual disruption of their own lives, which was associated with or was a consequence of parental illness, was the focus of their accounts, rather than the identification of parents' behaviors as sequelae of depressions. . . . They were clearly able to distinguish between themselves (and their own experiences) and their parents' illnesses. (Beardslee, 1990, p. 109)

Beardslee concluded that realistic appraisal, self-understanding, and separateness were psychological qualities associated with resilience of adolescent children of parents with affective disorders.

Factors in resilience are obviously an important target for research because they help to mitigate one of the most important stressors in family caregiving: the presence of vulnerable children and adolescents in the household. We turn now to the literature on the coping strategies developed to deal with family stress.

9

Families' Coping Strategies

Various theoretical approaches to family stress and coping are found in the literature, with schemas for assessing the adaptive capacities of individual families. These models take into account multiple variables, including vulnerabilities, capabilities, strengths, resistance factors, prior strains, competing demands, and management styles in the family's adaptation to stress (e.g., McCubbin & McCubbin, 1989). They offer typologies of familial characteristics, such as hardiness, resilience, coherence, and bonding, that may be crucial to any family's adjustment to the caregiving demands of mental illness.

For our purposes, however, a simpler definition and empirically derived typologies may be even more helpful. Coping has been defined by the pioneering theoreticians Pearlin and Schooler (1978) as "the things that people do to avoid being harmed by life strains" (p. 2). They state that coping behaviors can function to (a) eliminate or modify the conditions that give rise to problems, (b) perceptually control the meaning of the experience in a way that neutralizes its problematic aspects, or (c) keep the emotional consequences of problems within manageable bounds.

This broad-based conceptual framework is valuable for looking at the many tasks that families face in dealing with mental illness. Coping behaviors begin with, but go well beyond, caregivers' interactions with their mentally ill relatives. In fact, caregivers are involved with multiple communities in their struggles to modify problematic conditions, control the meaning of their experiences, and avoid adverse emotional consequences to themselves and their loved ones.

To help their loved one, caregivers may have to cope with the clinical, welfare, social security, legal, and sometimes the criminal justice systems. Caregivers' lives are influenced even more on an indirect basis by specific groups whose activities affect critical domains of the mental health

114

enterprise. One group is composed of service providers, practitioners, and clinical educators who determine the delivery and content of services. A second includes legislators, federal agencies, and mental health planning bodies that determine the parameters, funding, and distribution of services. A third group is composed of the legal community and citizen advocates who guard the civil liberties of persons with mental illnesses. Their work directly affects families' access to help in crisis situations. And last, caregivers' lives are increasingly influenced by the activities of their organized peers and by the evolving movements of primary consumers. The latter groups have become instrumental in providing new channels for coping with stressors at both familial and societal levels.

COPING WITH MENTAL ILLNESS IN THE FAMILY

Stages of Family Response

Both adaptive and maladaptive coping strategies are found in the nine stages of family response to mental illness empirically identified by Tessler, Killian, and Gubman (1987). These stages include the following:

1. Initial awareness of a problem without recognition of symptoms
2. Denial of mental illness
3. Labelling of the patient as mentally ill
4. Faith in mental health professionals, with expectations of quick cure
5. Recurrent crises—episodes of disturbed, aggressive behavior or suicidal attempts
6. Recognition of chronicity
7. Loss of faith in mental health professionals
8. Belief in the family's expertise
9. Worry about the future

The eighth stage illustrates the family's positive coping during much of the life course of the illness.

> After dealing with recurrent crises, living with the patient's problem for months or years, and having disillusioning experiences with professionals, the family members most intimately involved with the patient develop the perception that they themselves are experts. . . . There is sometimes a release during this period, at least some diminution of the family's burden. (p. 11)

During this phase also, some caregivers reassess the situation and are able to derive some gratification from their role, including the perception of strength in adversity. Some feel that coping with mental illness in the family has made them stronger persons, better able to cope with life's trials (Greenberg et al., 1994). This coping strategy is what Carver, Scheier, and Weintraub (1989) call "positive reinterpretation," or reappraisal of a distressful event as a learning or growth experience. This is categorized, however, as emotion-focused rather than problem-focused coping, a way of adapting rather than actively trying to change a situation that might indeed have the potential for alternative solutions.

In this reality-based typology, moreover, coping is not a progressive linear process. Even with positive reappraisal and faith in the family's expertise, it is the ninth stage that taxes the coping capacities of most caregivers. Concordant with our discussion of family burden within the life cycle perspective, the final stage means having to deal with the realities of the future of a loved one after the caregiver dies. Here the Pearlin and Schooler model becomes most germane. Unless there are siblings or other younger relatives willing to take over caregiving responsibilities, the task of modifying problematic conditions and avoiding emotional distress requires a whole process of caregiver education. It involves learning about financial management, entitlement benefits, everything the system has to offer in the way of residential programs or supported living, or all of these.

Terkelsen (1987) offers an evolutionary model of coping that overlaps but expands on the stages identified by Tessler et al. (1987). There are 10 distinct phases of familial response, as follows:

1. Ignoring what is coming, that is, noticing behavioral changes but denying mental illness
2. The first shock of recognition
3. Stalemate, in which the family's help-seeking efforts are obstructed by the patient's denial and recalcitrance
4. Containing the implications of the illness; in this phase, the family attempts to cope using various defensive maneuvers, such as minimization and rationalization, but still maintains optimism and hope

The ensuing phases take the family through recognition of the illness and dealing with the treatment system to a realistic appraisal and decision-making capability. These phases include the following:

5. Transformation to official patienthood
6. The search for causes
7. The search for treatment
8. The collapse of optimism
9. Surrendering the dream
10. Picking up the pieces

In this final phase, the family has learned to place the illness in perspective and effect a balancing of needs.

According to Terkelsen, this involves two interdependent processes. First, the family learns to compartmentalize the illness so that it is perceived as one of many challenges rather than the central problem in the family's life. Second, the family rediscovers activities unrelated to the illness and takes up other interests and concerns. Terkelsen notes the following, however:

> At present the solution is very frequently for one member of the family (the primary caregiver) to specialize in looking after the welfare of the affected person while the rest of the family pursue other interests. In this circumstance, compartmentalization is achieved at the expense of the capacity for redirection in the primary caregiver. (Terkelsen, 1987, p. 165)

To resolve caregiver stress, this author cautions that there is really no good way to bring about meaningful compartmentalization unless the mental health system offers adequate community programming, case management, and residential alternatives, as well as necessary hospital services.

Spaniol and Zipple (1994) offer a more parsimonious model that encompasses practical coping strategies, including ways to affect the mental health system. Their stages are based on a family recovery process that involves (a) *discovery-denial;* (b) *recognition-acceptance;* (c) *coping;* and, finally, (d) *personal and political advocacy.* In a prior paper, I also outlined stages of family response but gave far more weight to advocacy as a proactive coping mechanism. These stages included (a) *coming to terms,* or emotional adaptation; (b) *learning to negotiate and improve the provider system;* (c) *learning how to educate clinicians;* (d) *expanding the self-help networks;* and (e) *taking control of one's life through advocacy and resource development* (Lefley, 1987b).

All of these familial response paradigms follow a course in which denial changes to recognition and a search for causes and treatment, ultimately ending in some active attempt to adapt to living with the illness. All paradigms involve a process of reappraisal, in which families evaluate and come to terms with a situation that can no longer be ignored. Some families remain at the level of emotion-focused coping but a surprising number choose an action-focused coping style that may involve one or more of the following: self-education about mental illness, self-education about the treatment system, self-developed behavioral coping strategies, and, sometimes, joining other families in political advocacy. The stages of family response may thus contain both personal and collective coping strategies with both short-term and long-range benefits for consumers and caregivers.

Personal Coping Strategies

Spaniol and Zipple (1994) studied families who identified areas of concern and coping strategies they had personally used. They also conducted surveys of mental health consumers who identified their own coping needs and made suggestions about how they would like family members to respond when a mentally ill person was in crisis. Practical strategies were offered for dealing with bizarre behavior, aggression, self-destructive and suicidal behavior, social withdrawal, and problems with personal hygiene and grooming. They also discussed methods for eliciting cooperation with treatment and for personal stress management.

From interviews with siblings and adult children, Marsh, Appleby, et al. (1993) revealed a series of strategies that the respondents felt had helped them in coping with their relative's mental illness. "These include cognitive strategies (e.g., learning about mental illness, services, and resources); behavioral strategies (e.g., developing stress management skills); emotional strategies (e.g., seeking personal counseling); and social strategies (e.g., joining a support group)" (p. 29). The researchers also found that many respondents reported that they had not merely survived but had become better, stronger, and more compassionate people—a reaffirmation of the power of positive reinterpretation as a coping response.

Using Social Support

An important coping strategy is caregivers' recognition of the value of social support and their willingness to use this resource. Social support has been considered a strong factor in buffering caregiving stress in mental illness (Potasznik & Nelson, 1984). Research by Jed (1989) found that three aspects of social support for caregivers were significantly correlated with reduced rehospitalization of their relatives. These were (a) a larger number in the support network, (b) a larger number of good advisers, and (c) a smaller proportion of conflicted support. Solomon and Draine (1994a) investigated adaptive coping among individuals with a relative with serious mental illness and found that social support was the major contributing factor. Specifically, adaptive coping was associated with membership in an AMI support group or another support group for families, a larger social network, and more affirmative or respectful support from social network members. *Affirmative support* referred to the extent to which caregivers could confide in others in the social network and receive respect and validation of their ideas. Surprisingly, active instrumental support did not contribute significantly to this model. The authors noted, however, that membership in an AMI support group does offer instrumental ideas and techniques for coping with mental illness in a relative while also increasing the number of potential members of the caregiver's social network.

Joining a family support group is an extremely valuable coping strategy, especially for the isolated caregiver. The group experience provides education, emotional sharing, resource information, and problem-solving techniques. Long-standing members of these groups often develop a social support system that offers companionship and active help in crisis situations. As suggested by the research of Solomon and Draine (1994a) and even more by the multifamily work of McFarlane (1994), their members may become a supportive resource. McFarlane's work demonstrated that multiple-family psychoeducation was superior to individual family psychoeducation. This suggested that supportive elements of the group experience—the sharing, information exchange, and development of friendships—may be similar to those found in informal self-help groups.

There are various models of support groups, however. J. Johnson (1994) has developed an eight-stage model of personal healing for families and friends of the mentally ill. The similarities with 12-step self-help groups are purposive. The author is concerned with the caregiver or family member rather than the person with the illness. Her focus is on personal development rather than on specific problem-solving strategies. The healing stages are as follows:

1. *Awareness.* I explore the ways in which the relationship/family has affected my life.

2. *Validation.*   I identify my feelings and share them with others.

3. *Acceptance.*   I accept that I cannot control any other person's behavior and that I am ultimately responsible only for my own emotional well-being.

4. *Challenge.*   I examine my expectations of myself and others and make a commitment to challenge any negative expectations.

5. *Releasing guilt.*   I recognize mental illness as a disease and release the attitude of blame.

6. *Forgiveness.*   I forgive myself for any mistakes I have made. I forgive and release those who have harmed me.

7. *Self-esteem.*   I return the focus of my life to myself by appreciating my own worth, despite what may be going on around me.

8. *Growth.*   I reaffirm my accomplishments and set daily, monthly, and yearly goals. (J. Johnson, 1994, p. 159)

For some caregivers, J. Johnson's model appears to fulfill a need that is sometimes underemphasized in the sharing sessions of family support groups; these tend to focus on strengthening the family's ability to cope with patients' behavior and to develop decision-making skills that enhance their own lives. Family support groups, however, rarely emphasize the personal growth of the caregivers, who are typically the parents, or delve into the psychodynamic effect of the illness on their personalities and lives. Johnson's model permits this type of self-exploration. It has been particularly effective with NAMI's Sibling and Adult Children Network, the target group of the first edition of her book. Testimony from Moorman (1992), a sibling caregiver, indicates that this model may have significant effect in strengthening individual coping skills and freeing siblings and adult children of guilt.

COPING WITH THE MENTAL HEALTH SYSTEM

Family members have developed strategies for coping with a mental health system that is sometimes viewed as uncooperative and indifferent to their needs. These strategies have mixed effectiveness. Some coping methods seem clearly adaptive, such as collaboration with providers, providing needed input for treatment planning and cooperation in discharge planning. Other coping styles may appear to be maladaptive. If the criterion of successful coping is achieving a desirable outcome, however, some rather strange behaviors are often applied to that end. In fact, one of the reasons that so many clinicians have expressed negative opinions about their interactions with families is that some family members have learned over the years that antisocial or aversive behaviors sometimes accomplish more than niceness or compliance.

Strategies for Obtaining Treatment: Reframing Aversive Behaviors

Why do so many professionals seem to see families at their worst? For one thing, they are likely to interact with families during periods of crisis, which precipitate in most people lowered defenses and patent manifestations of psychological distress. But there may be other explanations as well. In many cases, the family's history of experience with providers has generated expectancies of evasiveness, dissembling, deflection of questions, or attitudinal rejection. We might ask, Do these expectancies produce anticipatory aggressive or demanding behavior in some families to receive answers or services? In other families, does the expected rejection reinforce a tendency to become overly submissive or compliant?

Contemporary clinical education still teaches variant views of etiology, including family pathogenesis. Unlike in previous years, there is a contemporary emphasis on biological factors. Regardless of when or how professionals have been trained, however, there is still a tendency to attribute pathological behavior in the patient to perceived abnormalities in family members. This is particularly likely when medications and psychotherapy seem to have little effect and the patient's symptoms fail to abate. The term *schizophrenogenic mother* is still heard in clinical case conferences, even with laughing disclaimers. Unlike its original meaning, the term may be applied to any parents who display excessive involvement or who are demanding or imperious with staff in their information-gathering efforts.

Unfortunately, clinicians receive almost no training in family burden, and many are insensitive to the trials and stresses of living with mental illness over a period of years. Survey data indicate significant differences between families and mental health professionals in perceptions of families' needs (McElroy, 1987). The tendency to see pathogenesis in families is reinforced when a patient's relatives demonstrate behaviors that are viewed as troublesome by treatment staff. Yet there are often good reasons for these behaviors. In fact, they may constitute adaptive coping strategies that achieve desired objectives for the patient or family. The following behaviors might be considered from that vantage point; they represent a recognizable typology of familial behaviors.

Aggressive Persistence

Families must often be aggressive in pursuit of help. Caregivers need information to fulfill their tasks appropriately. They need information on medications and side effects. They want a diagnosis so that they can go to the library and look up the disorder. They want to know the latest word on treatment modalities. They know they cannot develop appropriate expectations or plan effectively without this information.

Families often have to develop a thick skin to press providers for information or have them share the most innocuous information about a case in which they, the caregivers, have a vital interest. Some families have to be overly demanding, excessively persistent, pull strings, use influence, or appeal to higher authorities to get the information they need. Such relatives are bothersome and universally disliked by treatment staff. But from a functional viewpoint, their behaviors may be far more adaptive than those of more compliant families.

Anger

Angry family members often have a long history of being sloughed off or ignored. They are full of hostility toward those who rebuffed them, took their money, and did not improve the status of their loved one. Resentful at having to use the treatment system that failed them in the past, they may bear anticipatory hostility toward treatment staff. They no longer believe in the efficacy of treatment but have no other options. Many family members who are full of anger are high EE people. They may project their rage against fate or displace their anger toward the patient onto the service system.

It would seem more adaptive to make the treatment system, rather than the patient, the target of one's wrath. This projection may have both negative and positive effects. Some staff may generalize their dislike of the family to the patient. It is more likely, however, that staff will have rescue fantasies about protecting the good patient from the bad family and invest more energies in his or her treatment.

Defensive Humility

These families are defensive. Some have been treated like and feel like pariahs, and they sometimes act unduly humble with professionals. Depending on their level of awareness, they may retreat because they feel ignorant in the face of professional authority or they may assume a low profile to prove they are not intrusive or controlling. These families are likely to be viewed as tractable and compliant but some may appear detached. Staff may be motivated to speak with them and even to offer education to promote a higher level of involvement.

Acting Out

As a variant of identification with the aggressor, some family members may act out to fulfill provider expectations. An ordinarily gentle, nonintrusive woman described to me her interaction with a social worker: "She seemed to assume that I was an interfering mother, and I found myself meeting her needs." Other family members may deliberately act out as a technique for obtaining services. A sibling (S) proudly informed her support group of her strategy for obtaining inpatient services. After a florid psychotic episode, her sister (P) had been treated in the crisis emergency room of the local mental health center. There was a heavy demand for inpatient beds, so the psychiatrist had given an injection of prolixin and okayed P's discharge after a few hours in the crisis unit. On the basis of P's history, S did not believe her sister was stabilized and felt she clearly needed hospitalization.

> I knew they wouldn't do it unless I created a scene. I stood there and screamed that my sister was suicidal, that I would sue them, that I was the only one who cared about my sister and they didn't give a damn. I made myself so obnoxious that they were afraid to send her home with crazy me. So they admitted her.

In that particular case, they not only admitted P but kept her for 2 weeks, effecting legitimate stabilization and giving S a much needed rest.

Guilt as Control of Illness

Some families have subscribed to theories of family pathogenesis because this is the only strategy they have for controlling the illness. Terkelsen (1982) calls this "the magical aspect of the wish to be blamed. . . . If I made it happen, I can make it go away" (p. 183). Guilt can also be a mechanism for controlling the treatment. A father, who typically was calm and nurturant and maintained a democratic atmosphere in his home, described how he suddenly began to bully and order his son around in the presence of his son's psychiatrist. He felt this behavior was concordant with the therapist's expectation of familial culpability. He admitted thinking that he might actually be a domineering father underneath, although his bullying outburst was highly unlike his customary demeanor. But he also felt his unusual behavior was purposive. "I want to believe that I can control this terrible situation. My acting up also provides a rationale for my son's illness in the psychiatrist's eyes. So now maybe he can help him."

It is highly unlikely, however, that this rationale will actually help the patient. Kersker (1994a), a consumer writing about the concept of recovery, warns families about the perils of assuming responsibility for the illness. He states that clients must be responsible for their own behavior, and that family members' guilt takes control and mastery away from those who must act in their own behalf.

"Sabotage"

Sometimes, families will interfere with therapy or remove the patient just when the therapist thinks progress is being made. Progress in psychotherapy typically involves abreaction and often opens the floodgates of unresolved hostilities toward family members. Families do not see progress in the expression of negative feelings. It is humanly difficult to countenance hostility after great struggle and sacrifice on behalf of the patient. Caregivers may refuse to pay further therapy bills out of self-protectiveness or because they view the patient as getting worse rather than better. In many cases, what the practitioner perceives as familial sabotage may be an adaptive response to inept or potentially harmful interventions.

There is no evidence that expression of negative emotions improves the recovery potential of people with schizophrenia. The evidence suggests rather that so-called insight therapy may be countertherapeutic in this disorder (Drake & Sederer, 1986). Psychodynamic and inappropriately applied systemic approaches may raise stimulus levels intolerably, and the evoked reactions may indeed create a chasm between clients and their major support systems. A mother described a situation in which she was paying for private team care. Her son received medication from a psychiatrist and psychotherapy from an allied social worker. The mother is well educated and knowledgeable about psychodynamic therapy. She felt the social worker totally lacked training in working with clients with severe mental illness.

It was a matter of opinion and I felt I was right. The therapist apparently thought she was loosening her client's psychological dependency but actually she was reinforcing his anger and frustration about having to depend on his family for sustenance. My son's behavior became mean and vicious and finally intolerable. I stopped paying for private psychotherapy and sent him to a psychosocial rehabilitation program, where he's doing very well and learning new skills. Now he is really no longer dependent; he has a job!

Fear of Recovery

This is another familial response that requires reframing. Fear of recovery has traditionally been interpreted in terms of the family's need for the patients' symptoms. In this schema, the illness serves to maintain a maladaptive homeostasis. Lacking conjoint therapy, the patient's symptomatic improvement will disrupt that precarious balance and require a painful readjustment of the family system.

There are far more parsimonious explanations for this legitimate fear, much of it based on long experience. Because of the cyclical nature of most major disorders, families have typically encountered periods of remission. With a history of dashed expectations, they may be hesitant to invest hope in the continuity of the symptom-free state. Another basis for fear of recovery is the family's desire to protect the patient from pain—from grief about losses and anxieties about new expectations of performance. A related empirical concern is that the patient will be unable to cope with a new identity that may be fervently desired but anxiety provoking. The return to a premorbid cognitive state or observable improvement in functional level poses demands and frustrations. The person may feel incapable of coping with the new demands, generating an anticipatory failure experience.

Even more poignant is the shock of recognition of status. The delusions, hallucinations, and defensive maneuvers have been replaced by the cold insight that one is a mental patient and that years of life have been lost to this condition. Many families are aware that suicidal attempts occur not only during periods of darkest depression but on the upswing as well.

Emergence from a long period of dysfunction raises tremendous anxieties in individuals now contemplating their ability to assume more normal roles. The dramatic recoveries reported with the new atypical neuroleptics, such as clozapine, have confronted responsive patients with overwhelming new challenges. Many must now cope with the "Rip Van

Winkle" experience of awakening from a dissociated state into an unfamiliar new world. Individuals with long histories of illness have been unable to fulfill valuable developmental stages of learning. There are lost years to be mourned and recaptured. Old patterns of dependency and disability must now be abandoned. New socialization and vocational skills must be learned.

Caregivers may actually have to learn therapeutic techniques for dealing with recovery anxieties. There are other recovery issues, however, over which they have no control. First are pragmatic fears related to the loss of entitlement benefits. With cyclical illnesses, clients have often learned that if their remissions last too long but not long enough, they may pay a heavy price in terms of cut-offs of social security, disability, and Medicaid checks. The system exacts penalties when mentally ill persons fulfill productive roles in competitive employment for too long a period of time. Clients are often unskilled or incapable of full employment and they are subject to the vicissitudes of the job market as well as those of their illnesses. Thus families may be legitimately concerned about the loss of disability status of their loved ones without the presumption of psychological need for their disability.

Rehabilitation programs and supportive therapies may help clients adjust to the demands of these new identities. The consumer movements, with their focus on recovery and self-affirmation, are excellent vehicles for dealing with the challenges of attaining new skills and roles. Families who have been coping with fears for their loved ones and barriers in the service delivery system have been immeasurably helped by the new roles generated through political action and through reeducation of providers and practitioners.

Positive Coping at Individual and Societal Levels

In contrast to some of the reactive and potentially maladaptive coping strategies just outlined, family caregivers are now increasingly called on to aid the therapeutic enterprise in ways that are both efficacious and personally rewarding. This is occurring at both the individual case-centered and societal levels. These new opportunities for active coping are due in no small measure to the growing influence of the family movement, NAMI, and to its multiple initiatives for family-professional collaboration. These developments are discussed in greater detail in the forthcoming section on consumerism.

Caregiver Collaboration
at the Case-Centered Level

Many caregivers have now entered what Spaniol and Zipple (1994) have identified as the final stage of the family recovery process: personal and political advocacy. Personal advocacy may involve collaboration of caregivers in their relative's course of treatment. The extent of this collaboration depends on the openness of a particular provider to participation of the client's relatives in treatment and discharge planning and in case management. Most facilities welcome this involvement because it provides continuity of support and may save their staff many hours of work.

In outpatient settings, professionals' interactions with their patients rarely exceed 1 hour a week and typically are far less. Caregivers who live with their patients are able to observe diurnal rhythms, mood swings, stimuli that seem to precipitate adverse reactions, areas of fear and anxiety, and other behaviors that are germane to the course of treatment. Caregivers can usually recognize prodromal cues of decompensation. Their observations on medication effects and side effects are similarly valuable. More and more, we are seeing willingness of professionals to hear this information with the consent and involvement of the patient.

Confidentiality. In contrast to previous years, psychiatric practice guidelines and some agency policies indicate that they encourage families' involvement in treatment and discharge planning. This means that professionals must find new ways to deal with their fears of breaching confidentiality and disrupting the therapeutic alliance. The need to ask patients to consent to their caregivers' involvement may in itself comprise a therapeutic intervention. There are many ways of asking patients, conferring with them about the boundaries of information and honoring their wishes in ways that will be acceptable to them and to the family. There are some cases in which patients do not want familial involvement; those issues should be explored and the patient's decision respected. Many agencies, however, have a tradition of automatically withholding information as a matter of policy. The need to obtain consent puts the ownership of confidentiality back where it belongs, in the hands of the patients. This is a message of respect and control that is intrinsically therapeutic.

Involving the caregiver in discharge planning is an excellent way to provide training in aftercare and to otherwise ensure that the patient receives and benefits from all the relevant services offered by the local service delivery system. This process also educates family members about the resources available to them for dealing with crises, resolving their own needs, and balancing their multiple responsibilities.

Active Coping at the Societal Level

Some of the most important coping strategies are directed at enhancing our collective potential for knowledge building, systems planning, and social policy change. These efforts have long-range benefits for both consumers and families. It is only by improving the system that much of the pressure of individual case involvement may be relieved. The production of knowledge may lead to more effective treatments or to greater understanding of etiology. It is hoped that it may someday even lead to eliminating or preventing some of the major psychiatric disorders.

The political advocacy efforts of the AMI groups, to which many caregivers belong, are wide-ranging and multifaceted. They are generally for increased funding for programs, resources, and research initiatives, as well as for proper zoning and other types of needed legislative changes in mental health law. Included are mechanisms for ensuring continuing and expanding aid for community support programs, treatment facilities, and residential resources for persons with severe and persistent mental illnesses. There are initiatives for state and federal policies that will provide incentives for developing guardianship and trust programs without jeopardizing financial entitlements of the mentally disabled. Currently, there is lobbying for insurance parity for physical and mental illness, and efforts to ensure that managed care will not short-change the seriously mentally ill population. There are continuing initiatives for provider policies that encourage clear lines of communication with families, incentives for clinical training programs to encourage professionals to work with the chronic population, and public and private initiatives for large-scale funding of basic research on the major mental illnesses.

Through the local affiliates of NAMI, many family groups have already developed rehabilitative resources in geographic areas that previously lacked them. Substantial numbers of caregivers are members of agency governance or advisory boards or serve on local and state mental health planning bodies. Family members monitor and evaluate programs and participate in protection and advocacy efforts. These are massive coping efforts that go well beyond serving the specific needs of a loved one. They extend familial care and oversight to the universe of persons with severe mental illnesses. In the course of these activities, the skills, knowledge base, and self-efficacy of the concerned caregiver are greatly enhanced.

10

Services for Families

Services for families of persons with mental illness are based on both clinical and nonclinical models of intervention (Marsh, 1992). Chronologically, clinical models have included psychodynamic and family systems therapies and, later, psychoeducational interventions. Nonclinical models typically have offered family education, often combined with support groups. These modalities have also been included in various types of psychoeducational interventions administered by clinicians (Goldstein, 1981; McFarlane, 1994). Nonclinical services, however, often go far beyond therapeutic models. They may offer information and mechanisms for accessing resources, for negotiating barriers within the mental health system, or for developing new social support systems for both patients and families. They may even develop coping strategies that enable participants to develop new resources to meet their needs.

Nonclinical educational models largely derive from a paradigm of stress, coping, and adaptation (Hatfield & Lefley, 1987). As Hatfield (1994a) notes,

> The literature on stress and behavior lends itself to explaining the effects of catastrophic events on people's lives and why they react to these events as they do. . . . This point of view tends to normalize the strong reactions of families as something to be expected in the face of their devastating experiences. It precludes the need for pathological explanations for the family's pain and confusion and avoids the use of alienating language. (p. 4)

The normalization of familial response is one of the most comforting aspects of nonclinical family interventions. From many reports, it is both therapeutic and motivating for participants to learn that others have reacted in the same way and to learn the coping strategies that have worked for other families.

PROFESSIONAL SERVICES

According to Marsh (1994b), there has been a pronounced paradigm shift in professional practice with families, from a model of pathology to one of competence. In her view, we have gone from seeing families as pathogenic or dysfunctional to viewing families as basically or potentially competent, from an emphasis on weaknesses, liabilities, and illness to one of strengths, resources, and wellness. The role of professionals has changed from one of practitioners who provide psychotherapy to one of enabling agents who assist families in achieving their goals. The family's role has changed from client to collaborator. Old assessments were based on clinical typologies, new assessments on competencies and competence deficits. The goal of the intervention has changed from treating family pathology or dysfunction to one of empowering families to achieve mastery and control over their lives.

Marsh's statements may seem overly optimistic if we consider both families' assessments and the continued writings of some family therapists in the professional journals. A current study by Biegel, Li-yu, and Milligan (1995) indicates that many families continue to remain dissatisfied about the information and support they receive from professionals. Therapists of the Milan school are still writing about schizophrenia as a "family game" and claiming that manipulations of family process can achieve a cure (Selvini, 1992).

Indeed, it is ironic that although mental illness is a quintessential example of how the dysfunction of one member destabilizes a family system, traditional family therapy paradigms have been ineffectual and in fact counterproductive in treatment. As noted in Chapter 4, which discusses conceptual models, systems-oriented structural and strategic family therapies have largely been abandoned in major mental illnesses. Shaw (1987) has stated that techniques such as systemic, strategic, or structural family therapies have not proved beneficial because they are based on a *replacement* paradigm. This paradigm conflicts with the realities of schizophrenia as a chronic illness and a stress on the family. He points out that families respond much better to psychoeducational approaches, which are based on a *repair* paradigm. The repair paradigm is best suited to treatment of any type of family dealing with a chronic illness, with no presumption of antecedent pathology.

Nevertheless, some strategic family therapists, such as Jay Haley or systemic therapists of the Milan school, continue to work with families of persons with schizophrenia. Haley has been criticized by leading family therapists for his antibiological stance (e.g., Wynne, 1988) and for not providing any research data on outcome. The Milan school has been criticized by prominent family researchers for making unsubstantiated claims of effectiveness, and their model has failed replication efforts in other settings (Coleman, 1987). The telling blow to the efficacy of systemic family therapies in major psychiatric disorders, however, comes from families themselves. Many of them attest to having been harmed rather than helped in their coping efforts (Backlar, 1994; Hare-Mustin, 1980; Hatfield, 1983; Marsh, 1992; and many others).

Psychodynamic family therapies are less frequent than systemic models but family members have often used individual psychodynamic therapy to deal with anger, guilt, or unresolved issues of grieving and loss (Atkinson, 1994). The most common clinical models today, and the ones most concordant with families' expressed wishes, are psychoeducational interventions. In contrast to other models, these have been developed and evaluated as research projects and have well demonstrated their effectiveness in significantly improving patients' treatment compliance and retarding relapse (Lam, 1991; Mari & Streiner, 1994).

PSYCHOEDUCATIONAL INTERVENTIONS

Various psychoeducational models developed in the United Kingdom and the United States were first developed for schizophrenia and brought together by Goldstein (1981). The most prominent models were developed as research efforts by Anderson, Reiss, and Hogarty (1986); Falloon, Boyd, and McGill (1984); Robert Liberman and his associates (Liberman, Cardin, McGill, Falloon, & Evans, 1987; Mueser, Glynn, & Liberman, 1994), and William McFarlane and his associates (e.g., McFarlane, 1994). The psychoeducational model has been widely applied. A contemporary overview of the effectiveness of family interventions revealed 300 citations, permitting a random selection of 69 studies for meta-analysis (Mari & Streiner, 1994). Hatfield's (1994b) latest book on family interventions indicates wide applications of psychoeducational models across cultures, including Australia, Sweden, and India. Even in rural China, a controlled evaluation of psychoeducational family interventions in three townships indicated significantly better clinical and social outcomes in the trial group (Xiang, Ran, & Li, 1994).

Although psychoeducational models are essentially atheoretical, they all draw from social learning, behavioral, and cognitive theory. Although they vary in specific emphases, all have generic components. These include education about the illness, support for families, problem-solving strategies, and illness management techniques. Most focus on schizophrenia, although psychoeducation has also proved beneficial with families of persons with bipolar disorder (Goldstein & Miklowitz, 1994) and major depression (Holder & Anderson, 1990).

In schizophrenia, the educational component typically offers state-of-the-art information on what we know about etiology, diagnosis, psychotropic medications and their side effects, and antiparkinsonian drugs, and on the patient's difficulties with respect to attention, information processing, and stimulus overload. Instruction is provided on the person's likely psychophysiological response to environmental stress and overstimulation. There is an emphasis on the actual experience of mental illness—the hallucinations and delusions of psychosis, the miasma of depression, hypomanic or manic episodes, and the like. The disorder is presented as a biologically based, stress-related illness that leads to multiple problems in living. This includes intimate relationships, work, study, personal care, social and leisure pursuits, and interpersonal transactions with the outside world.

The educational component is intended to reduce guilt, confusion, helplessness, and overresponsibility in the family. In some but not all interventions, families are taught about the dangers of high expressed emotion. Reduction of confusion and guilt, however, typically enables family members to become less judgmental and critical. Family education also includes information on the adverse effects of street drugs and alcohol, on stress identification and control, on an expected slow rate of improvement, and on recognition of prodromal signs of decompensation. Patients are taught to reduce denial and accept their illness but are also encouraged to hope and plan for reasonable improvements. Visual aids, handouts, and diagrams are widely used.

Support and understanding for families are expressed through acknowledgment of the family's agony and burdens, as well as through traditional family therapy techniques of connecting, joining, and reframing. Family strengths are emphasized and maximized, however, and rules and expectation of treatment are established up front. In contrast to the dissembling that underlies some family therapy models, rules and expectations of treatment are specified in a genuine working partnership of families and practitioners.

Although psychoeducational interventions were developed by family systems therapists, there is no presumption of family psychopathology or dysfunction. In fact, low-EE families who have relatives as ill as their peers have sometimes been used as role models for high-EE families (Goldstein, 1981). Social learning paradigms are used to train skills through repeated role rehearsals, modeling, and social reinforcement. Cognitive theory aids in questioning assumptions about the meaning of symptoms or of the illness itself. Behavior modification techniques are widely applied. These include setting limits, time out, token economies, contingency contracting, shaping, and the like. Families are also taught to avoid focusing excessive attention on the patient, which may reinforce the sick role and unintentionally reduce motivation to recover.

Communication training is another basic component of psychoeducation. Families are taught verbal and nonverbal communication skills through repeated role rehearsal, with instructions, modeling, and social reinforcement. In Liberman's and Falloon's approach to nonverbal behavioral training, families are alerted to voice tone and volume, eye contact, and facial expression. The verbal content of the interaction is also emphasized. Family members are taught to reflect empathic listening, keep communication highly specific, simplify content, and avoid excessive delays in expressing both positive and negative emotions (Liberman et al., 1987; Strachan, 1992). In the model of Anderson et al. (1986), communication techniques involve avoiding excessive details or abstractions, describing events without interjecting feelings, accepting responsibility for one's own statements and allowing others to do the same, and making and acknowledging positive messages and supportive comments.

Problem-solving training includes identifying specific family problems or stressors and developing a structured, sequential approach to generating effective solutions (Falloon et al., 1984; McFarlane, 1994). After specifying the problem, a list of potential solutions is generated and evaluated and the most effective is chosen. After the solution is implemented, the status of the problem is reviewed. The important component of problem solving is engaging the entire family in joint planning to identify stressors and help resolve them. This removes the onus of being the sole problem bearer from the mentally ill family members. The process involves patients in identifying problems (which may or may not be related to their own behavior) and engages them in planning and implementing their resolution. In addition to teaching behavioral techniques for problem solving, engagement of patients in a mutual endeavor on a par with other family members is intrinsically respectful of their opinions and therapeutic for all.

A most important question relates to the inclusion or exclusion of patients in family psychoeducation. Families often find it impossible to ventilate their feelings and frustrations in front of their mentally ill relative, and, indeed, this can be harmful to persons who are already vulnerable to stress. Some practitioners resolve this dilemma with separate sessions. On the other hand, the therapeutic benefits of being involved in education and problem resolution with other family members militate against patients' exclusion.

In McFarlane's (1994) research-based psychoeducational model, each session includes a formal problem-solving process involving the patient. His overall approach emphasizes knowledge and coping skills, regulation of the patient's stimulus load, communication techniques, and establishing a clear hierarchy of family structure to facilitate caregiving functions. For professionals, the technical operations in McFarlane's psychoeducational model include assessment and engagement of the family and patient, evaluating the present crisis, eliciting family reactions to the illness and treatment system, evaluating the family and social system, and goal setting. Sessions are structured in phases that proceed from an initial educational workshop to reentry and social-vocational rehabilitation, emphasizing maintenance antipsychotic medication.

OTHER PROFESSIONAL INTERVENTIONS

Although most professional interventions have focused on parents, often with the inclusion of siblings, other models have been developed for other role relationships and for disorders other than schizophrenia. One example is preventive family intervention for children of parents with serious affective disorders (Beardslee, 1990). An intervention featuring specialized social-learning-based marital therapy combined with cognitive therapy has been developed for depressed patients and their spouses (Coffman & Jacobson, 1990).

Marsh (1994) notes that systemic family or marital therapy may be called for when preexisting family or marital problems, such as difficulties in communicating or conflict resolution, have been exacerbated by the circumstances of the illness. Traditional family therapy may also be called for when the family is unable to cope adequately with the mental illness of the family member or successful treatment of one individual requires the involvement of other family members. This author also gives the following caution, however:

> Potential risks of marital or family therapy include reduced autonomy, increased family disruption, loss of privacy, undermining of internal boundaries of family subsystems, and deflection from individual problems and concerns. There are additional risks associated with general prescriptions of family therapy that are based on assumptions of family dysfunction or pathogenesis and that do not take into account the needs, desires, and resources of particular family members. (Marsh, 1994, p. 51)

SUPPORTIVE FAMILY COUNSELING
AND FAMILY CONSULTATION

The risks and assumptions Marsh outlines are specifically eliminated from other clinical interventions, such as Bernheim's supportive family counseling (Bernheim & Lehman, 1985) and the family consultation model of Wynne, McDaniel, and Weber (1986). Bernheim (1994) states that the major goals of family interventions are to reduce familial distress and support the adaptive competencies of family members. The major components are as follows: (a) helping families identify and ventilate painful feelings; (b) normalizing and assisting with resolution of family conflicts; (c) focusing on mastery and competence rather than failure and pathology; (d) helping families with stress-management and problem solving strategies; (e) educating families about the illness, the mental health system, and their role in rehabilitation; (f) helping families develop realistic expectations; (g) teaching warning signs of impending relapse; (h) encouraging family members to reserve time and energy for their own activities; (i) helping family members explore what role they would like to play in rehabilitation and communicating their preferences assertively to the treatment team; (j) referring families to self-help organizations; and (k) maintaining availability for crisis assistance.

In Bernheim's supportive counseling, family members are treated as individuals with their own needs and are given the option of carving out their own roles in the caregiving and rehabilitation process. This is concordant with the model of family consultation. As Bernheim (1994) notes, there are substantive differences between family consultation and a therapeutic model of family interventions. First, family members are presumed competent and to have the right and ability to set a service agenda. "Unlike therapy, in which the therapist generally decides what is best for the patient(s), the family consultant behaves more like an attorney or accountant, laying out options and helping consultees assess the relative merits and risks of each" (p. 189). Bernheim states that power inequities are minimized in consultation, information and hypotheses are shared rather than withheld, and paradoxical and mystifying techniques are never appropriate in the consultative context. And there is no assumption of pathology.

> The family is not regarded as the unidentified patient. Rather, families with mentally ill relatives are assumed to be much like other families. Some cope extremely well most of the time, some cope quite poorly most of the time, and most exhibit coping skills in between these two extremes. Family interactions are conceptualized as a series of more or less adaptive responses to stress. Recognition of the effects of the patients' symptomatic behavior on other family members, as well as the effects on them of social stigmatization, social isolation, the complexity of the mental health maze, financial burden, and long-term caregiving responsibilities, is a prerequisite for adequate application of this model. Although the goal of therapy is to cure illness or at least to ameliorate symptoms, the goal of consultation is to empower and enhance problem-solving in persons who face extraordinary challenges. (Bernheim, 1994, p. 189)

Bernheim also notes that whereas the consultation model always provides education, it differs from a strictly educational model in offering specific advice and problem-solving assistance. Unlike the formal structure and group format of family education, consultation is more informal and focuses on the consultees' immediate agendas. The family consultant may also, of course, refer consultees to either clinical or nonclinical services, depending on the family's needs and desires.

NONCLINICAL INTERVENTIONS:
FAMILY EDUCATION AND SELF-HELP MODELS

Hatfield (1994a) has distinguished between clinical and nonclinical interventions in terms of message and target. Services administered by therapists and educators convey a different message. Despite their acausal model, even psychoeducational interventions may focus on remediation of some pathogenic influence that interferes with patient progress. This certainly characterizes those interventions whose major purpose has been to lower EE, although numerous families who need education do not have problems with high EE. Family education, on the other hand, is intended to increase knowledge. It remedies an informational rather than a psychological deficit.

Perhaps more important is the target of nonclinical services. Clinical services typically focus on what is presumed therapeutic for the patient. The aim of nonclinical services, including family education, is to improve the quality of life of families rather than to prevent decompensation in patients.

Lefley and Wasow (1994) similarly have suggested that the best way of helping families is to view them not as instrumental channels for healing the relative with mental illness but as valid recipients of aid in dealing with highly adverse life situations. The primary agenda should be to help families cope with the existential problems created by the illness. A major argument for family education programs is that they are focused primarily on family needs and not primarily on the psychoeducators' goal of reducing patients' rehospitalization. Although there is a large body of evidence that family psychoeducation indeed can deter relapse in patients, research findings are time limited and there is ample evidence that relapses recur over time (Lam, 1991; Mari & Streiner, 1994). Family education must include the skills for coping with psychoses that are often cyclical in nature and subject to psychosocial influences that are far beyond the family system. Furthermore, families may be taught skills that presumably reduce the probability of relapse, such as lowering EE, but research has also shown that the duration and stability of patients' response is time limited and unpredictable (Lefley, 1992a). Families must also be taught the skills for coping with relapse should it recur.

Various models of family education have been developed, typically by professionals associated with the National Alliance for the Mentally Ill (NAMI). Several of these are models for training trainers who are typically family members well educated in other fields. Dr. Agnes Hatfield, a professor emeritus of education at University of Maryland, devised a training series for NAMI family education specialists in every state, who now form a national network. Hatfield's (1990) book, *Family Education in Mental Illness,* has also become a widely used manual for professionals. Dr. Joyce Burland (1992), a clinical psychologist in Vermont, helped design the Journey of Hope, a 12-session family education course that is now administered in many states by specially trained NAMI members. Dr. Diane Marsh (1994), a professor of psychology at the University of Pittsburgh at Greensburg, developed a 10-week educational program for families. Manuals by Bisbee (1991) and Meisel and Mannion (1989) similarly provide well-designed curriculum materials for educating and teaching coping skills to families of persons with serious mental illnesses.

Most family education programs share common elements. Hatfield (1990) offers a comprehensive model that adds to core content a discussion of learning and instruction approaches as well as information on program development. Her curriculum materials include understanding mental illness (schizophrenia, major mood disorders, and other major disorders), the personal side of mental illness, treatment modalities, creating supportive environments, coping with crisis situations, and planning for the long range. Burland's (1992) Journey of Hope curriculum has specific classes on schizophrenia and mood disorders, including basics about brain biology, genetic research, environmental theories and family blaming, and vulnerability in postpsychotic periods. As in Hatfield's model, there is a session on "inside mental illness" to enable families to gain empathy and understanding of their loved one's experiences and identity problems. Classes also include medication review; problem-solving workshops; communications skills workshops; self-care (dealing with family burden, handling negative feelings, and effecting balance in one's life); psychiatric rehabilitation for patients and families (including new models of family support); and advocacy.

A recent book by researchers Mueser and Gingerich (1994) is a comprehensive hands-on guide for families coping with schizophrenia that covers most of the noted areas, including dealing with special problems such as alcohol and drug abuse. An innovative component is the provision of worksheets and charts that enable caregivers to record their own behaviors, their expectations of performance, and their assessment of their relative's actual ability to fulfill these expectations in ordinary household living. Families are also given step-by-step behavioral instructions for rule setting, establishing limits, and helping their relatives increase motivation and activity.

FAMILY SUPPORT GROUPS

Family support groups are an extremely important element of nonclinical interventions. In a nonstructured way, these provide crisis intervention for families, resource information, exchange of ideas for coping strategies, and above all, the sharing of pain and understanding by others who have lived through similar trials. Some are based on a variant of the AA model and target self-attitude change and personal growth on the part of the family member. J. Johnson (1994), a clinical social worker who pioneered the Siblings and Adult Children network of NAMI, has developed an eight-stage healing process that is now used by many AMI support groups. This model was described in detail in Chapter 9 as a structured coping strategy for caregivers.

Most support groups do not use a structured model, such as Johnson's, for self-healing and for removing emotional encumbrances to rational decision making. Nevertheless, the group process may have a similar effect. As an analogue of the therapeutic alliance that arises between patients and therapists, the support group offers a powerful alliance that often fulfills a need that cannot be met through any other means. This is when a desperate but reluctant parent is given permission by peers to do something that is unthinkable but necessary for survival.

Mrs W., a widow, has finally decided she can no longer live with her disruptive 30-year-old son and, on a meager income, she pays the rent for Don's apartment a mile away. Don stopped taking medications months ago and refuses to see a psychiatrist for medication renewal. He has become increasingly disheveled and irrational. For the past few months, Don has periodically been arriving at his mother's apartment in the early morning at 5:00 a.m. or 6:00 a.m., banging on the door and demanding to be let in. Once inside, he holds her hostage, threatens her, and demands that she fix him meals and give him money. He bars the doors and refuses to let her leave the apartment or even move from room to room. He hangs around watching TV and does not leave until after dinner. Mrs. W.'s only respite is at night. She explains that she cannot afford to refuse him admission. When she has tried this, his banging and threats are so loud that the neighbors have already called the police several times. The police did nothing because he always calmed down when they arrived, but the neighbors remained upset. She is afraid to let Don in but is also afraid that if he continues making noise, she will be evicted from her low-rent apartment. She read about the support group in the newspaper and hopes they can help her.

The families commiserate with Mrs. W.'s plight and suggest that she obtain an ex parte order for involuntary evaluation. She knows nothing about this procedure, so they explain where to get the court order and how to get Don to the clinic. One couple offers to accompany her. They normalize the experience by explaining that they have had to do the same thing under similar circumstances and felt as bad as she does. Mrs. W. admits that she is falling apart from stress but insists she cannot possibly commit her son. One woman tells

Mrs. W. that if she continues this way, she will be no help to Don, and he will end up psychotic and alone. She says, "Sometimes the only way you can be a good mother is to be a bad mother first."

Mrs. W. got the ex parte order. Don was admitted to Crisis and stabilized on psychotropic medication. He spent 2 weeks in the inpatient ward. The support group urged Mrs. W. to speak with the social worker and arrange for a contract as part of the discharge plan. The contract stipulated that Don would visit his mother twice a week for dinner, with the dates marked on a calendar, and that under no conditions would he come without an invitation. Limits were set on the requests that he could make of his mother. Stabilized on neuroleptics, Don kept to the contract, made some new friends at his apartment, and has since reduced his visits to one night a week.

This case illustrates the power of the group, both in providing important resource information and in granting permission for an emotionally difficult act. With both mother and son caught in a pathological spin, Mrs. W.'s action broke the momentum and equalized the balance of power. This provided therapeutic space for her mentally ill son to move on.

When patients are involved in psychoeducational interventions, a certain level of interest and commitment are required. In many cases, families come to support groups when their relatives deny their illness, refuse medications, or otherwise subsist in a decompensated mode. These reluctant individuals are rarely candidates for clinical interventions with the entire family. It is in these cases that the support group most clearly demonstrates its value. Family education on limit setting and behavior management techniques are extremely valuable, but the group consensus and support are often the critical ingredients in helping families cope.

Support groups typically have a variety of participants, of long- and short-term duration. Some families come during a crisis and leave when the crisis has been resolved. Some come and go, appearing on a fairly irregular basis. Others form a core group who come religiously for many years. This core group, typically made up of relatives of chronic patients, has become an extended family. The members know and support each other and they are the old hands who support incoming families.

ADVOCACY AS THERAPY

Although both professional services and self-help support groups may provide invaluable assistance, many families report a sense of frustration after they have resolved immediate problems. They have become tired of sharing and caring, crying and commiserating, ventilating grief and anger, and other emotional concerns. They have learned coping techniques, but the persistence of the illness is still a disturbing element in their lives. They want to advance to a higher level of activity. They want to do something—to eradicate mental illness, to change the system, to provide needed services, to fight stigma, to obtain a better quality of life for their loved ones. It is at this level that participation in an advocacy movement often becomes personally therapeutic as well as socially constructive. Action gives meaning and validity to families formerly preoccupied with tragedy. It changes the central core of their lives from one of misery to one of mission and purpose.

Sometimes, simply joining and participating in a NAMI affiliate can be an extremely therapeutic intervention for depressed or demoralized family members. The activities, the monthly lectures, and the community of caring members may fulfill a long-standing need. When a local affiliate of NAMI held its first anniversary meeting, a member stood up and spoke as follows:

I have had 14 years of experience with doctors, psychologists, psychiatrists, and hospitals. But last year at this time, I was still alone with my problem, totally miserable, and totally without answers. This year, I have finally found out what schizophrenia is and how it is treated. I have heard lectures about social security, mental health law, crisis management, and many other things I always needed to know. Now I have some answers, and if I need more, I know there are people who can help me. I cannot tell you what this means to me. It has given me life and hope. (Anonymous member, Community Alliance for the Mentally Ill, Dade County, Florida)

Research Findings on Family Interventions

Family Psychoeducation

Lam (1991) reviewed five major studies of family psychoeducational interventions in schizophrenia with 2-year outcomes (Falloon, McGill, Boyd, & Pederson, 1987; Hogarty et al., 1991; Leff et al., 1985, 1990; Tarrier et al., 1989). These studies, by different teams in different geographical sites, indicated that family interventions were significantly linked to reduced relapse rates at 9 months. The relapse rates of the family intervention groups ranged from 6% to 23% compared with 40% to 53%

in the no-intervention comparison groups. By 24 months, however, the relapse rate was less impressive, as about 40% of the patients had relapsed in the family intervention group. Lam pointed out that "it looks as if the existing intervention packages serve to delay rather than to prevent relapse in the longer term" (1991, p. 429). He noted, however, that with the exception of Falloon et al.'s (1987) study, which showed a favorable outcome of 17% relapse rate at 2-year follow-up, the therapeutic contact between the team and the patients was minimal or nonexistent after the initial 9 months.

A cost-benefit analysis by Cardin, McGill, and Falloon (1986) indicated that the cost of the family intervention group was 19% less than for the control group because the control patients needed more crisis management and hospitalization. Lam (1991) points out further benefits for the patients in not being disrupted by frequent hospital admissions, perhaps leading to less stigmatization and better self-esteem.

Schooler and Keith (1993) found no significant effects of an intensive in-home behavioral family management intervention combined with a monthly patient-family group (applied family management) when compared with a monthly family-patient group only (supportive family management). The family treatment strategies did not differ in terms of relapse and rehospitalization.

Mari and Streiner (1994) conducted a computer network search on the effectiveness of family interventions in decreasing relapse in schizophrenic patients. Six randomized controlled trials were included in a meta-analysis of 350 patients (181 in the control group and 169 in the experimental group). They found that the experimental group showed a significant increase in drug compliance and a significant reduction in hospitalizations over time. These outcomes were apparently not linked to a significant reduction of high EE in families, however. The authors note the limitations of using relapse as primary outcome in the assessment of efficacy and suggest other outcome measures, including reduction of family burden and relatives' distress.

In well-controlled studies with random assignment of patients and families both in New Jersey and in New York State, McFarlane (1994) found that psychoeducational multiple-family groups had a significantly longer time to first relapse than did single-family treatment. In the New Jersey study, at 4 years after discharge, the relapse rates were 50% for the psychoeducational multiple-family group, 57.1% for a psychodynamically oriented multiple-family group, and 76.5% for psychoeducational single-family treatment. Moreover, the psychoeducational multiple-family group registered the highest increase in patients' functional occupations. In New York, relapse rates at 2 years postdischarge were 28% for multiple-family and 42% for single-family psychoeducational groups. In fact, the results of multiple-family groups were so robust that MacFarlane (1994) states that treatment effects were comparable in magnitude to the effects of psychotropic medications. McFarlane suggests that in the multiple-family group format, the families begin to form a social network, providing a degree of social support unavailable in the single-family interventions.

Reduction of Family Burden

D. Johnson (1994) studied family interventions that did not include the relatives with mental illness and that focused on reduction of family burden. Three studies reported positive intervention effects, whereas three others reported no effects on burden. In a study contrasting a four-session educational program for an experimental group with mailed printed materials for a control group, Smith and Birchwood (1987) reported a nonspecific effect of reduction of family burden for both groups at 6-month follow-ups. Abramowitz and Coursey (1989) used a six-session educational support program, including problem solving and resource information, based on a stress-coping framework. There was a waiting list control group. At posttest, experimental group members were significantly less anxious and distressed and made more use of community resources but showed no differences in sense of efficacy or negative feelings toward the patient.

A large New Jersey project provided multiple services (which could include psychoeducation, respite, support groups, or individual consultation) to 376 families in eight community programs. An evaluation of 191 of these families found that individual consultation was preferred by 91% of the respondents. Family psychoeducation was used by 49% and the support group by 37% of the families, with respite care the least popular (14%). The researchers found significant reduction of burden on all measures. There were continuing concerns, however, related to needs for housing, the stigma of mental illness, and planning for the future. Worry about the ill member's future continued to be a major concern that could not be resolved by family interventions alone (Riesser, Minsky, & Schorske, 1991).

Riesser et al.'s (1991) findings of preference for individual consultation were not necessarily in conflict with McFarlane's (1994) multifamily findings because the package of services offered was not comparable in scope or intensity, and selection was based on families' presumptions of benefit. The data suggested, however, that (a) discrete needs may require specific answers from professionals or individual case managers and (b) there are some issues of burden that professionals cannot deal with. These are issues that require broader systemic change.

Self-Help Groups

D. Johnson (1994) states that despite the common perception that mutual support groups or advocacy organizations are effective in reducing family burden, there are almost no data on the independent effects of such participation. Nevertheless, membership does seem to have an effect on the emotional well-being of both families and patients. Biegel and Yamatani (1986, 1987) conducted a controlled study of self-help support groups for families of the mentally ill. Questionnaires were completed by 54 new members of 10 self-help groups, and 83% of the respondents completed a follow-up questionnaire after 6 months' participation. A comparison group of caregivers who were not members of a self-help group were also assessed. Data were also collected on the mentally ill relatives.

Self-help group caregivers reported high satisfaction with their experience, with almost two-thirds reporting that sharing experiences and interacting with others in the same situation was what they liked best. The perceived helpfulness of the program was significantly related to better patient functioning in terms of fewer hospitalizations and lower lengths of stay in a 12-month period, although no direction of effect was inferred from the data. (One of the problems with such correlations is that the families of sicker patients, those more likely to be rehospitalized, may gain greater benefit from the self-help group.)

A positive relationship was found between the rate of program participation and perceived helpfulness. The most frequently rated helping activities were empathy, catharsis, mutual affirmation, encouragement of sharing, explanation, normalization, and behavioral prescription (Biegel & Yamatani, 1987). The authors had noted that these activities related to the emotional, affirmational, and informational components of social support, whereas the least frequently occurring activities were behavioral techniques, such as rehearsal, punishment, extinction, confrontation, requesting feedback, and the like. They pointed out that

[These activities] tend to be more threatening, directive, structured, and focused on behavioral change. Although families of the mentally ill may require assistance in altering patterns of behavior and interaction with their mentally ill patient and in learning specific skills for coping with this chronic problem, they are unlikely to receive such assistance through their self-help group. . . . Professional assistance to families through structured educational and counseling activities may also be required. (Biegel & Yamatani, 1986, pp. 75-76)

The personal benefits of advocacy are inferred from such studies as those of Norton, Wandersman, and Goldman (1993). These investigators compared members of an AMI group with nonmember relatives of a random sample of clinic patients designated as chronically mentally ill. Their purpose was to assess the incentives and barriers to AMI membership, characterized as cost-benefit variables. Their typology was a trimotivational theory of incentives: material (concrete benefits), solidary [sic] (social or relational rewards), and purposive (improving welfare of others). Material benefits included solutions to problems, increased knowledge of mental illness, and increased coping ability. Solidary benefits were assessed by two items: a feeling of importance among friends and friendships with other members. Purposive benefits included a sense of helpfulness, increased influence in changing the mental health system, increased sense of responsibility and contributions to the organization, and providing a service to the mentally ill and their families. Factor analysis yielded only two factors, however: social-purposive and personal.

The investigators found major differences in racial and income composition of the member and nonmember groups but minimal correlations of race, income, and education with benefits and costs. The findings indicated that members perceived greater personal benefits (knowledge, coping ability, and solutions to problems) than nonmembers, but the groups did not differ in the social-purposive factor. Providing a useful service, a sense of responsibility, and helpfulness to others received the highest values in both groups, whereas feelings of importance were lowest. Both factor scores were significantly higher for more active members of AMI than less active members.

Members perceived significantly lower personal and social-organizational costs (e.g., energy drain, frustration at lack of group progress, disagreement with goals) than were imagined by nonmembers. The investigators concluded that overall, "clearly, members view the organization as offering tangible benefits" (p. 156).

In this chapter, we have discussed a range of services for family caregivers offered by mental health professionals and by trained educators. Clinical services include various types of family therapy, but the primary modality in recent years has been family psychoeducation. Psychoeducational interventions share common components of education, support, training in communication and problem-solving skills, and overall help for illness management. Other contemporary professional interventions, such as supportive family counseling and family consultation, share similar assumptions of family competence but are more oriented toward the specific needs of individual families.

Nonclinical interventions include structured family education modules delivered by educators trained for this purpose, with the aim of improving families' coping skills. Family support groups are another important type of nonclinical intervention. The self-help format involves sharing experiences and coping strategies with others who have lived through the same pain. The groups also offer information exchange, resource knowledge building, help with crises, and often an expanded social network. Some support groups target self-attitude change and personal growth. In contrast to clinical and educational interventions, support groups are ongoing and there are often several groups in a given locality. Support is almost always available in times of crisis. Membership in advocacy groups is also considered a nonclinical service that can be immensely helpful to persons who are oriented toward action in lieu of, or in addition to, ventilation, knowledge building, and crisis resolution.

The chapter's final section presents research findings on the effects of family services in terms of selected outcome indicators. Numerous controlled studies have demonstrated the efficacy of psychoeducational interventions in significantly prolonging the time until patients relapse. Other more family-focused research has demonstrated a reduction in family burden as well as improved emotional well-being among family members belonging to support groups. Membership in an AMI group seems to offer tangible benefits, both in terms of personal help and a sense of helping others. Yet some research findings suggest that although a range of interventions may deal with some individual problems and help participants feel better, worries still remain about issues that require systemic or cultural change. In the next section we turn to a discussion of the social context in which mental illness is experienced.

PART IV

The Social Context: The Future of Family Caregiving

11

Cross-Cultural Issues
in Family Caregiving

Familial caregiving is more than a matter of concern for the well-being of a loved one. It is also linked to societal concepts of personal and collective responsibility and particularly to notions of what is right and appropriate with respect to obligations to kin. The major premises underlying caregiving are related to (a) cultural conceptions of personhood, of the self in relation to others, and (b) cultural notions of interpersonal morality. In this chapter, I discuss how these concepts relate to the caregiving enterprise in Western and non-Western countries as well as to caregiving among different ethnic groups in the United States.

THE PERSON IN INDIVIDUALISTIC
AND SOCIOCENTRIC CULTURES

Much anthropological discussion has been devoted to cultural variation in conceptions of the self. As Miller (1994) notes,

> the self-sufficient individual tends to be accorded paramount value in modern western thought. . . . In this view the individual is treated as prior to and more fundamental than the social order, with the social order existing only as a means of realization of individual ends. (p. 13)

Cross-cultural research comparing Western (American) and non-Western (Hindu Indian) populations supported Miller's hypothesis that Americans have an individually oriented interpersonal moral code that stresses personal freedom of choice and individual responsibility, whereas Indians have a duty-based interpersonal moral code. This code emphasizes mandatory responsibilities based on one's position vis-à-vis another in the social matrix.

Miller's (1994) study adds to the body of anthropological research that distinguishes individualistic cultures (typically designated as Western or modern) from sociocentric or group-oriented cultures (typically designated as non-Western or traditional). These very different cultural styles are highly relevant to caregiving in mental illness. First, traditional cultures typically have both an interpersonal moral code that stresses responsibilities to kin and clear gender distinctions that impose a noncareer-oriented, homemaking, caregiving role on women. This makes it much more natural to maintain ill members in the household—for a lifetime, if necessary. Caregiving tasks are also likely to be perceived as less burdensome in cultures that view this as a natural role commitment. Because the vast majority of caregivers throughout the world are female, caregiving has become a feminist issue in Western cultures (Ascher-Svanum & Sobel, 1989; Cook, 1988; Thurer, 1983). In modern societies, women are no longer culturally valued for sacrificing their own needs to serve others. There are clear frustrations and few secondary gains when mothers, wives, or daughters have to abandon other interests or even competing career choices to fulfill a caregiving role.

Another factor, suggested by Hooley (1987), is that notions of personal responsibility may be related to the significant cultural variations in high or low expressed emotion (EE) indicated in Chapter 5. Hooley has noted that the high EE so normative in Western cultures appears to reflect familial attributions in which mentally ill persons are perceived as being in control of symptomatic behavior. Individualistic thinking may well underlie the prevalence and acceptability of critical remarks aimed at relatives who are considered accountable for their symptoms and capable of change. Last, as we will discuss further, notions of individual rights and personal and collective responsibility distinguish the family and consumer movements in their ongoing discussion of rights versus needs. This argument, in turn, is having a pronounced effect on the type and direction of services and caregiving resources available for persons with severe mental illness.

Cultural concepts of selfhood, views of dependency and disability, and professionals' attitudes toward patients' families are interrelated with how a society cares for its disabled, dysfunctional, and dependent citizens. Cultural norms determine the rights and prerogatives of these individuals, the society's obligations to care for them, and the type of mental health system developed to serve them. Cultures with few mental health resources depend on families to care for their mentally ill loved ones, and professionals tend to accept families as allies and collaborators (Shankar & Menon, 1991). In some cases, nonindustrialized nations that lack local clinics have developed services that are in many ways superior to our own—such as the integration of medical and mental health care at the village level combined with home visits from workers trained precisely to monitor the needs of mentally ill constituents (Lefley, 1994a).

WORLD HEALTH ORGANIZATION FINDINGS: IMPLICATIONS FOR CAREGIVING

The World Health Organization (WHO) has conducted a number of international studies that appear to demonstrate that extended families as well as cultural belief systems may be important factors in the prognosis for schizophrenia. Specifically, the WHO international pilot study of schizophrenia (IPSS), which demonstrated diagnostic uniformity in nine different cultures, found that outcome was significantly better in the developing countries than in the industrialized West 2 years after the first treated schizophrenic episode. At that time, remissions ranged from 58% in Nigeria to 8% in Denmark. A further epidemiological study of first-episode patients in 10 countries found a uniform annual incidence rate (1 per 10,000) but a continuing difference in outcome favoring the developing nations (Jablensky et al., 1991).

In the literature interpreting the WHO findings, common themes are that traditional cultures offer (a) cultural belief systems that externalize causality, freeing the patients and families of blame; (b) greater opportunities for social reintegration and normalized work roles in agrarian economies, and (c) more human resources to buffer the effects of the illness on the patients' caregivers (Leff, 1988; Lefley, 1990b). Lin and Kleinman (1988) suggest that compared with Western nations, there is less social isolation and a more benign family milieu in traditional sociocentric cultures, which are characterized by long-term social relationships and extended kinship networks. Leff and Vaughn (1985) have speculated that family structure may explain the cultural differences in EE. They suggest that the criticism, hostile remarks, or emotional over-involvement of high EE are more likely to be found in the overwhelmed nuclear family, whereas extended kinship networks are better able to diffuse burden and provide multiple caregivers.

In a WHO study of family burden in developing countries, Giel et al. (1983) indicated that culture determines the conceptualization of mental illness, its causes, and expectations regarding the effects of modern health care. Religion influences attitudes toward people with mental illness, and these authors state that Islam is probably the most explicitly tolerant toward people considered mentally ill. The political system is also part of the cultural influence because government is responsible for the type and availability of health care systems, whether or not they are free, and where they are concentrated. Leadership, group cohesion, and reciprocity at the community level are factors involved in treatment and caregiving. Other cultural factors that influence the functioning of the family are its socio-economic viability, its composition, its stage in the life cycle, and its housing conditions.

In subsistence-level village life, Giel et al. (1983) found that psychotic disturbance in an important member of the household can gradually destroy the socioeconomic prospects of the family unit as a whole. On the other hand, in contrast to most communities in an industrial society, the stable and reciprocal pattern of village family life appeared to have prevented the breaking up of the family unit for many years. In a Nigerian study, Martyns-Yellowe (1992) reported that rural families actually experienced more burden than urban families. Significantly greater financial burden in the rural sample appeared to be related to significantly greater anxiety and depression vis-à-vis the urban comparison group. Higher burden scores were related to poorer economic circumstances of the family and patient characteristics of male sex and an age range that encompasses the peak working years. The role and responsibilities of afflicted family members, rather than their behavior alone, seem to be the major issue in family burden in developing countries. Yet despite the higher tolerance levels, it appears that severe, chronic psychotic behavior may lead to maltreatment by villagers and sometimes abandonment by families (Cohen, 1992).

El-Islam (1982) studied patterns of care among nuclear and extended families of 540 Arab schizophrenic outpatients in Qatar. He reported that the extended family seemed to show greater emotional commitment to each other's well-being.

> The extended family is more tolerant of patients' minor behavioral abnormalities and temporary protective withdrawals. It is more helpful in the supervision of patients' medication and their social adjustment and leisure time occupation. . . . Extended family members are less likely than nuclear family mem-

bers to tax the patients' emotional resources and limited repertoire of social skills. (p. 112)

These findings seem in good accord with Leff and Vaughn's (1985) notion of the buffering effects of the extended family vis à vis the burden of caregiving in the nuclear family.

ETHNIC GROUP DIFFERENCES
IN THE UNITED STATES

Cultural diversity deals with the traditional value orientations, belief systems, behavioral practices, and world views that typically define particular ethnolinguistic groups. In modern industrial societies, ethnicity often overlaps and is confounded with socioeconomic status, minority group status, and immigrant or refugee status. As we have noted previously, sociocultural variables affect service needs and service delivery in multiple ways, including diagnostic practices, referral patterns, and selection of treatment modalities (Lefley, 1990b, 1994b). Cultural factors are related to both accessibility of services and service use, reflecting barriers that respectively may be institutional or self-imposed. The structure and cultural appropriateness of services and their acceptability to different ethnic groups may reflect different expectations of providers and consumers.

Milstein et al. (1994) studied cultural conceptions of mental illness among African American, European American, and Hispanic American family caregivers. Their premise was that these conceptions play a role in whether or not a relative will be referred to the mental health system as well as in the ways the family will care for that person. They were also interested in whether the medical model used in psychoeducational curricula was culturally acceptable to different ethnic groups. They found that Hispanic Americans were more likely to see their relatives' problems as emotional, whereas African Americans and European Americans preferred a medical explanation ("mental failure or chemical imbalance"). However, European Americans were more likely to attribute the medical condition to heredity or family history as the most important factor. The most significant difference was in prognosis. African Americans and Hispanics felt there would someday be a cure, whereas European Americans felt that a cure would not be found. Overall, the researchers concluded that in contrast to European Americans, ethnic minorities do not seem to view mental illness from the perspective of clinicians nor are they as ready to involve their relatives in professional care. Cultural variables also relate to the resources and informal systems of care available in different ethnic communities. Almost all cultural groups have traditional methods and adaptive resources for coping with illness. Families may choose to use their own indigenous healing and support networks, to use the professional mental health system, or, more typically, to combine the two. Caregivers rarely rely on traditional healers alone when there is a history of persistent mental illness. There is some evidence that native healers recognize the symptoms of major psychiatric disorders and encourage the use of mental health professionals along with their own spiritual resources, and that families and patients assign a separate function to each source of healing (Lefley, Sandoval, & Charles, in press). There is inadequate research at this point to assess the extent of use of alternative healers and whether this practice has a significant effect on use of services of the mainstream mental health system.

RACIAL-ETHNIC PATTERNS IN SERVICE NEEDS AND UTILIZATION

The population of most concern to caregivers is composed of persons with serious mental illness, defined in terms of diagnosis, duration, and disability (Barker et al., 1992). The government's National Health Interview Survey, providing the most current data on adults with serious mental illness in the general household population, showed a rate per 1,000 of 18.3 for whites and 19.7 for blacks. Among persons currently limited in their activities by serious mental illness, the figures are 78% for whites and 82.8% for blacks (Barker et al., 1992).

This national study also found that black adults with serious mental illness were more than twice as likely to receive SSI disability payments despite the fact that black applicants were less likely to be awarded benefits than white applicants. A higher proportion of black adults with serious mental illness were unable to work because of their disability. They were also more likely to live in poverty and to have less education and poorer health than white persons with serious mental illness.

Despite these differences, the summary of the household study of serious mental illness (Barker et al., 1992) points out that neither the prevalence of serious mental illness nor the proportion of persons with resulting current disability is significantly different for black or white persons. The prevalence rate among "other" races, however, is about one-half that of black or white persons, a factor of considerable interest when we consider the data that follow.

CULTURAL DIFFERENCES AMONG MINORITY GROUPS

For many years, national statistics have shown significantly higher psychiatric hospital admission rates for nonwhites ("blacks and other races") than for whites, and this dichotomous reporting pattern continues today (Manderscheid & Sonnenschein, 1992). In one annual report, however, *Mental Health United States, 1987,* rates were given per 100,000 population for American Indian-Alaska Native, Asian, black, Hispanic origin, and white admissions to all inpatient psychiatric services. This report showed highly significant differences among minority groups. Relative to population distributions, African Americans and American Indians had significantly higher admission rates than all other racial-ethnic groups to all inpatient facilities. The rates for African Americans were more than double the rates for Hispanics and more than three times greater than the rates for Asians (Manderscheid & Barrett, 1987, Table 3, p. 76).

Compounding this picture were the inverse ratios of admissions and length of stay. There seemed to be little relation between need for hospitalization and level of disability. Groups with lowest inpatient admission rates (Asians, Hispanics, and whites) had considerably higher median inpatient stays than did African American or American Indian patients (Manderscheid & Barrett, 1987, Table 3.5, p. 80). As may be seen in Table 11.1, for persons diagnosed with schizophrenia—the primary diagnosis requiring inpatient admission—Hispanics and Asians had considerably higher median inpatient stays than did African Americans and American Indians.

One explanation for these paradoxical figures is that perhaps Hispanic and Asian families are more likely to keep their relatives at home and to present them for hospitalization at an advanced stage of illness, when they would require longer hospital stays. Perhaps these groups are reluctant to use the mental health system because there are insufficient staff who speak their language. Perhaps they are more likely to use indigenous healers

Table 11.1. Admission per 100,000 Population to Inpatient Psychiatric
Services and Median Days of Inpatient Stays for Schizophrenia
and Substance Abuse by Race and Hispanic Origin

| | Admissions to State and County Hospitals | Median Days | | Total Admissions to All Inpatient Facilities |
		SCZ	SA	
Blacks	364.2	32	12	931.8
American Indians or Alaska Natives	306.4	20	12	818.7
Hispanics	146.0	54	13	451.4
Whites	136.8	48	12	550.0
Asians	75.4	52	16	268.1
Total	163.6	42	12	592.0

SOURCE: Adapted from Manderscheid and Barrett (1987, p. 76, Table 3.1; p. 80, Table 3.5).
SCZ = schizophrenia; SA = substance abuse.
NOTE 1. Schizophrenia and substance abuse are the only diagnoses for which there is full reporting for
all ethnic groups. Data on median length of stays for these diagnoses are available only for admissions
to state and county mental health hospitals.
NOTE 2. Total admissions include state and county, veterans' administration, general (nonfederal), and
private psychiatric hospitals.

before turning to the professional system. Yet the latter variables might
also apply to American Indians, and, overall, they seem inadequate dis-
criminants of differential practices among racial-ethnic groups. Snowden
and Cheung (1990) have noted that we really have no hard data on these
types of cultural differences and that involuntary commitment practices
and diagnostic error should be looked into. They also suggest that admissions staff may have a tendency to view greater psychopathology in
African Americans and Native Americans but may have a "minimizing
bias" (p. 354) in judging psychopathology in Asian and white patients.

Asians appear to be distinct from other ethnic groups in their inpatient
use and readmission rates in the United Kingdom as well as in the United
States. An outcome study in England used the WHO findings as the basis
for hypotheses about relapse in first episode schizophrenia (Birchwood
et al., 1992). The authors felt that the Asian community still manifested
many of the features related to positive outcome in the developing
countries, such as extended family structure, greater opportunities for
social integration, and more positive constructions of mental illness. An
exploratory study found a lower rate of relapse-readmission in the first
12 months after discharge among Asian (16%) as opposed to white (30%)

and Afro-Caribbean (49%) patients. Available evidence suggested that speed of access to care, living with a family, and employment opportunities may account for this effect. They noted that medication compliance may have contributed to differences in relapse among white and Afro-Caribbean patients but was not a factor influencing the low rate among Asians. The investigators also found significant differences in family caregiving patterns, however. The percentages of patients discharged to their family homes were 90% for Asians, 70% for whites, and 31% for Afro-Caribbeans. When the researchers controlled for differences in the integrity of family structure, group differences in relapse-readmission rates were no longer significant.

CULTURAL PATTERNS
OF RESIDENTIAL CAREGIVING

A major item of importance in looking at racial-ethnic issues in family caregiving is to note the significant differences in the percentages of mentally ill persons living at home with their families. Most studies of samples that are predominantly white European American have found that about 38% to 40% of persons with severe and persistent mental illness live at home at any given time (Lefley, 1987a; Skinner, Steinwachs, & Kasper, 1992). Most of the earlier studies were done of families who were members of the National Alliance for the Mentally Ill (NAMI), which is predominantly a white, middle-class organization. Studies of families of lower socioeconomic status, however, recruited through users of public mental health services, show a similar pattern for white European American families. A major ethnographic study by Guarnaccia and his associates (in press) of families of community mental health center patients with an average age of 34 to 40 years (similar to those in the NAMI samples) reported that about one third of European American families lived with their mentally ill relatives, in contrast to three quarters of the Hispanic American and 60% of the African American families. The authors noted that patients from European American families generally lived in residential programs or lived on their own in the community. They felt that these differences reflected both the families' preferences and the relatively lower availability of residential programs to minority families.

Nevertheless, there are strong mandates for publicly funded mental health programs to serve minority clients, and residential programs tend to actively solicit nonwhite or ethnically diverse members. Thus it is likely that cultural preferences prevailed among clients and families and the authors themselves suggest this was the main motivation. The racial-ethnic differences reported by Guarnaccia et al., however, require replication in other areas. In contrast to their findings, a study by Biegel, Milligan, & Putnam (1991), which carefully controlled for socioeconomic status of caregivers, had found no significant differences in living status by race.

In this same triethnic sample, Milstein et al. (1994) found significant differences in residential preferences of caregivers. As indicated, most of the European American patients already lived outside the home but of the remaining families, only a small percentage wanted their relative to continue living at home. Most Hispanic American patients lived at home and were expected to continue living there. As a group, the African American and Hispanic American families whose relatives lived with them did not want their family member to live elsewhere. Patterns of response in family support groups also tend to support the notion that residential caregiving is a strong cultural differentiator, particularly among immigrant families. Lefley (1990a) found in observations of support groups that immigrants from traditional cultures often found household density uncomfortable in the small apartments they were able to rent in the urban areas to which they were translocated, without the commensurate outdoors space to which they were accustomed. They also missed the extended kinship network as an emotional resource and as a support system for caregiving. Uncomfortable household arrangements combined with acculturative stress aggravated the burdens of living with the disturbances of mental illness. Yet these families found it alien to cultural mores to have a mentally ill family member live away from them in a residential program or board-and-care home affiliated with a treatment center. Interactions with mainstream European American families in support groups enabled them to think differently about the situation. In effect, they were given permission from older American families to do the unthinkable, with the message that they would actually be helping their loved ones by enabling them to live on their own outside of the household.

In their study, Guarnaccia and his colleagues (in press) found differences with respect to the decision to hospitalize the mentally ill member. For Hispanic families, the decision was as often made by a medical professional as by the family. This was rarely the case with the other groups. However, the police were more likely to be involved in hospitalizing African American or European American clients.

All families reported deep frustrations with the processes of commitment. After the initial hospitalization, many families stated that their family members were discharged to them, often on medication, with little or no guidance as to follow-up arrangements or how to deal with the clients' resistance. With respect to other differences, African American clients were the most involved in day programs, and European American clients made the most use of residential services, whereas Hispanic families did not use residential programs at all and used day treatment the least of the three ethnic groups. The investigators felt that the low use of day treatment programs by Hispanics was because of a lack of bilingual-bicultural programs.

SOCIAL NETWORKS AND KINSHIP ROLES

The Guarnaccia study (in press) also indicated that minority families tended to have larger social networks than white Americans and these networks included more kin. African Americans and Hispanic Americans sought out other family members for advice, whereas Europeans turned more to mental health professionals. Europeans reported the greatest effects on their physical and mental health as a result of caregiving, even though the minority families had more contact. The authors attributed this greater perceived stress to the lack of social support networks. The investigators also note, however, that when caregiving is viewed as culturally normative, there is a tendency for caregivers to deny subjective burden.

Some preliminary data from the Family Impact Study at New York State Psychiatric Institute suggest that there may be cultural differences in the kinship roles of primary caregivers of psychiatric patients. A hospital-recruited sample of 180 caregivers indicated that parents were the caregivers for 72% of white patients, 53% of black patients, and 34% of Hispanic patients (Struening & Steuve, 1994). The lower percentages of parental caregiving may be due to greater separation and dispersion of the patients' families of origin. Minority populations often migrate to seek better economic opportunities, leaving older people behind. But the differences are even more likely related to the previously cited finding of larger kinship networks on which to draw for caregiving. If replicated, this pattern may indicate substantially greater involvement of siblings and other relatives as caregivers in minority groups.

These findings are highly germane to the international literature on the course of illness in schizophrenia and the EE research. Social support network—the availability of helping kin—is one of the major explanatory models for the IPSS (Jablensky et al., 1991) findings on the more benign course of illness in developing countries. The Guarnaccia et al. (in press) findings that African American and European American families were more likely to report that their family member's problem stemmed from negative personality traits—a high EE response—is congruent with the findings of higher EE in these populations in comparison with low-EE Hispanic families (Jenkins & Karno, 1992; Lefley, 1992a).

ETHNICITY AND
CAREGIVING BURDEN

In a study of parental caregiving burden, Cook et al. (1994) found that ethnicity was a significant factor in differentiating various types of burden. Minority parents reported greater cognitive preoccupations and feelings of ultimate responsibility with regard to their ill child, whereas white parents reported greater distress over their child's behavior. This is in contrast to prior research, which found greater burden from children's behavioral problems among African American families (Tessler, Fisher, & Gamache, 1990). The Tessler research group found that in African American families, the greatest burden was associated with violence and disruptive behavior, whereas white families reported greater distress from their family member's poor functioning and inability to fulfill role responsibilities. In a study of a program for homeless mentally ill adults, Lefley et al. (1992) found that African American clients were more likely to report extrusion from their homes because of violent and disruptive behavior related to substance abuse. These respondents felt their families were justified in evicting them. They were also more likely to be in contact with their families than were white homeless mentally ill adults.

Guarnaccia et al. (in press) noted that among Hispanic families, caregiving is viewed as culturally normative; thus there is a tendency to deny subjective burden. They also noted that despite greater contact with the patient, minority families reported fewer effects on their physical and mental health as a result of caregiving. The authors attributed this to the greater availability of social support networks. There are other possible explanations, however. As Noh and Turner (1987) have demonstrated, the family's perception of mastery and control of a situation seems to be associated with less subjective burden. When caregiving is viewed as a natural responsibility and there is no perception of inordinate demands, mastery may be implicit in the caregiver's task.

Pickett, Vraniak, Cook, and Cohler (1993) compared the coping mastery ability and self-esteem scores of 24 black and 185 white parents of severely mentally ill adults to determine the effects of caregiving. These investigators used a strengths rather than a deficit model in assessing responses to family burden. They were particularly interested in determining the effect of caregiving on parents' feelings of self-worth, postulating that when caregivers were able to cope successfully with frequent crises and trauma, this would validate their own capability and value as well as build confidence and self-esteem. Their findings were that black parents had significantly higher levels of overall coping mastery ability and significantly higher self-esteem than did white parents. Surprisingly, the availability of a greater number of potential social supports, including church resources, was negatively related to coping mastery and self-esteem in black parents. This contrasted sharply with Guarnaccia et al.'s (in press) assumption of the positive effects of social support. Pickett et al. (1993) felt that potential supportive resources may sometimes have an adverse effect. First, having more children or extended family nearby may bring a greater number of additional problems and more strain. Second, church members may not be as supportive of mental illness as of other disabilities and may resent the religious delusions of psychiatrically disabled persons. Third, the principle of reciprocity may involve too many demands. Caregivers may be reluctant to call on family and friends because they know they will have to give assistance in return. Also, family and friends may feel they know what is best and may be resentful when their advice is not followed, with additional burden imposed by the ensuing friction.

Pickett and her colleagues (1993) also found different psychodynamics in the adaptation of black and white parents to their child's disability. They found that the relationship between parental ratings of their ill child's age-appropriate behavior and feelings of self-worth was opposite for black and white caregivers. Black mothers and fathers adjusted their expectations according to their child's level of psychiatric disability, whereas white parents appeared unable to accommodate themselves to diminished expectations.

White parents may hold some abstracted normative development expectations regarding age-appropriate behavior that may cause them to be disappointed.

As a result, white parents rate their offspring's behavior as greatly delayed and in turn experience greater levels of depression and lower levels of self-worth. (Pickett et al., 1993, p. 465)

A study by Biegel, Milligan, and Putnam (1991) found remarkably similar findings to those of Pickett et al. (1993) in both the perceptions of support from family networks and in emotional response. They found that black caregivers reported that their network of family members provided significantly less support than that reported by white caregivers. The frequency of clients' behavioral problems was a significant predictor of caregiver burden for both black and white respondents. The most frequently reported items by both black and white caregivers were related to clients' dependency, caregiver strain (overall worry and lack of client appreciation), and family disruption due to the stress of multiple role responsibilities. In contrast to other studies, these investigators found that caregiving burden among black families was predicted not only by a greater number of clients' behavioral problems but by lack of perceived support from other family members in caring for the person with mental illness. Yet, despite similarity in most areas of caregiver burden, black caregivers reported significantly lower levels of depression than did white caregivers.

Obviously, there are many variables involved in these responses and many questions that should be asked with respect to reference points. Do black families perceive less support in the case of mental illness as compared with a typically higher standard of family support in other life exigencies? Do they experience less depression because of more realistic expectations, as Pickett and her colleagues have suggested? Cook et al. (1994) have noted the contradictions of some studies finding burden higher for minority families and others reporting greater burden for white families. They believe that varying definitions of the concept of burden may explain the inconsistency. Thus burden related to disruptive behavior may be different from internal conflicts over behavioral management issues. Substance abusing members, especially those who are dually diagnosed with mental illness, may shake the very foundations of families already beset by multiple economic problems, inadequate social resources, and competing caregiving responsibilities. The economic dependency and destructive activities of these individuals may be intolerably damaging to already weakened family systems.

Conversely, in chaotic family systems with multiple stressors, the passive negative symptoms of schizophrenia may seem quite tolerable when compared with substance abuse, violence, or criminality in other members of the household. There also may be relative gratifications for a poor family with multiple household members, many of whom are not working, when the mentally ill relative can support himself or herself with a monthly disability check.

It is evident that ethnicity interacts with and may be confounded with socioeconomic status. Comparisons of ethnic groups may indeed reflect cultural caregiving norms, but unless there are careful controls, the findings may reflect the realities of poverty and social deprivation rather than cultural practice. Cook et al. (1994) note the importance of including minority status and education as factors in caregiving burden. Socioeconomic status, of which education is only one component, should always be controlled, but family structure and household composition may also reveal other demands that contribute to caregiving stress.

CULTURAL APPROPRIATENESS OF CLINICAL AND NONCLINICAL SERVICES

Rivera (1988) has applied psychoeducational interventions with low-income Hispanic families and indicated that in the main, they are beneficial and acceptable to this population. She has some useful comments on the cultural appropriateness of various components of the psychoeducational approach:

Compatible With Hispanic Culture: including families in the patient's treatment, providing concrete information on mental illness, using comprehensible treatment modalities such as medications and explicit behavioral instructions, alleviating families' sense of blame or stigma.

Incompatible With Hispanic Culture: use of an egalitarian problem-solving paradigm, lack of attention to spiritual factors, possible misinterpretations of spiritual beliefs as psychosis, the concept of emotional overinvolvement.

Rivera suggests that culturally different professionals must be cautious in assessing what constitutes overinvolvement with an ill family member in Hispanic culture. She also feels that Hispanic families must have some hope that the person can get better. So education about an illness such as chronic schizophrenia should not imply that the symptoms are not likely to improve and that families must accept the current level of incapacity.

Another point is that Hispanic families have natural support systems. Self-help groups, such as those offered by AMI, will not fulfill the same functions and provide the same supports that they do for white European American families. Rivera points out that most psychoeducational groups are built on groups of unrelated individuals with a similar problem. She states that culturally sensitive psychoeducation for Hispanic families should be built on larger family networks that share ties of kinship or community membership.

The same point might be made about other ethnic minority groups such as African Americans, American Indians, and Asians. Kinship-based psychoeducational groups are probably difficult to implement for migrating or lower socioeconomic families who are likely to have experienced ruptured family networks and broken ties. One approach would be to integrate them with other family networks of the same cultural background or to offer psychoeducation in local churches and other community institutions.

Fowler (1992) has found psychoeducational interventions culturally appropriate for families of Caribbean patients in New York City. Both Fowler and Rivera have added social activities to their psychoeducational meetings, thus expanding the social networks within culturally homogeneous groups. They also encourage continuing participation in support groups following the termination of formal clinical education.

The composition of support groups continues to be predominantly white middle-class. In a study of 225 families with mentally ill relatives recruited in an East coast metropolitan area, Mannion et al. (1994) found that of those participating in support groups, 84% were white, 15.6% African American, and 0.4% Asian. Nonclinical interventions are offered in the support groups developed by AMI affiliates serving specific ethnic populations. NAMI now has numerous affiliates in various parts of the country that are predominantly African American, Hispanic, mixed Caribbean, Asian, or American Indian. In some of the AMI support groups on Indian reservations, "family" means all members of the patient's clan. Thus attendance at a support group meeting may include many more people than simply nuclear family members. This expansion of the social support network is highly desirable, of course. It provides psychological and often economic support as well as resources for respite caregiving and often vocational assistance to the patient. When the extended family is involved in shared education, moreover, this tends to diminish the burden of prejudicial judgment, misinformation, and bad advice so often imposed by well-meaning but ignorant relatives.

ASSESSMENT OF SERVICE NEEDS

Studies of families of hospitalized patients show few differences among cultural groups in their assessment of specific service needs for their relatives. Solomon and Marcenko (1992b) studied caregivers' concerns regarding community placement of their relatives following hospitalization in a predominantly African American sample (54%). They found that family concerns at discharge were consistent across ethnic groups, regardless of the race, sex, or age of the mentally ill relative. The mean age of the caregivers was 60 years; the relatives' mean age was 38. Although three quarters of the caregivers felt they had seen some progress, most were concerned that their relatives might have to live in an unsafe neighborhood (72%), would not stay on medication (78%), could not support themselves financially (75%), and, above all, would not get needed services (80%). A year later, their concerns had expanded. They were afraid their relatives would cause conflict in the family and not be able to control their use of alcohol or drugs.

These investigators also studied families' satisfaction with inpatient and outpatient treatment (Solomon & Marcenko, 1992a). Across ethnic groups, families indicated greater satisfaction with services to their relatives than to themselves. The greatest areas of dissatisfaction related to case managers' failing to discuss future plans for their relatives, provide caregivers with emotional support, give practical advice, and teach them about medications. Caregivers indicated a need for family education and guidelines on how to motivate their mentally ill relative. They felt, however, that case managers helped them more than hospital staff in providing information. With respect to meeting caregiver needs, approximately half felt dissatisfaction in some areas. Family members were more satisfied with mental health agencies than with hospitals but ranked case managers above agencies in responding to at least some of their needs (Solomon, 1994).

CONCLUSIONS ON FINDINGS

Overall, the burden and clinical data tend to support the heterogeneity among ethnic groups indicated in the differential statistics on hospital admissions. Ethnic groups in the United States as well as other countries may share minority status and often comparable levels of poverty but they vary greatly in familial cohesiveness, attitudes toward mental illness, and service use patterns. There are some suggestions of strengths in adversity, as Pickett et al. (1993) put it. Minority caregivers appear, in some cases at least, to show less depression than their mainstream white American counterparts—arguably, because they have more realistic expectations, more familiarity with adversity, and social support as a buffering mechanism within their own ethnic communities.

Lacking equal access to the larger society, ethnic minority groups are often required to fall back on their own resources, maintaining and strengthening internal support systems that have often been eroded among mainstream Americans or Europeans. Ethnic minority groups still tend to maintain active membership in churches and some subscribe to supernatural belief systems that provide human as well as spiritual sustenance. Often, they have extended families with traditions of reciprocal assistance in times of need. Nevertheless, the research suggests that the scope of the social networks is not always indicative of support. Larger social networks can sometimes be detrimental by not fulfilling expectations of reciprocity. Relatives and friends may exacerbate an already stressful situation by imposing misinformation, criticism, and poor advice. When shame and secrecy preclude the sharing of family burdens, the social network may become a hindrance rather than a help in coping. The data indicate that affirmative support for the caregiver's efforts is at least as important as instrumental aid for effective coping. Although minority families may show less subjective distress, it seems apparent that all caregivers need acknowledgment of their burdens as well as education and illness management techniques.

12

The Effects of Advocacy Movements on Caregivers

In the United States, there have long been organized constituencies of patients, families, and others concerned with specific diseases or disabilities. Their organizations generally have been devoted to advocacy for research, public information resources, and expanded services. Until recent years, mental illness has been different from these other disabilities in the composition of its advocacy groups. Under the broad rubric of safeguarding human rights and the global promotion of mental health, advocacy for persons with severe psychiatric disorders had primarily been the domain of interested citizens rather than of stakeholders whose own lives were invested in treatment, care, and cure. Former patients and family members who participated in these organizations generally maintained a low profile, perhaps due to internalization of societal (and often professional) stigma. Officers in these movements rarely acknowledged any personal connection with mental illness in public advocacy or leadership roles. The experiences and expertise of stakeholders were thus little publicized until the advent of national family and consumer organizations about 15 years ago.

In this chapter, we describe a small number of advocacy groups whose activities have had an effect on the lives and destinies of persons with mental illness and their caregivers. This includes citizen advocates who have devoted some of their activities to public education, destigmatization, and legislative lobbying. Included also are organizations whose primary task involves protection of the civil liberties of persons with mental illness. Our major focus, however, is on the activities and emerging social influence of the family and consumer organizations.

CITIZEN ADVOCACY GROUPS

The National Mental Health Association (NMHA)

Prior to the era of consumerism, the NMHA had been the major citizen advocacy group for persons with mental illness. Despite its founding by a former mental hospital patient, Clifford Beers, the NMHA has had a limited emphasis on the most seriously impaired population. Rather, the NMHA has had the broad-based mission of improving mental health in the population at large. Mental Health Association (MHA) branches have focused on such activities as befriending troubled schoolchildren, working with disaster victims, training police to deal with interethnic conflict, running conferences on sexuality, and the like. MHA branches have served as umbrella organizations linking professionals with citizens interested in mental health. Since 1987, the Mental Health Information Center has been the NMHA clearinghouse to disseminate information on a wide range of mental health topics.

MHA branches have also sponsored support groups for families of persons with mental illness but, in contrast to self-help groups, these have typically been led by volunteer professionals. In recent years, MHAs have begun to offer resources to psychiatric consumer groups as well.

It should be emphasized that despite their broad-based interests, MHA groups have actively lobbied for legislation for persons with serious mental and developmental disabilities at both state and national levels. For many years, they were the major citizen voice in conjunction with professional societies and persons interested in mental health law and patients' rights.

The Judge David L. Bazelon Center for Mental Health Law

The Bazelon Center was formerly called the Mental Health Law Project. Organized in 1972, its purpose was to halt abuse and neglect in state mental hospitals and training schools for persons with mental and developmental disabilities and to prevent exclusion of disabled children from public schools. Over the years, the project's agenda has become more comprehensive to encompass the demands of deinstitutionalization and the era of community-based care. In addition to its basic focus on protecting the civil liberties of persons with mental illness, the Bazelon Center provides legal resources to combat exclusionary zoning and rental policies and to ensure access to health care, social services, and income support. Legal aid is also directed toward reforming state systems and generating a continuum of community services for persons with psychiatric and developmental disabilities. Attorneys of the Bazelon Center work in the courts and in legislative and policy arenas and offer legal assistance to other advocacy groups, consumers, and policymakers.

State Protection and Advocacy (P&A) Centers

The P&As are federally mandated to protect disabled persons from neglect and abuse and to guard their rights in institutional and other residential settings. Protection and advocacy legislation was initially passed by the U.S. Congress in 1986, and reauthorized in 1988 and again in 1991 (PL102-173), as the Protection and Advocacy for Individuals with Mental Illness (PAIMI) Act. PAIMI extends to persons with mental illness rights already afforded to persons with developmental disabilities. All 50 states, the District of Columbia, and five territories have established PAIMI programs. Under current reauthorization, the P&As' jurisdiction will be extended to community care facilities, including nursing homes, board-and-care homes, facilities for the homeless, and jails and prisons. State P&A Centers are members of the National Association of Protection and Advocacy Systems (NAPAS).

Much of the P&A work involves grievance casework for individuals as well as initiating lawsuits to upgrade institutional conditions. Many P&As also view their mission as reforming the service delivery system, which may include shifting resources from institutional to community providers. P&As have been criticized for choosing to advocate in court for the expressed choice rather than for the best interests of mentally disabled persons, a policy that has been incorporated in the mission statements of many states. According to Isaac and Armat (1990), a fixed adherence to this policy has sometimes led to highly unfortunate consequences for the individuals and their caregivers.

THE RISE AND INFLUENCE OF
STAKEHOLDER ORGANIZATIONS

Arguably, the most important influence on family caregiving in mental illness has been the rise of the family movement, the National Alliance for the Mentally Ill (NAMI). NAMI provides direct assistance for caregivers in the form of education and support groups and indirect assistance through its influence on the political process. Numerous factors beyond the control of caregivers, and about which they may have little knowledge, clearly impinge on their lives and those of their loved ones. These factors range from the availability and structure of services to medications that may vastly improve symptomatology and level of functioning. They involve the accessibility of community housing and the ease with which persons with severe and persistent mental illness may obtain entitlements. NAMI has provided a support mechanism for caregivers, a powerful national initiative for public education on mental illness, a vehicle for political action and antistigma campaigns, and an important lobbying capability to influence funding for services and research.

The consumer movement has also affected caregivers' lives. Their local organizations provide outlets for socialization and skill building and for personal therapeutic growth. They may provide a range of alternative services and even alternative caregiving resources. Consumer groups have many positive effects, enriching the lives, goals, and self-concept of persons with mental illness. Above all, the consumer philosophy offers many persons with mental illness a vision of empowerment that counters self-stigmatization and reinforces their belief in themselves and their aspirations to live independently (Deegan, 1992).

Consumers have been vigilant in protecting the rights of persons with mental illness. This is in accord with a major emphasis in NAMI. The philosophy of total empowerment may be highly therapeutic for some individuals and countertherapeutic for others, however, depending on their level of cognitive impairment and capacity for reasoned choice. Some members of the consumer movement, particularly those who define themselves as survivors or ex-inmates, may have a negative effect on caregivers' lives. With a political agenda that is essentially antipsychiatry, some survivors have influenced the reduction of state hospital beds and made it more difficult to hospitalize persons for protracted periods of time, even when long-term sheltered care is clearly needed. Along with advocates from the field of mental health law, former psychiatric patients who dispute the validity of mental illness have made it more difficult for caregivers to obtain involuntary treatment for persons undergoing florid psychotic episodes and temporarily incapable of informed consent. In some cases, legal constraints against involuntary interventions have resulted in the need for caregivers to press charges and to criminalize illness to obtain needed treatment for loved ones.

Organization of Families

Local family support groups in various states had been organized in the 1960s, and at least one state family federation existed in 1971 (Shetler, 1986). These groups had developed almost spontaneously from profound mutual need. One woman, for example, described how she was waiting, feeling miserable and alone, in the office of her adolescent son's psychiatrist. Looking up, she saw another woman, a stranger, whom she immediately felt shared a similar problem.

> I went over and talked to her and told her I had a son with schizophrenia. She did too. We went out for coffee and poured out our hearts. We decided to set up a meeting and advertised it in the papers for all families with a mentally ill relative. That's how our group got started. (Anonymous AMI member, personal communication, July 1981)

Her group became one of the pillars of the emergent national family organization.

THE NATIONAL ALLIANCE FOR THE MENTALLY ILL (NAMI)

A major psychiatric textbook has termed the organization of NAMI one of the most important events in the history of U.S. psychiatry (Kaplan & Sadock, 1991). The authors have described the organization as "the most vigorous citizens group in America, advocating the problems of the mentally ill to legislators and the public" (p. 846). A former director of the National Institute of Mental Health, Herbert Pardes, has hailed the political influence of NAMI as "the single most positive event in the history of mental illness" (Flynn, 1993, p. 8). This is because for the first time, the major psychiatric disorders have an important national political presence, a grass roots constituency of families with a profound commitment to improving services, research, and public awareness.

NAMI was founded in 1979 when 284 family members from various states convened at the University of Wisconsin in Madison, with backing from the Community Support Program of the National Institute of Mental Health (NIMH). In a little more than a decade, NAMI has grown at this writing to 150,000 members with 1,090 affiliates in all 50 states, as well as Puerto Rico and the Virgin Islands.

National Networks and
State Organizations

Today, there is a well-functioning NAMI office disseminating information and lobbying for research and services at the national level. State Association for the Mentally Ill (AMI) organizations work for improved services in their individual states. Specialized national networks focused on mentally ill subpopulations—children and adolescents, forensic patients, homeless persons, and patients from culturally diverse backgrounds. NAMI networks have included the Homeless and Missing Persons Network, Curriculum and Training Network, Child and Adolescent Network, Multicultural Concerns Council, Forensic Network, Religious Outreach Network, National Plan Network, Consumer Council, Siblings and Adult Children Council, Veterans Council, Hospital and Long-Term Care Network, Legal Alliance, Legislative Network, Literature Committee. In addition, NAMI has a health care coordinator in every state and a network of family education specialists throughout the country.

Support and Education

Like most organizations that are formed by stakeholders rather than interested outsiders, NAMI merges self-help and advocacy. Thus the basic armature in all localities is mutual support groups and membership education about all aspects of major mental illnesses. Professional educators within NAMI have developed models for training family education specialists. NAMI's multiple activities also include resource development, public education, and antistigma campaigns.

Antistigma Initiatives

NAMI has actively enlisted the aid of media experts (including some who are themselves members of NAMI) in combating stigma against the mentally ill. The organization has been influential in the development of television movies and other programs depicting realistically the lives and problems of people with schizophrenia. A committee monitors the media and advertising for negative portrayals or insulting references to people with mental illness. On several occasions, NAMI representatives have convinced an advertiser to remove an offensive ad or a negative commercial. In some cases, an advertiser has not only apologized but made a substantial contribution to further the organization's work. NAMI has also been successful in enlisting the services of actors, sports figures, and other celebrities who are willing to speak publicly about their own experiences with mental illness and offer open reassurance of the possibility of recovery.

*Mental Health Planning
and Professional Training*

NAMI members serve on mental health planning, policy, and governance boards and focus on legislative advocacy. Family members and consumers are trained as effective lobbyists and patient advocates. NAMI has also had an effect on clinical training. The NAMI Curriculum and Training Network had two major goals: (a) to interest mental health professionals in working with persons with severe mental illness and (b) to ensure that clinical training programs provide current, state-of-the-art, research-based education on the major psychiatric disorders, from preservice to continuing education levels. Several national conferences cosponsored by NAMI and NIMH have brought together leading clinical educators, researchers, and practitioner-family members for concept development and curriculum planning in the core professions (Lefley & Johnson, 1990; National Institute of Mental Health, 1990).

Publications

NAMI lists an array of carefully reviewed resource materials on mental illness for caregivers and for the lay public. Specialized NAMI-sponsored publications have also had a substantial influence on mental health service providers. These include *Care of the Seriously Mentally Ill: A Rating of State Programs* (Torrey, Wolfe, & Flynn, 1990), which is regularly updated and revised, and *Criminalizing the Seriously Mentally Ill: The Abuse of Jails as Mental Hospitals* (Torrey, Wolfe, & Flynn, 1992). In collaboration with the Center for Psychiatric Rehabilitation at Boston University, NAMI began publishing in 1990 the scholarly journal *Innovations and Research* with a focus on clinical services, community support, and rehabilitation for persons with severe and persistent mental illness. Other publications include the bimonthly *NAMI Advocate* and the highly respected *Journal of the California Alliance for the Mentally Ill.*

Research Promotion

The family constituency has been powerfully influential in raising research dollars for mental illness. NAMI has successfully lobbied for substantial increases in congressional appropriations for NIMH research on the major psychiatric disorders and helped launch the National Schizophrenia and Brain Research Campaign. NAMI members helped launch two private foundations for research on serious mental illness. They cofounded the National Alliance for Research on Schizophrenia and Depression (NARSAD) in 1985 and have made available more than one million dollars in research awards through the Ted and Vida Stanley Foundation. Members have also worked to ensure continuity of research, demonstration, and service programs such as the Community Support Program of the Center for Mental Health Services, inducing Congress to override the zero-funding that had been recommended by previous administrations.

Legislative Advocacy

A number of members of Congress themselves have mentally ill family members, and the family organization has been a natural matrix for coordinating efforts to initiate and promote federal legislation favorable to the mentally ill. For example, NAMI's influence was strong in attaining enactment of the 1984 Social Security Act amendments to restore eligibility to mentally ill and other disabled individuals. With a major personal stake, NAMI members were active in promoting passage of Public Law 99-660, which required all 50 states to develop a comprehensive mental health plan, including provision of community care to persons with serious mental illness. The legislation for the first time required family and consumer participation on a state advisory council. Reauthorization language linked the approved state plans to the federal block grant, and local AMI groups became active in monitoring their state's compliance with the plan's objectives. They joined with other disability interest groups to pass the 1990 Americans with Disabilities Act, which now protects persons with mental illness from various forms of discrimination. Currently, NAMI is actively working for equitable coverage for mental illness on a par with other physical health problems in private insurance and in any forthcoming plan for health care reform.

NAMI had also worked vigorously to obtain the P&A legislation previously described. At the urging of NAMI members, the law was amended to require increased representation from family members and consumers on P&A governing boards and advisory councils as well as training for advocates on the nature of serious mental illness. The new P&A formulations may help ease a situation that has disturbed a number of family members. According to Isaac and Armat (1990), in certain states some AMI groups feel the following:

> P&As for the mentally ill [are] staffed largely by the mental health bar, militant ex-patients, and anti-psychiatric patient advocates. . . . They have found that many of the P&A staff see treatment itself as an abuse from which the patient needs protection. (p. 268)

The balancing of patients' rights with patients' needs for housing and treatment is an ongoing debate in the advocacy movement and, as we shall see, consumers themselves are divided on many of these issues.

CONSUMER SELF-HELP
AND ADVOCACY ORGANIZATIONS

The NAMI Consumer Council is a group of primary consumers who function as a separate organization within NAMI, with substantial representation on the NAMI Board of Directors. Some members have the dual status of consumers and family members. Members of the Consumer Council generally support the NAMI agenda. They tend to have a biological view of mental illness and agree with the various research, service, and other legislative initiatives proposed by the larger organization. Many, however, also have overlapping affiliations and common interests with other consumer organizations.

All consumer self-help organizations offer their members mutual support. Some, however, tend to focus on one of two major objectives: personal problem resolution and growth, or political advocacy. A study of 104 self-help groups of present and former psychiatric patients identified two major service models that the author differentiated as social movement versus individual therapy (Emerick, 1990). The social movement groups were oriented toward broad social change; they offered public education, legal advocacy, information-referral, networking, and technical assistance to other consumers. The individual therapy groups offered more "inner-focused" individual change through mutual support meetings and various types of "alternative therapy." The research found that almost two-thirds of the groups were social movement models.

The National Depressive and Manic-Depressive Association (NDMDA) is a major consumer organization that combines both social movement and therapeutic functions. The NDMDA consists of 250 chapters serving more than 35,000 patients and families. Chapters may have multiple area support groups. Like NAMI, the NDMDA views major affective disorders as biogenic, disseminates public education on the biochemical nature of depressive illnesses, holds annual conferences with professional presentations, and tries to fight stigma and promote basic research with a variety of advocacy efforts. In its public presence and influence, the NDMDA is the consumer organization that is most comparable to national organizations of persons suffering from major physical disabilites.

The Nonpolitical Self-Help Model

Therapeutic support group models generally offer fellowship, support, and information. Many are based on 6- or 12-step programs. Schizophrenics Anonymous (SA), founded in 1985 with more than 70 chapters, is organized and run by people with a schizophrenia-related disorder. SA focuses on recovery and uses a six-step program, along with medication and professional help. GROW is an international organization with more than 100 groups in the United States. It has a 12-step program to provide skills for avoiding and recovering from a breakdown. They offer a caring and sharing community to attain emotional maturity, personal responsibility, and recovery from mental illness. Recovery, Inc. has 850 chapters nationally and offers "a self-help method of will training; a system of techniques for controlling temperamental behavior and changing attitudes toward nervous symptoms and fears" (White & Madara, 1992, p. 109). All of these groups provide helpful experiences and social outlets for people with mental illness.

The Political Advocacy Model

The era of deinstitutionalization was accompanied by formation of protest organizations with such names as the Insane Liberation Front or the Mental Patients Liberation Project. These groups of former psychiatric patients were angry at a mental health system that they felt had abused and dehumanized them rather than helped them. They tended to have strong antipsychiatry views and were vehemently opposed to electroconvulsive therapy and often to psychotropic medications as well. Many felt that the only valid help for persons who were "psychiatrically labelled" would come from peers who had also experienced a history of psychiatric hospitalization but had later rejected professional care. Many of the pioneers of the consumer movements developed and provided models for today's consumer-operated services (Chamberlin, 1978; Zinman, Harp, & Budd, 1987).

Ideological Divisions

Although the contemporary consumer movements have a common agenda of self-determination and empowerment, former psychiatric patients seem to be divided ideologically about the nature of mental illness. Although some prefer to view mental illness as psychogenic or as a social construct, rejecting biogenesis, most seem to accept a diathesis-stress model, and many describe themselves as having a brain disease or a chemical imbalance (Beall, 1994; Frese, 1993; Hatfield & Lefley, 1993; Kersker, 1994a). Some consumers are totally opposed to any kind of forced treatment, whereas others have suggested that without it, some friends might not be alive today (S. Rogers, 1994). A few members of the consumer movement feel that hospitalization is harmful and would like to close all hospital beds; others oppose hospital closing and premature discharge (Kersker, 1994b). The view that hospitalization is harmful was not supported empirically in a scientific study of psychiatric clients designed and conducted by consumers and directed by a professional researcher who is also a consumer. In the California Well-Being Survey, more than 50% of the respondents felt their hospitalization had been helpful, 22% reported both positive and negative aspects, and only 20% found hospitalization harmful (Campbell, 1989).

These differing viewpoints are reflected in the major consumer advocacy organizations. The more radical National Association of Psychiatric Survivors (NAPS) retains an essential protest orientation. They reject the name "consumers" and identify themselves as survivors. This term is typically construed as survivors of the mental health system rather than as survivors of psychiatric disorders. Many indeed have highly negative recollections of their experiences in treatment (Hatfield & Lefley, 1993). Most members would like to outlaw electroconvulsive therapy, and many reject psychotropic medications and hospitalization as well. NAPS has taken a formal position opposing any kind of involuntary treatment. The more moderate National Mental Health Consumers' Association

(NMHCA) has taken no formal position on forced treatment (Frese, 1993). They clearly agree with the goal of consumer empowerment, however. Their most recent mission statement states the following:

> Recovery and healing, not social control, must be the goal and outcome of the mental health system; therefore, the mental health system must be client-driven. . . . We support the full and sustained funding and development of user-run alternatives and additions to the traditional mental health system, self-determined and governed by and for members, in every community. (National Mental Health Consumers Association, 1992, p. 1)

NMHCA members acknowledge the validity of mental illness and the need for treatment and have a larger and seemingly more diversified membership than NAPS.

Many NMHCA members also belong to the NAMI Consumer Council. These consumers also espouse the empowerment and recovery doctrines but within the framework of acknowledging the validity and personal agony of their experiences with mental illness. They endorse etiological research and applaud new psychopharmacological advances. A Consumer Council member who writes a column for the *NAMI Advocate* describes receiving almost 500 letters, mostly from consumers, agreeing with NAMI's biological view of mental illness. Many consumers shared their hopes of recovery because of positive experiences with new medications such as clozapine and risperidone (Beall, 1994).

Roles of Federal and State
Governments in Consumerism

A major catalyst in the organization of both family and consumer movements is the Community Support Program (CSP) of the federal government. Initially under the National Institute of Mental Health and now part of the government's Center for Mental Health Services, the CSP was organized in 1978 to deal with problems of deinstitutionalization. The federal program focused on developing in each locality a comprehensive continuum of care for deinstitutionalized patients that would include all needed resources for survival, treatment, rehabilitation, and, hopefully, a satisfactory quality of life (Stroul, 1989). Through targeted grants to state administrations, the CSP fostered public-academic linkages and funded research and demonstration grants for model rehabilitative programs for persons with severe and persistent mental illness.

The CSP has also aided the development of state and local self-help and advocacy groups and facilitated dissemination of their ideas on a national basis. Through the years, the program promoted "learning community conferences" to bring together researchers, service providers, family advocates, and primary consumers. In recent years, the CSP has helped develop annual "alternatives conferences," which bring together members of primary consumer organizations from all over the United States to discuss national goals. The CSP has been a major catalyst in the development of services in which former psychiatric patients are participants or primary providers.

Several other national bodies funded by the federal government play an important role in consumer affairs. The National Mental Health Consumer Self-Help Clearinghouse in Philadelphia, Pennsylvania, encourages the development of consumer self-help groups and provides information, materials, and referrals on fundraising and program development. The National Empowerment Center in Lawrence, Massachusetts, provides technical assistance to mental health self-help groups. Two self-help research centers at the University of California, Berkeley, and the University of Michigan, Ann Arbor, have been federally funded to conduct studies on self-help initiatives of persons with mental illnesses. Consumers are totally involved in all phases of the research, including design, instrument development, interviewing, and analysis. Additional studies are being conducted by consumer-researchers in Massachusetts, Missouri, and New York.

Consumer-researchers have also been involved in developing appropriate outcome measures used in CMHS-funded services research. A concept-mapping project resulted in a publication by the National Association of State Mental Health Program Directors (NASMHPD) entitled *Mapping Mental Health Outcomes from the Perspective of Mental Health Consumers* (Trochim, Dumont, & Campbell, 1993). This project generated recommendations to the mental health research community on outcome measures of greatest interest to consumers in a future research agenda.

By the late 1980s, NASMHPD had developed a position paper that specifically outlined the role of "expatients-consumers" in state mental health systems. "Their contribution should be valued and sought in areas of program development, policy formation, program evaluation, quality assurance, system design, education of mental health service providers, and the provision of direct services (as employees of the provider system)" (National Association of State Mental Health Program Directors, 1989, p. 1).

A survey commissioned by NASMHPD reported that in 1993, 65.5% of state mental health agencies provided financial resources to consumer-run and family-run programs and 19 states had consumer offices or definite plans to start a program within the year (National Association of State Mental Health Program Directors, 1993). The most commonly supported activities were peer or mutual support, advocacy, and promotion of positive public attitudes. Most of the programs were stimulated by CSP incentive funding but some continue with state support.

Resource Development by Family and Consumer Groups

Almost from the beginning of NAMI, affiliate groups in various localities started developing resources to fill in gaps in their service delivery systems. Included were multiple housing facilities, employment opportunities ranging from thrift shops to furniture workshops, psychosocial rehabilitation programs, and even a psychiatric hospital. Resource development, however, requires a large investment of time, effort, and money in services that can serve only a limited number of people. Many NAMI members are opposed to volunteer initiatives that relieve local governments of their obligations to the disabled. Some feel that these resources may be targeted to the developers' relatives and generate an inequitable system of care. Although individual initiatives are continuing, many AMI members feel that families should be investing their energies in legislative advocacy for the universe of persons with severe mental illness rather than in the development of new services.

Most consumer advocacy movements have a different view of their role in services. Their goals are to use the experiences and skills of former psychiatric patients both within the system and as operators of consumer-run alternatives. Many CSP initiatives have been devoted to helping consumers achieve that end through the funding of research and demonstration projects and other inducements to state administrations. Consumer-run enterprises include housing facilities, residential placement services, case management, peer companion programs, social centers, employment services including consumer businesses, crisis respite houses, and special programs for the homeless. Fourteen CSP-funded demonstration projects include a variety of consumer enterprises. In most states today, there is a

Mental Health Consumer Affairs Office organized and staffed by one or more former psychiatric patients.

Almost all states have networks of drop-in centers that provide socialization outlets and interest workshops outside of the traditional mental health system. The state of Florida, for example, has 32 drop-in centers well distributed across the state, which are maintained and operated by consumers. The centers are members of the Florida Drop-In Center Association Inc., which publishes a newsletter and coordinates political lobbying activities. Many states offer sponsorship of consumer drop-in centers by state hospitals and community agencies. Typically, maximum independence is afforded to the consumer group.

Research on Consumers
as Service Providers

Researchers are beginning to show good outcomes in some of these early consumer efforts. One study looked at patients discharged from a state psychiatric hospital who participated in a community network development (CND) self-help program. The research found that 10 months after discharge, CND participants required 50% less rehospitalization and two-thirds fewer inpatient days than a comparable group of nonparticipating patients. A significantly smaller percentage of CND ex-patients required community mental health center services than the comparison group (Gordon, Edmunson, & Bedell, 1982). Mind-Empowered Inc. (MEI) is an assertive case management-supported housing program in Oregon that is completely run by consumers. Operating successfully for several years, MEI received a county contract to bring 30 persons out of the state hospital and keep them in the community. Preliminary data indicated that during the first 6 months of the program's operation, only two clients returned to the hospital (Nikkel, Smith, & Edwards, 1992).

An evaluation of six consumer-run drop-in centers in Michigan found that the centers were meeting their programs' goals of providing acceptance, social support, and problem-solving help. The study found high levels of consumer satisfaction together with the reported feeling of the members that they actually ran their centers (Mowbray, Chamberlain, Jennings, & Reed, 1988). A 6-month survey of nine consumer-operated drop-in centers in Pennsylvania similarly found a high level of member satisfaction (Kaufmann, Ward-Colasante, & Farmer, 1993). An inherent source of bias in such studies, however, is that the samples are typically drawn from continuing participants, so less-satisfied participants who may have dropped out are usually not counted.

Nevertheless, there are other objective sources of satisfaction with consumer-run programs. In California, a project that used former patients as peer counselors on locked inpatient wards received enthusiastic evaluations from clinical staff. Most staff wanted the program to be extended. The peer counselors themselves indicated that they had experienced personal benefits in terms of greater self-confidence, increased empathy, and feelings of being needed and responsible (McGill & Patterson, 1990).

Family members participating in a randomized trial of consumer versus nonconsumer case management teams reported equal satisfaction with the capabilities of consumer case managers. Because many studies do not report on ethnicity, it is of interest that 86% of the respondents were African Americans (Solomon & Draine, 1994b). A randomized evaluation of consumer versus nonconsumer training of state mental health service providers found positive reactions to the use of consumers as trainers (Cook, Jonikas, & Razzano, 1993).

There are many concerns about job stress and the stability of former psychiatric patients as mental health service providers. A project in Denver, Colorado, trained consumers as case management aides in a psychiatric rehabilitation program. Of 25 trainees, 18 completed the program and 17 were employed as case management aides. At 2-year follow-up, the 15 trainees who were still employed had required a total of only 2 bed-days of psychiatric hospitalization (Sherman & Porter, 1991).

Other CSP research demonstration projects based on consumer services are currently being evaluated for outcome. Consumers seem to be doing well on many of the evaluated programs, but there are some problematic findings as well. Sometimes the findings are contrary to hypotheses about expected consumer behavior. For example, research in Chicago, Illinois, compared trained consumer and nonconsumer staff on mobile outreach teams for persons manifesting psychotic behavior. The findings showed that contrary to expectations, consumers were significantly more likely than nonconsumer staff to certify clients for involuntary hospitalization (Lyons, Cook, Ruth, Karver, & Slagg, 1993). It is unknown whether consumers were less capable of handling psychotic behavior or whether they were more knowledgeable about the limitations of trying to obtain voluntary consent for treatment.

According to an evaluator for the Community Support Program, consumer alternatives were never envisioned to serve as substitutes for mental health services. Rather, their purpose was to empower consumers to gain some control over their lives. An analysis based on systematic observations of consumer-run services found that consumers often tried unsuccessfully to replicate services provided by the local mental health clinic rather than to offer self-help alternatives, and that power conflicts and hierarchies developed in many programs (McLean, 1994). Negative findings are rarely reported in the literature, so it is uncertain at this point which consumer enterprises were unable to fulfill their missions and which variables related to failure. In the evaluations required of grants supporting consumer-run services, it was not necessary to prove that consumers were superior to nonconsumer staff but only that they did not differ significantly in effectiveness. In many of the published findings, this effectiveness has been demonstrated.

Families and Consumers as Advocates

There is no doubt that the consumer movement has brought enormous benefits and new insights to the treatment of persons with serious mental illness. As McLean (1994) has suggested, the most important element is not an attempt at replicating professional treatment but the message of personal worth and empowerment. Peer supports, role models, meaningful work opportunities, and, above all, a voice in the political process are extremely powerful therapeutic modalities for persons who have felt diminished and stigmatized by society. Some of the so-called negative symptoms of withdrawal and apathy, as well as aggressive and acting-out behavior, may be attributable to learned helplessness or to anger at devalued identity. In such cases, the consumer message of empowerment has the potential for reversing behaviors that may well be reactions rather than symptoms of a disease process. These are empirical issues that are yet to be explored.

Meanwhile, the message of self-determination has also generated internecine conflict and, in some cases, a purposive avoidance of collaboration with other advocacy groups. One of the basic arguments regarding empowerment is the insistence of some members of the survivor movement that NAMI cannot speak for psychiatric patients, that only the consumer-survivors or those defined as "ex-inmates" may do so (Chamberlin, 1984). Yet there is fervent defense of NAMI from other individuals with these credentials. Beall (1994), a member of the NAMI Board of Directors, represents the opposite view to the antipsychiatry arm of the consumer movement and verbalizes the conflict of those who disagree.

Consumers recounted how they were not welcome in "psychiatric-survivor" organizations because they believed in the biological basis of their mental illnesses. The "survivors" went out of their way to assure them that NAMI was very anti-consumer. This shocked me. (p. 15)

Beall went on to say how she had always been welcomed at her local and state AMI, how they had helped form a depressive and manic depressive group, paid for their facilitator's training, and actively worked for a support group for persons with schizophrenia. "I believe our shoulder-to-shoulder work has made us all stronger and more effective advocates. Together we are an unbeatable team" (Beall, 1994, p. 15).

The differing viewpoints on the biological nature of mental illness, the efficacy of professional treatment, and the question of who speaks for persons with mental illness are more than academic. The issues are presented here because they have a continuing relationship to the nature and structure of services and a profound effect on the availability of involuntary interventions during times of crisis. Essentially, the issues relate to the heterogeneity of the disorders that are lumped under the rubric of serious mental illness. They involve the degree of independent functioning that may be expected of particular types of individuals and the therapeutic strategies that may be most effective for these individuals to attain their own levels of what has been termed *recovery vision* in mental illness (Anthony, 1993). These issues are discussed in greater detail in the forthcoming chapter.

13

Patients' Rights Versus Treatment Needs

The Family Dilemma

A member of the Board of Directors of NAMI and of the New York Friends and Advocates of the Mentally Ill relates a typical help line call to the latter organization.

> Hello. My son is locked in his room and afraid the devil will get him if he leaves. The hospital said if he won't come in voluntarily, there's nothing they can do. The police said he's not a danger to himself or others, so they left without doing anything. Can you help me? He has schizophrenia. (Jaffe, 1994, p. 16)

The scenario of the person who is obviously in a psychotic state but refuses any kind of intervention—including interventions from sympathetic consumers—is a nightmare for families who do not know what to do. Even when a family is able to obtain a court order for psychiatric evaluation, legal obstacles to involuntary treatment reinforce an increasing reluctance of crisis emergency rooms to do anything more than stabilize an overtly psychotic person and then discharge him to the home. Lacking private insurance, families often find it almost impossible to admit their loved one for inpatient care. Legal barriers go hand in hand with fiscal constraints and are often the excuse for refusal of needed services.

The frustrations of finding services and being able to hospitalize a mentally ill family member are a ubiquitous complaint. This is a common theme at NAMI conferences and is found at all levels of culture, ethnicity, and socioeconomic status. Many families that once had private insurance covering their mentally ill relative have long ago reached the cap for psychiatric disorders and are now forced to seek admission in public sector facilities. The frustration at having one's own observations and experiences minimized by admitting staff is verbalized in some of the reports collected in a multicultural study of families of long-term mental health system clients.

> Many families, in discussing their experience with hospitalizing family members, reported deep frustrations with the processes of commitment. Their own experience with and assessment of the patient was discounted by hospital staff and admission refused in spite of the families' feeling that significant deterioration has occurred. . . . They made several attempts to convince their family member to go to the hospital before they were successful. When they arrived . . . they were told their ill family member did not meet the criteria for psychiatric commitment and sent home without further help. (Guarnaccia et al., in press)

This story is repeatedly heard in support group meetings throughout the United States. As in the cited study, the trip to the hospital typically occurs only after exhaustive efforts and extensive pleading with the mentally ill family member to agree to go for help. The degree of stress endured through the behavioral deterioration, psychotic episode, attempts to convince the person of the need for help, spending hours in a clinic waiting room, and finally being denied admission without further help is self-evident. It is truly remarkable that family members have been able to endure these trials without decompensating themselves.

CAREGIVERS' DILEMMAS
WITH FORCED TREATMENT

Families' experiences with coercive treatment are painful, filled with ambivalence, and are lacking in viable options. They are faced with an unresponsive treatment system and a legal system that places them in an adversarial posture against a loved one. Families must balance the right to autonomy of a relative with mental illness against their own rights to protect themselves from acute personal suffering and possible danger to themselves or to other family members, including the relative in question. If an involuntary intervention is the only option, they must balance indignity to a loved one against his or her own self-destructive behavior, threats to themselves or others, the very real possibility of self-neglect or even death on the streets, or the criminalization of illness. They themselves feel coerced by a system that offers inadequate resources and makes it difficult to help persons during a critical period, when they are perceived as incapable of helping themselves.

Like members of the consumer-survivor movements, family caregivers would greatly prefer alternatives to involuntary interventions. Forced treatment has an adverse effect not only on the self-concept and integrity of the individuals involved but on the well-being of family members and on their relationship with a person they value. A family's need to obtain a court order for psychiatric assessment may lead to short-term gains, if any, but generate long-term resentment on the part of a loved one who may feel angry and betrayed.

In general, family members view the involuntary intervention as an undesirable but essential safety net. But there are a number of experiences that differentiate the family's perspective from that of consumers, legal advocates, and service providers. Family members are the ones most likely to be aware of, and to be personally affected by, the behaviors leading up to the need for involuntary treatment of a particular individual.

Precursors of Involuntary Interventions

Involuntary interventions are usually preceded by psychotic episodes —sometimes exacerbated by family conflict, but most typically because a person who needs medications has stopped taking them for a protracted period of time. In fact, because the majority of persons with severe mental illness do not live with their families on a regular basis, most involuntary admissions are likely to originate outside the family home. When a psychotic episode does occur in the family setting, however, the person may become delusional, paranoid, aggressive, or manic. Displaced hostility toward family members often alternates with acute guilt for nameless crimes. There may be profound depression and suicidal threats that the family may have good reason to fear, but it is difficult to obtain treatment until an actual attempt has been made.

There are many cases of persons in a manic state charging huge bills or selling off property for a pittance, impoverishing not only themselves but their spouses and children. There are situations where paranoid delusions generate abusive accusations or threats against vulnerable family members, such as young children or elderly parents. There are instances of self-mutilation, serious property destruction, and attempts at arson. In most of these cases, the family is helpless to act unless these behaviors occur in the presence of police or they are willing to press charges when the police come. All in all, the psychotic episode elicits bewilderment, terror, and anguish in family members and may leave the family exhausted and depleted of coping resources.

If the psychotic episode occurs outside the household, the family is usually expected to manage it. Even within the mental health system, many programs or boarding house operators will try to get the family to take the problem off their hands. Family members have received calls from residential managers stating they are evicting the client because of assaultive behavior toward other more vulnerable clients who are also mentally ill and who need to be protected. In one case, a boarding home resident threw boiling coffee on another resident, was evicted bodily by the manager, and was running in the middle of traffic on a busy boulevard when the family came. They took him to a crisis emergency unit, where he signed himself in voluntarily, but he walked out the next day. Ironically, the press for voluntary consent, which is presumed to safeguard the person's perception of individual autonomy, often has countertherapeutic consequences without fulfilling its basic premise. Research indicates that patients may perceive as much coercion in voluntary treatment situations as in involuntary ones (Hoge et al., 1993).

Elopement against medical advice is a constant danger with voluntary admissions, although the latter are often favored by hospital personnel. In families' experience, the policy often generates a self-perpetuating cycle of decompensation, brief stabilization, noncompliance, and recurrent psychosis. Paradoxically, a supreme court decision militates against voluntary admission signatures, which are typically pro forma among psychotic individuals lacking capacity for informed consent. In *Zinermon v. Burch* (1990), the court essentially held that the rights of a psychotic individual are breached, rather than upheld, by consent that is uninformed and given when incompetent.

Despite accelerating psychotic behavior, family members are almost always reluctant to call the police and even more reluctant to initiate involuntary commitment procedures. Both of these not only are humiliating and dehumanizing to a loved one but can also have consequences that are counterproductive. The police must personally observe dangerous behavior to take someone to a crisis emergency unit against his will, but often by the time they come, an assaultive person has calmed down. The police leave, accelerating a cycle of repeated assaultive or destructive behavior with no further recourse for the family. After going through the agony of obtaining a court order and enduring an involuntary commitment procedure, families may see a patient discharged within a few days, still symptomatic but now angry and alienated from his or her major support system.

GAINS AND PROBLEMS
OF MENTAL HEALTH LAW

Over the years, numerous advances have been made in protection and advocacy legislation for persons with mental illness. Because of the long history of "snake pit" conditions in mental hospitals, caregivers have a vital interest in making sure that their loved ones will be helped and not mistreated when they require institutional care. Largely due to the efforts of mental health legal advocates, there are now safeguards with respect to the use of restraints and seclusion in crisis and inpatient facilities. Strict regulations are intended to ensure that (a) patients may be subjected to restraints or seclusion, or both, only when no other options are available to deter dangerous uncontrollable behavior; (b) patients may be kept under these conditions for limited periods of time and must be released as soon as the behaviors have abated; and (c) their well-being must be monitored by staff so that patients are not left to languish alone. Conditions are supposed to be scrutinized carefully to confirm that temperatures are adequate and that patients do not suffer unduly because of removal of furniture, mattresses, or clothing that may be used in suicidal attempts.

Facilities are monitored by various regulatory agencies to make sure that patients are not mistreated. Staff must be trained to adhere to these regulations, treat patients respectfully, and keep careful documentation of all critical incidents. For any coercive intervention, comprehensive case notes must be available to provide backup demonstration of need. Despite these safeguards, violations sometimes occur. All mental health facilities are required to have risk management and quality assurance-quality improvement mechanisms to ensure that these violations are appropriately handled and that they do not recur. The system is still far from perfect, but long-needed controls are finally in place.

THE PAINFUL QUESTION OF
INVOLUNTARY INTERVENTIONS

The imposition of seclusion and restraints, even when justifiable, tend to reinforce the negative attitudes of many persons with psychiatric disabilities toward crisis or inpatient treatment. Despite the heroic attempts of advocates to provide safeguards against inappropriate use, the very availability and legality of these options offend many people. To date, no one has been able to come up with acceptable alternatives when an individual is acutely psychotic, dangerous, and seemingly uncontrollable. The argument that has been advanced so many times that violent behaviors can be soothed away with the right kind of humane interventions has never been demonstrated empirically.

Involuntary Treatment and
the Nature of Mental Illness

This argument has similarly been advanced in the interests of doing away altogether with any kind of involuntary intervention. Embedded in this argument is a basic issue raised throughout this book: fundamentally differing conceptions of the nature and reality of mental illness.

Persons who view major psychiatric disorders as legitimate illnesses that are largely biologically based tend to accept the remedy of involuntary treatment as an undesirable but essential safety net. Opponents of involuntary interventions tend to believe that the psychotic behaviors leading to commitment are psychological responses to overwhelming external stress. Their premise is that most psychotic episodes are terrified perceptions of threat. They feel that sympathetic others, preferably persons who have shared a similar experience, may be able to convey a real understanding of the terror and transmit a message of reassurance that the person will not be harmed. From this perspective, psychotic episodes are preventable if one is able to recognize the events that trigger the terror. Physical or chemical restraints only reinforce the conviction that one is in danger of being harmed. A medical ambience and psychotropic drugs are likely to exacerbate rather than reduce the person's fears.

From the biogenic perspective, however, internal stimuli can also generate psychotic episodes that involve a threat to oneself or others. These episodes may be triggered by street drugs, excessive alcohol, or malfunctioning neurons. In schizophrenia, for example, internal life is disorganized and fragmented by brain dysfunctions, which are manifested behaviorally in aberrant thinking, misinterpretations of stimuli, and associated terrors. The outside world responds to these behaviors with misunderstanding and confusion, generating a spiralling negative feedback loop that reinforces and exacerbates the terror.

> Consider the effects of psychotic behavior. Neurotransmitter dysfunction leads to paranoid ideation, which is projected onto another patient, a family member, a case manager, or just someone on the street. The paranoid thought triggers an angry gesture or curse directed toward the object person. The latter feels threatened or offended and reacts with anger. The schizophrenic person feels attacked and decompensates into further paranoid fantasies and perhaps further acting-out behavior. The internal stressor, which is physiologically based, has triggered a maladaptive attempt to restore equilibrium by contesting a perceived threat, generating a series of social behaviors with unfortunate consequences. (Hatfield & Lefley, 1993, p. 14)

In any treatment setting, whether operated by professionals or consumers, calming behavior and attempts to understand what the patient is trying to say always constitute the preferred approach. In some cases, this, indeed, may be enough to allay the terror and mitigate, if not eliminate, the psychotic ideation. Whether humane, sympathetic treatment is adequate, without psychotropic medications, remains to be demonstrated empirically. Also demanding further research is the issue of whether and under what conditions psychotic episodes can be prevented. Although there is some empirical evidence of stressful life events in the 3-week period preceding decompensations (Day et al., 1987), the presumed linkages have little predictive validity for future episodes. Indeed, the international research of Day et al. (1987) indicates great heterogeneity in the types of antecedent stressful experiences as well as their relative disturbance value when evaluated from a normative viewpoint. Most of these stressors occur in daily life and rarely, if ever, elicit psychotic responses in the general population.

Given our present state of knowledge, the field is not yet able to distinguish between psychological and biological precursors of psychotic behavior or to ascertain the salience and predictive value of a wide range of idiosyncratic stressors. We have no means of distinguishing between those crisis episodes that can be defused with appropriate psychological interventions and those that cannot be controlled under any circumstances without physical restraint. An example of the latter is a substance-induced psychosis involving command hallucinations to harm oneself or others. It is doubtful that cocaine-induced paranoia can be talked away.

Philosophical and Ethical Objections to Coercive Interventions

The problem remains as to how to deal with psychotic behaviors that appear to pose a threat to the self or others. The question of involuntary treatment embodies some of the most critical philosophical, clinical, and political issues in any society. Primary among these are the rights of the individual versus those of the group, the latter embodying the rights of the individual's family as well as the social good. Also involved are the responsibilities of society to protect the individual from self-damage and the tension between the rights and the needs of persons with presumably impaired judgment.

The spectrum of opinions ranges from a totally civil libertarian view that no one can be deprived of his or her liberty without clear demonstration of a crime (not for imminent dangerousness) to the concept of the state as *parens patriae,* fulfilling a protective role for persons who are too disabled to function in their own best interests. The issues have been discussed in numerous forums as well as in the professional journals of the legal and mental health professions. Questions of defining and assessing dangerousness and empirical studies of civil commitment have been reviewed (Monahan, 1977). The diagnoses that satisfy a state's definition of "mental disorder" and grave disability have been assessed among judges and investigators of civil commitment (McFarland, Faulkner, Bloom, Hallaux, & Bray, 1989). Also in relation to civil commitment are comprehensive legal and psychological analyses of the meaning of personal autonomy in a democratic society (Winick, 1992). Some people are totally opposed to involuntary treatment under any conditions. Others give guarded approval to civil commitment as an intervention that simultaneously protects both the patient and society. Some practitioners even view forced treatment as therapeutic. In this perspective, psychotic episodes may be a call for help, and the availability of involuntary treatment provides reassurance that a person will not be allowed to do harm when he or she is in an uncontrollable state. Indeed, a substantial number of persons have expressed relief that at one time or another they were hospitalized against their will. Recalling the events leading up to their hospitalization, they have stated that they probably would have been dead or in jail if civil commitment had not been available. The tension between recognition of the adverse aspects of involuntary treatment and the conflicting demands of suicidal risk are manifested in the statement of a consumer speaking at a national conference on these issues.

> There are people in this room that have been forced-treated and that are categorically opposed to forced treatment under any circumstances. And I like some of these people very much, and I would love to be able to take that position in order to make myself popular with them. But I can't do it, because people's lives are at stake. (Rogers, 1994, p. 6)

Outpatient Commitment

One of the most perplexing issues for caregivers and service providers is what to do about the subset of patients who manifest the revolving door syndrome. This is the familiar cycle of patients who are discharged from the hospital, stop taking their medications, decompensate, and are readmitted involuntarily. Again they are stabilized, are discharged, and stop taking their medications.

> One possible solution that has always seemed tantalizingly simple is to extend the state's civil commitment powers to compel patients to take their medications and continue contact with a therapist after discharge. . . . [This] may be attractive to civil libertarians who see it as the "least restrictive alternative" to inpatient hospitalization. (Appelbaum, 1986, p. 1270)

This is outpatient commitment, which according to Appelbaum (1986), has had uneven and relatively unsuccessful applications.

Slobogin (1994) discusses three major legal mechanisms for providing involuntary community treatment. About half the states permit *outpatient commitment* as a less restrictive alternative to hospitalization. *Preventive commitment,* which exists in only a few states, permits commitment to outpatient and sometimes inpatient treatment of people who do not yet meet the usual commitment criteria; that is, they are not currently dangerous but are expected to be dangerous if there is no intervention. The criterion for both outpatient and preventive commitment is called a "predicted deterioration" standard. Although this seems to curtail civil liberties more than a criterion of outright dangerousness, it is sometimes a safety valve for persons with a history of violence and a mechanism for averting tragedy. The third type of involuntary community treatment is a *conditional release,* available in about 40 states, which involves continued supervision of a person released from the hospital. Violation of conditional release may trigger rehospitalization after a hearing (Slobogin, 1994).

Criminalizing Mental Illness

Some former patients, particularly those who view themselves as survivors, have stated that jail is a less dehumanizing alternative to civil commitment (Blanch & Parrish, 1991). One must question why some consumer-survivors consider involuntary imprisonment preferable to involuntary hospitalization. Jail often fulfills the most terrifying fears of the person in psychosis—that one has committed nameless crimes for which the most awful penalties must be exacted. Moreover, any jail experience, with its potential for physical assault from criminal offenders, is likely to be far more cruel and unusual punishment than involuntary hospitalization. In the national survey by NAMI and the Public Citizens' Health Research Group of mentally ill persons in the criminal justice system, 40% of the jail officials reported that inmates with mental illness were abused by other inmates (Torrey, Wolfe, & Flynn, 1992).

Moreover, jail personnel themselves may be anything but protective. According to the survey by Torrey et al. (1992), criminal justice systems nationwide typically house more inmates with severe psychiatric disabilities than are found in existing mental health facilities. In 1993, the jails of Dade County, Florida, held more mentally ill people than any hospital or institution in the county. Many were held for such minor charges that they were unlikely to be prosecuted. Conditions for mentally ill inmates were described as follows:

> The jail strips them naked and locks them in a cold cell, with a bare metal shelf for a bed and a toilet to sit on. . . . Men deemed suicide risks huddle naked in cells stripped even of toilet paper. Other mentally troubled inmates mill about cramped day rooms, where heavily medicated people nap on the floors. At night, they sleep two or three to a tiny cell. The lights are never dimmed. (Rogers, 1993, p. 1A)

According to the report, jail authorities kept the cells chilled to keep the inmates more subdued. All clothing and toilet paper were removed and lights were left on to prevent suicide attempts. The assistant state attorney was reported to have said, "I've had psychiatrists tell me they had difficulty interviewing inmates because the inmates were so cold, they're shivering" (Rogers, 1993, p. 17A).

Conditions were exposed in the media only because of the death of an inmate. Found screaming obscenities on the street, he had been taken to jail despite the intercession of an aunt who claimed she told officers his history of mental illness. The inmate was charged with resisting arrest, refusing to put his hands behind his back, and disorderly conduct. In jail, he apparently was stripped, placed naked in a cold cell, and allegedly hosed down and beaten. An autopsy revealed pneumonia and fractured ribs (Rogers, 1993).

The national report by Torrey, Wolfe, and Flynn (1992) suggests that criminalizing mental illness is by no means an isolated event. In the Miami situation, a minor misdemeanor led to a person's death. But police officers are frequently forced to make judgments and dispositions that are best left to mental health professionals. They are often confronted with misdemeanants about whom a quick decision must be made: jail or involuntary evaluation in a crisis facility. Involuntary civil dispositions are often cumbersome and time-consuming, requiring careful paper work for the courts. There may also be a spontaneous hostile reaction to someone screaming obscenities and resisting arrest, eliciting a wish to punish rather than to treat. Few police academies offer comprehensive training on how to deal with persons exhibiting psychotic behavior, particularly when this is happening in the street and passers-by feel threatened. For house calls, this type of intervention is sometimes handled by a few well-trained warrant officers, provided the municipality is fortunate enough to have developed this special resource. In other localities, a mobile crisis team may divert the case from unnecessary police involvement. This is an area in which the critical needs of mentally ill persons and their caregivers frequently come into conflict with local norms and regulations surrounding the process of seeking involuntary treatment.

Disagreements Among Consumers

Considering the dangers to mentally ill people from predatory inmates and the system itself, why do some consumer-survivors prefer involuntary incarceration in jails to involuntary commitment in hospitals? Perhaps it is precisely this presumption of vulnerability that is so offensive to persons trying to repair and reestablish their insulted autonomy. Perhaps jail is less threatening to the ego integrity of individuals who have felt diminished and humiliated by the treatment system. Imprisonment suggests that the inmate was in control of what he or she was doing and was the architect of the consequences. Involuntary hospitalization, on the other hand, conveys the paternalistic message that one is not responsible for one's own actions and must be cared for by others, reinforcing feelings of helplessness. This is a core issue, again relating to the nature of mental illness and the degree of accountability to which one should be held for one's own behavior. Consumers-survivors espousing self-determination and autonomy suggest that they and their peers should be willing to take the consequences for antisocial behaviors. They suggest that feelings of helplessness may indeed be at the root of many of the problems that are subsequently manifested as psychotic behavior and that forced treatment only confirms their helplessness. They argue that seclusion, restraints, and other types of coercive practices are not treatment but social control and that the term *involuntary treatment* is an oxymoron. They contend that no interventions can be considered therapeutic without the informed consent of the individual.

What precipitates a psychotic episode? Many consumers feel that the underlying motivation is a communication of needs. Thus abusive or destructive behaviors may reflect frustration at not being understood or even listened to by others. Sometimes, indeed, episodes may be triggered by arguments in which the persons with mental illness make demands for things perceived as vital needs and then feel that their needs are ignored by others. Sometimes family members trigger resentment by being too critical about issues such as self-care, money management, or household responsibilities. Research indicates that ordinary family dynamics may elicit unusual psychophysiological arousal in persons with the hypersensitivities of schizophrenia or related disorders (Lefley, 1992a). But most caregivers are not aware of this. If treatment systems offered adequate education to patients and families on the major mental disorders and their management, many conflict situations and possible relapses might be avoided. Family members often know from experience, however, that psychotic episodes are not always responses to observable interpersonal events. Violent behaviors often appear to be triggered by fearful hallucinations or delusions. The terror of decompensating persons may be exacerbated by anger that their perceptions of danger are not recognized or are discounted by other people. Caregivers are ready targets for anger. Sometimes this type of reaction may indeed be "talked away" by supportive persons, particularly those who have experienced similar terrors or who know how to validate the perception and at the same time defuse the accompanying fear. But in many cases, particularly when hallucinations are exacerbated by substance abuse or in substance-induced psychoses, people are likely to be completely out of control, unusually strong, and quite dangerous to themselves and others. As has been indicated, some members of the expatient-survivor movement have suggested that in such situations, the people be taken to jail.

Other consumers, however, are vigorously opposed to jail as a solution. They are also opposed to social policies that close state hospital beds without adequately controlled community placements, precisely because this policy often generates situations in which people end up in jail. For example, the director of the Florida Consumer Drop-In Center Association has written about severely mentally ill friends who against their wishes were discharged from the controlled environment of the state hospital.

> [They] are now controlled through our state prison system. . . . I think it is wrong to shift people from state hospitals to community placement and then put responsibility on the former patients for control and management of their illness. Some are not able to make the transition from a controlled and stable environment into the freedom and lifestyle of the community. The issue is not dangerousness. The issue is the wrongful imprisonment of persons with severe psychiatric illnesses in jails. (Kersker, 1994b, p. 2)

The indication here that some people actually want to stay in the hospital and are discharged against their will to community placements is an issue that has not been given much thought by protection and advocacy systems that espouse expressed choice. Typically, the advocacy is to permit discharge of individuals who want to leave, sometimes against medical advice (Isaac & Armat, 1990). Yet it is probable that at least as many people fear the destabilization of discharge as those who fear involuntary commitment. Lewis et al. (1991), who studied 313 Illinois patients discharged from four state hospitals, found that of those who returned to mental institutions, 97% did so voluntarily. In today's service system, premature discharge is far more likely to occur than forced admissions to inpatient facilities. Although most states have initiated case management systems, the psychological and logistical aspects of preparing patients and monitoring their community reentry are still inadequately handled in most clinical facilities.

Social and Legal Implications

Above all, the "normalization" of psychotic behavior by declaring it criminal rather than sick perpetuates the myth that mental illness is a myth and adds powerful reinforcement to its stigmatization. A very real concern with normalizing psychosis by declaring it criminal is the implication for the so-called insanity defense. Consumers today speak for a whole body of individuals, many of whom are extremely ill and subject to command hallucinations or other failures of impulse control. Mental illnesses are not only highly diverse, but also highly variable. Delusional or manic states can alternate with completely rational behavior. In 1994, the U.S. Supreme Court declined to review the conviction of a person diagnosed with paranoid schizophrenia who had been sentenced to 60 years in state prison for assault (*Cowan v. Montana,* 1994). The jury felt he had knowingly committed the crime because his delusional behavior seemed to come and go. The defense of "not guilty by reason of insanity" has already been eliminated in several states, including Montana, Idaho, and Utah, and may be dispensed with in others. The term *insanity* is a dubious legal term, subject to multiple interpretations. The elimination of this defense, however, would mean that people who commit crimes because of their mental illness may spend many years in prison cells rather than in treatment facilities. This is a possibility of grave concern to the community of persons with mental illness and to their families as well.

THE DIVIDING ISSUE OF HETEROGENEITY

The opposition of persons who have lived through civil commitments must be respected and taken seriously. The very logic and articulateness of their arguments highlight the role of cognitive impairment in differentiating categories of mental illness and ability to give informed consent, however. Is there not a contradiction in expecting informed consent from someone whose behavior is so disordered that forced treatment is being considered? Do patients differ diagnostically in their capacity for rational thought and judgment even under these circumstances? Furthermore, are all individuals diagnosed with mental illnesses equally susceptible to the types of psychotic episodes that may lead to civil commitment?

What about responsibility for these episodes? Are there some individuals who presumably may be held accountable because the episodes requiring intervention were generated by their own behaviors—such as those who refuse to take the prescribed drugs that have previously stabilized them or, conversely, insist on taking street drugs that result in disordered thinking and affect? Are there individuals who simply cannot be held responsible under any circumstances because their psychotic behavior is unpredictable and not under willful control? Do we jail those people who are accountable and hospitalize those who are not? And what do these distinctions mean in terms of diversion from involuntary treatment?

Clinical depressions so profound that they generate suicidal risk are difficult to deal with outside a clinical setting. It is uncertain to what extent interpersonal or cognitive therapies, intense peer support, or other interventions can remedy depressions without the patient's willingness to take antidepressant medications. If the person is noncompliant and suicidal, can we say that personal autonomy and the right to control one's own body take precedence over society's self-assigned mandate to prevent people from taking their lives? Do families have rights to protect themselves from pain and loss of a loved one?

Differences in Levels of Functioning

Heterogeneity of diagnosis and function is a critical issue in the relations of the consumer and family advocacy movements. Consumer organizations purposively use a broad definition and accept into their midst anyone who has ever used the mental health system, although the membership largely consists of persons who have endured at least some psychiatric hospitalization. In contrast, members of the family organization typically represent the most chronic population. A scientific study of the composition of NAMI suggests a preponderance of mentally ill relatives with schizophrenia and, to a lesser extent, bipolar disorder, long-term disability, and fairly severe levels of impairment (Skinner et al., 1992). The diagnostic distribution and baseline functional levels of members of the consumer political advocacy movements are unlikely ever to be assessed as a matter of principle. These external clinical issues are either in disrepute or considered irrelevant to the mission of the membership.

Some NAMI members have pointed out the differences between the remarkably articulate consumers they see at conferences, or whose writings they read in journals, and the grossly disabled, disoriented individuals they see at home. There is no doubt that many of the consumers-survivors have suffered great pain, and some have experienced gross injustices in their previous hospitalization experiences. Yet observing the functional capabilities of these consumers, many AMI caregivers feel that at the present time, their own relatives are much more likely to need involuntary interventions.

Although the NAMI Consumer Council also tends to be composed of highly functioning, articulate consumers, many acknowledge the need to maintain civil commitment as a last resort for family caregivers who are related to persons with more severe mental illness. Yet none of these groups may adequately reflect the need. Despite increasing representation of minority members and formation of culturally diverse affiliates, both NAMI and the consumer movements remain predominantly white, middle-class organizations. Given racial-ethnic differences in national statistics on mental hospital admission rates (Manderscheid & Barrett, 1987), and in involuntary commitments (Snowden & Cheung, 1990), it is likely that the existing advocacy and self-help organizations underrepresent the populations most in need of services and political influence.

The differing views in the consumer and family movements are paralleled by the difficulties of theoreticians, clinicians, and statisticians to arrive at a common definition of "serious mental illness." Mandated by congressional legislation to provide a definition for needs assessment purposes, panels of experts and stakeholders elected to include almost all of the then current DSM-III-R disorders with the exception of V codes (no mental disorder) and a few categories covered by other data sets. Their definition emphasized functional disability, rather than diagnosis, as the major criterion. Although the intent of the legislation was to assess service needs of persons with chronic mental illnesses, in large measure this all-inclusive definition was an attempt to avert inevitable battles with third party payers for coverage of excluded diagnoses. This expanded the population deemed eligible for parity with physical disorders in insurance coverage. In an effort to attain parity for persons with the most severe and persistent mental illness, NAMI had tried to limit the definition of serious mental illness to syndromes with demonstrable, research-supported biological substrates and a chronic course. Presumably, these are the syndromes that are most likely to be involved in involuntary interventions.

ATTEMPTED SOLUTIONS
TO FORCED TREATMENT

Beginning in 1990, the federal Community Support Program (CSP) sponsored three major roundtable discussions of alternatives to involuntary interventions. There was a first meeting with consumers and a second with family members, psychiatrists, and attorneys specializing in mental health law. A third meeting included mental health administrators and policy planners. A large national conference with representatives from all constituencies was held in Houston, Texas, in May 1994, and initiatives are expected to continue. Although the stakeholders continue to be highly divided on the issue of whether society can totally eliminate involuntary treatment, all participants agree on the need to seek a range of alternative options.

Advance Directives

Advance directives can eliminate the coercive aspects of involuntary interventions by putting patients in charge of the decisions that affect their lives. During periods when people who suffer from serious mental illnesses are competent, they can execute directed care documents that specify how decisions about treatment will be made in the event of later incompetence. One mechanism is the formal designation by the patient of a health proxy or surrogate who is empowered to make treatment decisions on the patient's behalf. Another alternative is for the patient to execute a living will that gives written instructions with respect to acceptable care.

Medical living wills are typically proscriptive, prohibiting heroic efforts in the event of terminal illness. Psychiatric living wills are oriented toward recovery. They focus on persons whose illnesses frequently involve a history of cyclical incapacity for rational judgment and whose treatment presumably will reinstate that capacity. Advance directives may be *prescriptive,* offering prior consent to authorize psychiatric interventions, or they may be *proscriptive* statements intended to prevent specific interventions that the person finds offensive or countertherapeutic. Both prescriptive and proscriptive consumers' viewpoints were presented in two contrasting articles on psychiatric living wills in *Schizophrenia Bulletin.* Rosenson and Kasten (1991) endorsed prior consent agreements called "Ulysses contracts." According to legend, Ulysses had ordered his crew to bind him to the mast, stop up his ears, and ignore his pleas for release so as to avoid being lured to destruction by the sirens. The Ulysses contract was perceived as a proactive attempt by a stabilized individual to plan ahead for a crisis, as "autonomy based on enlightened self-interest" (p. 1). The article described how the leader of a large metropolitan chapter of the National Depressive and Manic-Depressive Association had given her psychiatrist prior informed consent for electroconvulsive therapy in the event of an acute episode. She later described this intervention as a "lifesaver."

The proscriptive viewpoint, presented by Rogers and Centifanti (1991), rejected prior consent as a form of self-paternalism. As an alternative to the Ulysses contract, which they viewed as "giving away our rights to choose and refuse in advance" (p. 9), these consumers advocated for the "Mill's Will," based on John Stuart Mill's philosophy that individuals do not have the right to relinquish their liberties. Mill held that the only time a state has the right to exercise power over citizens against their will is to protect others, not to protect the subjects from themselves. Rogers and Centifanti proposed more comprehensive documents that included a list of treatment choices, prescriptive and proscriptive; a related treatment history; and statements indicating the authors' understanding of their rights and a caveat that their wishes are not to be discounted in favor of their "best interests." It should be emphasized that there is nothing inherent in either Ulysses contracts or Mill's wills that prevents both endorsement or rejection of specific treatments. The person's response to psychotropic medications and known side effects are also valuable information in the document. Developing directed care documents may be an excellent opportunity for education and joint planning by a patient, psychiatrist, and family members.

According to Appelbaum (1991), who has written widely on this subject, the major drawback of psychiatric living wills is that they cannot anticipate future needs and take all contingencies into account. Proxy directives have a clear advantage because they are not constrained by events that cannot be foretold. There are two other advantages of the proxy, according to Appelbaum. First, patients can discuss their desires and values in depth with their designated health surrogate and establish specific principles to be applied if they become incapacitated. Second, if the proxy is appointed as the ultimate decision maker, this precludes conflicts about the proper way to proceed among the patients' friends and relatives.

Alternative and Preventive Measures

Legal and technical obstacles make it unlikely that advance directives can offer a global solution to the problem of involuntary interventions in psychiatric emergencies. The essential goals are to develop alternatives to interventions against the patient's will, and, even more important, to reduce the conditions conducive to relapse. "Safe houses" and respite facilities, preferably consumer staffed, are alternatives for persons in crisis. Preventive efforts involve collaborative work with patients, clinicians, and caregivers on complying with medication, avoiding street drugs, reporting prodromal cures of decompensation, and reinforcing participation in rehabilitation programs.

Other preventive approaches may involve special training for police as well as educating caregivers, other relatives, and friends in how to calmly manage hallucinating or abusive individuals or how to defuse crises in the home. Mental health systems need to ensure continuity of care with "no reject-no eject" policies. The rejection or eviction of difficult patients from programs or boarding homes is highly likely to lead to decompensated behavior and the need for forced stabilization. Development of mobile crisis teams for on-site stabilization is an important mechanism gaining wide appeal. Applications of intensive case management or assertive community treatment, such as the Program of Assertive Community Treatment (PACT) model (Stein & Test, 1980), are guards against decompensation. Finally, providing referrals to consumer self-help groups for peer supports can also help avert the need for involuntary interventions.

CAN WE ELIMINATE THE
NEED FOR CIVIL COMMITMENT?

As was indicated in the CSP meetings, most families would be happy to see viable alternatives to involuntary commitment. Family members firmly support, and have even helped found, projects involving mobile crisis teams or other types of diversion programs so that their loved ones can avoid the humiliations of police calls, restraints, and other insults to their humanity. AMI members have been very responsive to the idea of crisis interventions in which consumers can help their loved ones calm down and become stabilized. Yet diversion programs and alternative options are not the major answer to this overwhelming social and personal dilemma. The major question is whether the need for forced treatment can be anticipated and prevented.

Who are the people with mental illness most likely to be involved in involuntary treatment? Along with persons who self-medicate with street drugs and those who are homeless, hungry, and self-neglectful are other persons who are homebound. As indicated in the descriptive case at the beginning of this chapter, these are people who lock themselves in their

rooms, reject medications, refuse to participate in any treatment programs, and avoid social interactions. The family is the only resource there
for them and must watch their loved ones decompensate without being
able to access the system on their behalf. Many of these people are likely
to end up in a florid psychotic episode and require involuntary hospitalization. These individuals require outreach teams, preferably other consumers, to motivate them to change and start them on the path toward
recovery.

Needed Directions for Research

Currently, there is an enormous emphasis on the recovery vision
(Anthony, 1993). The position of the consumer movements is that respect
and encouragement of autonomy are the major therapeutic modalities that
will lead to mood or symptom alleviation and to improvement of one's
quality of life. Indeed, these arguments make intuitive sense if one accepts
the premise that both positive and negative symptoms may reflect defensive responses to diminished self-worth—introjections of societal labeling of persons as mental patients (Link & Cullen, 1990). Here, the issue
of heterogeneity becomes paramount as one assesses the extent of psychophysiological vulnerability in the individual patient. For example, a
substantial body of research has indicated the therapeutic value of teaching families that high expressed emotion (hostile criticism or emotional
involvement) should be avoided (Lam, 1991). Families are taught alternative ways of responding to provocative or disruptive behaviors that
would normally evoke indignation. Clinicians, also, have spoken of the
dangers of too many demands and overstimulating environments for
persons with the core deficits of schizophrenia. They have distinguished
between patients who thrive and others who decompensate when confronted with high-expectancy programs and have called for different
rehabilitation models geared to the needs of individual patients (Pepper
& Ryglewicz, 1987).

But these protective strategies are counter to the ideas of many consumer-survivors that persons labeled mentally ill are autonomous individuals and accountable for their own behaviors. In this conceptual
system, psychoeducational interventions that teach family members to
change their communication styles or lower expressed emotion may be
interpreted as manipulative efforts to change the patient's behavior. In this
value system, also, clinical outreach to convince homeless mentally ill

people to accept services or seek shelter is sometimes viewed as disrespect for presumptive expressed choice and self-determination.

In the series of meetings on involuntary treatment held by the CSP, there were several areas of disagreement between family and consumer participants (Blanch & Parrish, 1991). Families contested the assumption that involuntary commitment for nondangerous behaviors—that is, behaviors that are merely bizarre or deviant—is fairly common. This may have been the case in some consumers' past experiences with the system. Certainly, there have been outrageous injustices and the position of family members should in no way be construed as minimizing the pain of unjust commitments and dehumanizing treatment. In the experience of most families today, however, it is extremely difficult to obtain court orders or to initiate procedures for involuntary evaluation, let alone involuntary treatment, even for behaviors that are extremely threatening and potentially dangerous to the person or to the family members. The suggestion that involuntary interventions are arbitrary or that persons can be committed against their will for trivial reasons is simply contrary to most families' experience.

There are both philosophical and empirical issues involved in these discussions. The research evidence suggests that there is a subset of persons with severe and persistent mental illnesses—probably as many as one third—who are highly incapacitated, have poor impulse control, and are likely to respond to various types of internal stimuli that may generate behaviors potentially destructive to the self or others. There is some evidence also that calm, benign, nondemanding, and stable environments may deter the types of psychotic decompensation that lead to involuntary interventions, particularly if vulnerable individuals take their medications and stay off street drugs. Consumer support networks, crisis respite houses, and consumer roles in mobile crisis teams may indeed provide viable alternatives for some of these individuals. Overall, however, these are empirical issues that should be determined by empirical means. So far, there is little solid outcome data on crisis alternatives. I have indicated previously that research on consumer and nonconsumer crisis workers on mobile outreach teams showed that consumer staff were significantly more rather than less likely than nonconsumer staff to certify clients for involuntary hospitalization (Lyons et al., 1993). A comprehensive research project in California found that persons who are involuntarily committed are at elevated risk of violence (Catalano & McConnell, 1993). The same study also showed, however, that adding capacity to the mental health system to perform civil commitments will not necessarily reduce violence. Other options are needed.

Despite the philosophical and political momentum to eliminate involuntary treatment, it is clear that social policy cannot be changed on the basis of ideology alone. Mental health planners clearly need sound methodological studies and appropriate sampling to explore whether alternatives work. Consumer subject pools are seriously skewed because they contain few minority respondents, despite the fact that a disproportionate number of minority members, primarily African Americans, have been involved in the involuntary treatment system (Snowden & Cheung, 1990). We need to know the specific kinds of behaviors that lead to involuntary interventions and how to prevent them.

We also need to learn the variables that differentiate those consumers who feel abused from those who feel benefited. For example, what are the characteristics of persons who reject all involuntary treatment and those of persons who favor Ulysses contracts because they do not trust their judgment to consent during psychotic episodes? We need empirical data to determine what kind of patients are actually helped or harmed in terms of objective operational measures so that predictive models can be developed and tested. We particularly need to assess what happens when someone who is sick enough to require involuntary treatment is not treated. Do those persons recover from their psychoses or are they, as hypothesized, shunted into far worse dispositions? Last, we need information on the effect of advance directives on these issues and whether particular kinds of directives help or hinder recovery from psychosis.

Above all, we need further research on alternative intervention models, the types of clients who actually can be diverted, and the types for whom involuntary interventions seem to be a necessary option. It is hoped that we will find that fewer people than anticipated need this option—that almost everyone can be successfully helped by voluntary models of care that do not strip away dignity and self-determination. That would indeed be the most hopeful solution of all.

14

Social Change, Mental Health Policy, and Future Directions

If present trends continue, there is both good news and potentially bad news for family caregivers of persons with mental illness. Some of the good news relates to ever-better relationships of families with mental health professionals and service providers. Professionals are discovering that families are a critically valuable resource in legislative advocacy initiatives. There is increasing involvement of consumers and family members in treatment and rehabilitation, in clinical training, and in mental health planning at municipal and state levels. Although still highly inadequate, efforts are also being made by some service agencies to reach out to families, provide some form of psychoeducation, offer space and resources for support groups, and provide other types of help and supports.

There is good news also in the growing strength of the National Alliance for the Mentally Ill (NAMI) and its network of resources for family caregivers. We have previously noted the story of the local AMI member who, despite numerous interactions with clinicians, had struggled alone with her problem for 14 years. In amazed gratitude she found that after a single year of her affiliate's existence, she now knew people, both lay and professional, who could answer her questions and help her cope. The human and educational resources, the understanding support groups, and the opportunities for action to exert some control over one's destiny are incalculably beneficial to caregivers who have often felt isolated and helpless to change their lives.

An extremely important source of good news for caregivers is the potential of the consumer movement for offering help to loved ones and an alternative caregiving capability. The consumer movement began with residential alternatives to professional services, and these may also be desirable substitutes for living with family members. The peer supports, role models, opportunities for training and work, and the affirmative message of the recovery vision enrich the lives of persons with mental illness. The consumer movement offers a message of personal self-worth that reframes the value and potential of individuals who have been diminished both by their illnesses and by society. Their empowerment message counters the view of mentally ill persons as damaged and ineffectual; the recovery vision urges people not to give up on themselves and to work toward goals that will release them from dependency on others.

A message of positive expectations from peers, especially higher functioning role models, is a relatively new development in the treatment of mental illness. For people with severe mental illness, expectations of significant progress cannot be fulfilled in many cases. For others, the pace of change will be extremely slow. Yet overall, for persons with psychiatric disabilities, these new vistas and opportunities for both consumer-providers and consumer-recipients may prove to be the most significant addition to our armamentarium of therapeutic resources.

In most localities, service delivery systems have gone beyond the basic clinical armamentarium and recognized the need for wraparound care and rehabilitation services for persons with severe and persistent mental illness. Case management and supported housing are now considered standard components in many systems. The Program of Assertive Community Treatment (PACT) model developed by Stein and Test (1980) has received increasing endorsement. Many states are now trying to replicate the intensive case management and training in community living program created and comprehensively evaluated by these researchers. Case managers can relieve the objective burden of family caregivers and also provide continuity of contact with the treatment facility. And there are staff members with whom families can communicate on a regular basis. Some systems even have respite facilities that reduce caregiver burden.

But many problems remain. At this point it is difficult to assess how caregivers' need for speedy access to crisis services will be resolved vis-à-vis the growing antagonism toward any form of involuntary interventions. Perhaps advance directives will gain more currency as an acceptable solution. Perhaps systems will pay more attention to creating alternative diversion programs that may head off the need for forced treatment. The important development is that the major parties are involved in a dialogue about these issues.

The potentially bad news for persons with mental illness and their caregivers relates to the possibility of further erosion of the service delivery system. Continuing deinstitutionalization policy has involved both decreases in long-term hospital beds and restricted access to short-term beds without commensurate increases in community-based services. Fiscal constraints threaten loss or attrition of independent living arrangements offered by mental health programs. There are also prospects of diminished rehabilitative resources in an era of managed care and portents of reductions in federal entitlement benefits. Yet as Lewis et al. (1991) have found in their research on deinstitutionalized patients, clinical services alone cannot improve functioning or reduce the number of rehospitalizations. What are needed are family, jobs, sources of income, support, and intimacy.

CHANGING RELATIONS OF FAMILIES AND MENTAL HEALTH PROFESSIONALS

Terkelsen (1990) has stated that three powerful forces in U.S. social thought gave rise to negative relationships between mental health professionals and families of their mentally ill patients. The first was a remnant of policies that first occurred during the mid-19th century, when asylums developed as a more humane approach to treatment of persons with mental illness. As indicated in Chapter 2, asylum policies deliberately separated patients from families as well as from other outsiders to reduce the presumably toxic effects of excessive urban stimulation. These policies also institutionalized patients for such long periods of time, in such isolated hard-to-reach settings, as to make them strangers to their relatives. Second, this estrangement was exacerbated by psychoanalytic ideas about the etiology of psychoses and their correlative treatment approaches. Last, the era of deinstitutionalization brought efforts to discharge patients to their relatives without preparing caregivers for this task. Barriers of confidentiality and vestigial blaming attitudes toward families added immeasurably to family burden.

Happily, the contemporary era has been accompanied by a sea change in the viewpoints of many practitioners. The empirical successes of psychoeducational interventions, which have no preconceptions of family pathology; the proliferating evidence on the biological bases of many of the major mental disorders; the research on family burden; an increasing emphasis on families' coping strengths in the current literature; and the pragmatic needs of deinstitutionalization have all been factors in changing professional attitudes. Above all, the increasing political influence of

NAMI as a grass roots advocacy movement for mutually desired service and research goals has elicited respect and valued partnership roles. Active participation by state and local AMI members in monitoring and governance bodies have cast families in entirely different status roles vis-à-vis service providers. Clinical training programs also have changed many of their curricula from an emphasis on family deficit models to methods for involving the family in treatment planning. In contrast to the earlier professional tasks of assessment and remediation of family pathology, current models emphasize partnership roles in managing the illness. A current textbook for social workers, for example, gives the following guidelines for working with families of persons with chronic mental illness.

1. See families as soon as possible and involve them in treatment planning. . . . Families should be involved in the development of short- and long-term treatment plans. It is they who live with the patient and will be largely responsible for ensuring that the treatment plan will be implemented.
2. Treat families as you would partners. We should have no preconceptions about any family. Families of the chronic mentally ill are not villains, martyrs, or saints. Each is likely to be a cross-section of all families, containing a mixture of strengths and frailties, of good and bad qualities. . . . What most will expect of the mental health professional is that they be treated with respect, taken seriously, and occasionally relieved of their caretaking responsibilities.
3. Link families to support groups. . . . Through self-help and support groups, families can develop new friendships, share experiences and advice, and participate in class advocacy. The largest and most influential of the self-help organizations is the National Alliance for the Mentally Ill (NAMI).
4. Make ongoing professional supports available. The gains of one-shot crisis-oriented help can soon become dissipated. Just as most chronic mentally ill persons require some form of help, for an indeterminate time, families too may need occasional emotional and concrete support, advice, and guidance. Of course, when families request more intensive interventions for their own problems we should comply with the request. But such therapy should never be foisted on a family, even if well intended. (Gerhart, 1990, pp. 248-249)

The latter injunction is far removed from families' reports of having been catapulted into family therapy against their will and acquiescing only because of fear their relatives would otherwise not receive optimal care (McElroy, 1987). The entire directive, in fact, is responsive to accounts of past interactions with professionals in which families reported feeling ignored, demeaned, or coerced without any explanation from those treating their loved ones. Respectful treatment of families is similarly urged in all of the new books for professionals indicated in Chapter 1.

THE SERVICE DELIVERY SYSTEM: FISCAL ISSUES AND FAMILY CAREGIVING

During the past decade, we have seen dramatic changes in the mental health service delivery system. Public sector hospital beds are now being reduced at an accelerating rate. The federal Center for Mental Health Services (CMHS) released a study reporting that the number of patients in state and county mental hospitals showed a sharp decrease in 1990 nationally, following relatively small decreases in the preceding 5 years. The CMHS report stated that the magnitude of the decrease (9%) was unexpected because the decrease between 1984 and 1989 averaged only 2.5% per year. There was a drop not only in census but in number of hospitals as well. State hospitals decreased from 290 in 1989 to 281 in 1990 (Center for Mental Health Services, 1993).

The closing of state hospital beds has not always been accompanied by the flow of dollars into community replacement services, even in states with presumably advanced service delivery systems. In New York, for example, it was not until 1993 that state legislation was passed and reported on by the *New York Times* in these terms:

[This law] for the first time requires that the state invest a substantial portion of the money it saves by closing down state mental hospitals into community mental health services. The state and city are now planning how to spend that money, which experts say will only begin to put a dent in meeting the needs of the mentally ill. (Dugger, 1994, p. 13)

This came a good 30 years after the federal government had enacted legislation for a nationwide network of community mental health centers that presumably would meet the needs of deinstitutionalization.

Information from Ohio demonstrates that even when state legislatures direct that savings from inpatient hospital use go to community services, this does not always happen. In 1988, the state legislature of Ohio passed a major piece of reform legislation called the "Mental Health Act of 1988." A fundamental principle of the legislation was that savings from reduced use of state psychiatric hospitals would be redistributed to local mental health boards and community service providers. A committee report concluded, however, that about 39 cents of every dollar made available from reduced state hospital use failed to go to community care systems. Instead, these dollars went out of the state mental health system budget to the Ohio general revenue fund (Ohio Study Committee on Mental Health Services, 1993).

The failure of state hospitals to make adequate provisions for their discharged patients has been the subject of numerous lawsuits. It has also been the subject of battles between cities and states over the locus of responsibility for the care of these patients. At this writing, in a ruling attempting to force New York City to deal with housing literally thousands of mentally ill persons discharged from city-run hospitals, a state court judge had ordered 90 days of follow-up care to ensure that the patients have proper residential placements. The ruling would apply not only to homeless mentally ill persons but to all 14,000 patients discharged annually from city hospitals. City officials announced their decision to appeal the order, claiming it would impose too costly a burden on the city (Dugger, 1994). Under these conditions, a concerted effort to convince families to house their mentally ill relatives might have a strong appeal to state and local officials. If families are unable to provide caregiving, it is possible that some states might develop a means test and require families to contribute financially to the care of their disabled relatives in community housing. Billing families for services is a practice that has already been applied in many state hospitals and other public sector service programs, particularly in cases of spousal financial responsibility. For parents of persons whose mental illness began in adolescence or early adulthood, financial contributions to services and housing might impose severe economic burden over the many years of disability and adversely affect the lives of siblings. The threat of homelessness of loved ones or of paying for alternative housing might also have the effect of coercing home caregiving by families reluctant to fulfill this role.

Managed Care

Although there have been efforts to reassure families that persons with severe mental illness will be adequately served under health care reform, there are serious misgivings about the effect of managed care systems. These systems are oriented toward persons with acute, short-term illness rather than chronic conditions. They are concerned with medical treatment, brief hospitalization, or limited psychotherapy, not with long-term rehabilitative needs.

In many states, community mental health centers are being urged to contract with HMOs with capitated Medicaid funding. In most cases, the annual capitation is simply not enough to meet the needs of persons with serious mental illness. An increasing number of states have received, applied for, or are considering Medicaid waivers to change their public mental health system to managed care models. Psychiatrists are already doing battle with managed care firms that restrict hospitalization and demand premature discharge of even severely psychotic people. Seemingly arbitrary caps are imposed for inpatient days following emergency admissions. Physicians are incensed when their clinical judgment is questioned by persons whose credentials are vastly inferior to their own and whose decisions are based on book regulations rather than the needs of the individual case.

Disclosures of Privileged Information

Psychiatric residents have informed this writer that they are particularly outraged when they must share privileged information on the patient with managed care staff in the interests of cost containment, whereas they are forbidden to share the same information with caregivers in the interests of patient welfare.

Patients' confidentiality is constantly breached. The former airtight barriers to sharing any kind of personal information on a patient's case are now extremely vulnerable. For example, for workers receiving psychiatric care or psychological counseling from an employee assistance program (EAP), personal information may be released not only to managed care firms but to the patient's employers. In fact, this may be part of the managed care firm's contractual obligations to the employers who hire them to administer the programs. According to a staff member of the American Psychological Association's *Monitor,* "some psychologists who work for EAPs write less-than-complete notes for fear a patient's employer will demand them" (Sleek, 1995). Availability of sensitive psychiatric information to insurers, present or potential employers, attorneys, or other interested parties is potentially damaging to anyone but extremely dangerous for persons with a diagnosed mental illness and a history of psychiatric hospitalization. Use of the protections of the Americans with Disabilities Act depends on the resources and energies available to an emotionally disturbed or cognitively impaired individual to obtain legal representation and fight what may be a protracted battle for justice. If such an individual lacks these protections, a history of mental illness can be used to deny employment and housing or to infer culpability in various situations involving civil or criminal law. In some managed care situations, these preexisting conditions may be used to deny insurance for medical as well as mental health care.

People with severe mental illnesses require a range of psychiatric, medical, and nonmedical services, including housing, psychosocial rehabilitation, vocational training, and case management. These are not uniformly covered by managed health care providers. Families and patients often require educational interventions, support groups, and other services not usually considered part of the treatment armamentarium. This decade has seen the rise of consumer-operated services, many of them initially funded by research and demonstration grants of the CMHS. The CMHS will no longer be able to fund these services, and state funding is sporadic at best. Will consumer-providers be remunerated by managed care entities for such therapeutic endeavors as drop-in centers or job-finding programs? Will consumers without academic degrees be credentialed as staff members in traditional programs?

Federal Policy and Entitlements

The 104th Congress that convened on January 4, 1995, grappled with the Republican "Contract with America," which contains 10 bills with profound implications for people with mental illness. According to a legislative alert from the Judge David L. Bazelon Center for Mental Health Law (1994), these bills propose tax cuts that must be offset by cuts in income support, health, and other programs relied on by millions of people with disabilities. Federal programs for people with mental illness, developmental disabilities, and substance abuse disorders will face deep cuts in funding and limits on their coverage. The Bazelon Center predicts that if the Contract with America is approved, the most drastic changes for people with mental disabilities or substance abuse disorders will be in basic entitlement programs: Supplemental Security Income (SSI) and Medicaid. Millions of adults are dependent on SSI for basic income, and even more rely on Medicaid for health care. Cuts of $10 billion or more in Medicaid are under discussion.

The Contract proposes to change SSI from an entitlement and cap its expenditures. As a result, people with mental illness would no longer be entitled to a basic level of income or to Medicaid even if they meet federal criteria for disability. Instead, funding for these programs would be contingent on annual congressional decisions. Federal cuts in social programs will also have an effect on state budgets. These cuts will squeeze state funding, and the states in turn may target mental health programs as a way to save dollars. The Bazelon Center predicts that the proposed caps on basic entitlements could lead to a new wave of homelessness, further increasing the burden of states and municipalities.

Regardless of the decisions taken by the 104th Congress, it is evident that the basic livelihood as well as the services for persons with mental disorders rest on a fragile base. Family caregivers may have to stretch their resources even further, finding ways to augment payments for the psychotropic medications now being covered by Medicaid. For many families in poverty, the loss of federal entitlements for disabled members may create inordinate stress, particularly if there is simultaneous reduction of other welfare benefits. Above all, the loss of an independent source of income, no matter how small, will undoubtedly have a psychological as well as economic effect on disabled persons who cannot support themselves and who already experience their lives as diminished by their dependency on others.

THE FUTURE OF FAMILY CAREGIVING
IN MENTAL ILLNESS

Individual lives are invariably shaped by larger social forces. Current sociopolitical developments in the United States predict the possibility of erosion or even abandonment of government's responsibilities to its disabled citizens. Meanwhile, there is increasing recognition of the objective burdens and subjective distress incurred when these obligations are shifted to families. The literature on family burden reviewed in this book barely touches the surface of the multiple problems faced by families living with serious mental illness. Even more important, there is practically no literature on the functional value of caregiving to the recipients. Both the social and personal cost-benefit ratios of family caregiving are unknown. Two researchers on schizophrenia give the following opinion regarding caregiving and the rights of families to be free of this responsibility.

While there is a long history of family involvement in the care of sick members, few other illnesses have an onset age as early in adulthood and a course as disabling and extended as schizophrenia. . . . The care for persons with schizophrenia is a general societal responsibility and not the responsibility of families. Whereas archaic theories of schizophrenia blamed the family for causing the illness, current policies continue this policy of inappropriately shifting responsibility. There is nothing abnormal about relatives of people with schizophrenia wanting to live their own lives. (Keefe & Harvey, 1994, p. 187)

There are similar observations on family caregiving from other noted researchers:

Mental health programs have frequently looked for new locations to house the chronically mentally ill from state hospitals to nursing homes. Families cannot be expected to become the new "back wards" of the community. The goal of family treatment should be to promote independent living functions. The family is an available instrument for encouraging positive change and should not be expected to play the role of chronic care giver. Failure to recognize this essential point may lead to "burnout" either because the family is asked to do too much for too long or simply because the family, the parents, become too old to provide the necessary care. (Schooler & Keith, 1993, pp. 439-440)

The international and cross-cultural research suggests that family caregiving is an artifact of two interrelated variables: societal resources and cultural norms. Cultural norms arise from past and existing social structures and inform their further development. Traditional cultures generally coexist with a low level of industrial development and relatively few alternatives to family caregiving. With no other options, families continue this role despite evidence of severe economic strain and other types of objective family burden (Giel, 1983; Martyns-Yellowe, 1992). In countries with more resources, families feel freer to pursue other possibilities. As we have indicated also, caregiving is typically performed by women, and in cultures that offer a greater variety of life choices, females may be less willing to assume a perceived sacrificial role.

In modern industrial societies, most families seem to prefer residential alternatives to home caregiving. We have previously noted that in Australia, for example, 78% of a sample of caregivers preferred that the mentally ill relative not live at home with them (Winefield & Harvey, 1994). Responses of 308 families to a questionnaire at a NAMI convention indicated that 97% felt their relative should live outside the family home (Hatfield, 1994c). In the United States, some substantial differences have been reported by Guarnaccia et al. (in press) in the percentages of home caregiving in European American (33% to 40%), African American (60%), and Hispanic American (75%) families. Biegel et al. (1991) failed to find any black-white differences, however. With increasing acculturation or exposure to middle-class expectations, differential percentages due to cultural differences may well equal out. The most recent report on demographic variables and their relation to family burden indicated that an Ohio client-based sample was similar in many respects to the NAMI national sample: The majority of caregivers were females taking care of young males. Caregivers were at high risk for family burden, particularly those living with male clients who threatened suicide (Jones, Roth, & Jones, 1995).

In contemporary life, the need for all family members to work and values of personal autonomy and self-actualization are all factors that militate against an unpaid caregiving role. Traditional cultures will also have to develop new structures for caregiving as they become industrialized and enter the nuclear family age.

In nuclear family settings, we have also noted the large number of elderly parents involved in caring for middle-aged adult children. A few elderly parents find gratification in the companionship and physical assistance of their mentally ill offspring. There is no doubt, however, that this companionship is experienced in a context that is developmentally skewed and psychologically undesirable and that both parties would have preferred a more normal lifestyle for the person who is mentally ill. Despite ongoing initiatives to deal with the "when I am gone" dilemma, we still have no current solutions for the aging issue—what happens to dependent dysfunctional adults when their parental caregivers die. We don't know the extent to which a home caregiving arrangement develops skills in daily living for the person with mental illness—the research suggests that this occurs in a very small number—or actually deprives individuals of skills they might have learned in comprehensive residential programs.

There may be wrenching psychological difficulties and a real threat of decompensation when an adult with mental illness has to suffer not only the death of a caregiving parent but translocation from the home he or she has known for many years. Indeed, a move to another setting may be necessitated by the illness or incapacitation of the primary caregiver. Research conducted among families in Maryland suggests that even when parents are still alive, the separation process itself can elicit great anxiety in caregiver and offspring (Hatfield, 1992). Hatfield recommends gradual separation while the parents are still alive to prepare mentally ill persons for the inevitable change in their lives.

We are now entering an era of accelerating sandwich generation responsibilities. The U.S. Census predicts that by the year 2030, the cohort of people more than age 65 will triple. With the expansion of the elderly population, substantial numbers of middle-aged caregivers of mentally ill adult children will also have to cope with caregiving for aged parents, many with senile dementias. Unless there are viable supplemental or alternative resources, this type of role strain almost inevitably will cause emotional stress and perhaps damage the health of exhausted caregivers.

The major thesis of this book has been that family caregiving in mental illness is not a desirable alternative to rehabilitative residential facilities or to any programs that prepare an individual for independent living. From a therapeutic viewpoint, home caregiving is not a favored option when a person could benefit from available supported housing with intensive case management, PACT programs, or congregate living arrangements that foster group activities and socialization with peers. Family caregiving is counterindicated when individuals are so sick or disruptive that their presence threatens the stability of the household. It is not a solution to a state's decision to reduce its hospital beds. From a social policy perspective, this solves one problem by creating another with the potential for profoundly damaging ripple effects.

Family caregiving is valuable only under certain circumstances. This practice is indicated when it is culturally normative and expected by family and patient alike and when there is every prospect of continuity if the primary caregiver dies. In rural areas with no residential alternatives, family caregiving may be necessary to keep mentally ill persons with their kinship network and supports and ensure their accessibility to treatment. Family caregiving is valuable when it has therapeutic benefits, when a loving, supportive family ambience helps the person with mental illness adjust to the disorder and ensures a decent quality of life. Family caregiving is beneficial when the mentally ill person has a clearly assigned function—whether it is attending a day treatment program, holding a job, or fulfilling productive tasks within the household. In cases where there is reciprocity and mutual gratification from this arrangement, everyone benefits because the person with mental illness then has a socially useful role. The main goal is to allow the person being cared for to contribute, to not feel dependent and diminished by the demands of the illness.

Although we have focused on caregiving primarily in coresidential terms, there is no doubt that the broader aspects of caregiving prevail among loving families living apart. Over the life cycle, families are the major support system for loved ones with mental illness. They continue to provide companionship and financial aid, supplementing meager resources with food, clothing, and other necessities even when housing and supervision are provided by the mental health system (Clark & Drake, 1994). Families are typically the only source of luxury items. They are the unpaid case managers, the transportation providers, the social outlets, the ones who can be called on for assistance when problems arise. Functionally, families serve best as an adjunctive resource to the treatment system to facilitate independence and growth. Psychologically, they provide the backdrop of continuity and security that all human beings need. Even when family ties are disrupted, researchers have discovered a pattern of "accordion relations"—a pulling apart and coming together again—with mentally ill persons returning to and being welcomed by their formerly estranged families (Stoneall, 1983). Thus, whether or not they are physical caregivers or involved in continuous loving relationships, families seem to be viewed as a permanent source of caring.

Meanwhile, the struggle to ensure adequate residential caregiving of persons with severe and persistent mental illness continues. Family members' struggles in the years ahead may well focus on increasing the resources available in the private as well as the public sectors, including facilities operated by consumers. As advocates, families continue to press legislatures to adequately fund a wide array of needed services as well as basic research. From the laboratories of scientists and from clinical studies, we as a society look for answers that may ultimately eliminate or modify the effects of severe psychiatric conditions. From consumers and their allies we look to the recovery vision to impart its message of hope and its motivation for growth among those persons who are currently impaired. As citizens involved in public education and stigma reduction, caregivers participate in the task of increasing society's knowledge about the causes, precipitants, treatment, and appropriate conceptualization of major mental illnesses. In this total, interrelated process, family members' contributions as advocates may not only help themselves and their loved ones but ultimately obviate the need for the caregiving role.

References

Abramowitz, I. A., & Coursey, R. D. (1989). Impact of an educational support group on family participants who take care of their schizophrenic relatives. *Journal of Consulting & Clinical Psychology, 57,* 232-236.

American Psychiatric Association. (1994). *Diagnostic and statistical manual of mental disorders* (4th ed.). Washington, DC: Author.

Anderson, C. M., Reiss, D. J., & Hogarty, G. E. (1986). *Schizophrenia and the family.* New York: Guilford.

Anthony, E. J. (1970). The impact of mental and physical illness on family life. *American Journal of Psychiatry, 127,* 136-143.

Anthony, E. J., & Cohler, B. J. (Eds.). (1987). *The invulnerable child.* New York: Clifford.

Anthony, W. A. (1993). Recovery from mental illness: The guiding vision of the mental health service system of the 1990s. *Innovations & Research, 2*(3), 17-24.

Apfel, R. J., & Handel, M. H. (1993). *Madness and the loss of motherhood.* Washington, DC: American Psychiatric Press.

Appelbaum, P. (1986). Outpatient commitment: The problems and the promise. *American Journal of Psychiatry, 143,* 1270-1272.

Appelbaum, P. (1991). Advance directives for psychiatric treatment. *Hospital & Community Psychiatry, 42,* 983-984.

Arnoff, F. N. (1975). Social consequences of policy toward mental illness. *Science, 188,* 1277-1281.

Ascher-Svanum, H., & Sobel, T. S. (1989). Caregivers of mentally ill adults: A women's agenda. *Hospital & Community Psychiatry, 40,* 843-845.

Atkinson, S. D. (1994). Grieving and loss in parents with a schizophrenia child. *American Journal of Psychiatry, 151,* 1137-1139.

Bachrach, L. L. (1988). Defining mental illness: A concept paper. *Hospital & Community Psychiatry, 39,* 383-388.

Backlar, P. (1994). *The family face of schizophrenia.* New York: Tarcher/Putnam.

Barker, P. R., Manderscheid, R. W., Hendershot, G. E., Jack, S. S., Schoenborn, C. A., & Goldstrom, I. (1992). Serious mental illness and disability in the adult household population: United States, 1989. In R. W. Manderscheid & M. A. Sonnenschein (Eds.), *Mental Health, United States, 1992* (DHHS Publication No. SMA 92-1942, pp. 255-261). Washington, DC: U.S. Government Printing Office.

Barrett, R. J. (1988). Interpretations of schizophrenia. *Culture, Medicine, and Psychiatry, 12,* 357-388.

Barrowclough, C., & Tarrier, N. (1992). *Families of schizophrenic patients: Cognitive behavioral interventions*. London: Chapman & Hall.

Bateson, G., Jackson, D. D., Haley, J., & Weakland, J. H. (1956). Toward a theory of schizophrenia. *Behavioral Science, 1*, 251-264.

Beall, M. A. (1994, July/August). Just between us. *NAMI Advocate, 16*(1), 15.

Beardslee, W. R. (1990). Development of a preventive intervention for families in which parents have a severe affective disorder. In G. I. Keitner (Ed.), *Depression and families: Impact and treatment* (pp. 101-120). Washington, DC: American Psychiatric Press.

Bernheim, K. F. (1994). Skills and strategies for working with families. In D. T. Marsh (Ed.), *New directions in the psychological treatment of serious mental illness* (pp. 186-198). Westport, CT: Praeger.

Bernheim, K. F., & Lehman, A. F. (1985). *Working with families of the mentally ill*. New York: Norton.

Biegel, D. E., Li-yu, S., & Milligan, S. E. (1995). A comparative analysis of family caregivers' perceived relationships with mental health professionals. *Psychiatric Services, 46*, 477-482.

Biegel, D. E., Milligan, S., & Putnam, P. (1991). The role of race in family caregiving with persons with mental illness: Predictors of caregiver burden. In *NASHMHPD Research Institute Inc. Second Annual Conference on State Mental Health Agency Services Research, October 2-4, 1991* (pp. 236-246). Arlington, VA: National Association of State Mental Health Program Directors.

Biegel, D. E., & Yamatani, H. (1986). Self-help groups for families of the mentally ill: Research perspectives. In M. Z. Goldstein (Ed.), *Family involvement in the treatment of schizophrenia* (pp. 57-80). Washington, DC: American Psychiatric Press.

Biegel, D. E., & Yamatani, H. (1987). Help-giving in self-help groups. *Hospital & Community Psychiatry, 38*, 1195-1197.

Birchwood, M., Cochrane, R., Macmillan, F., Copestake, S., Kucharska, J., & Cariss, M. (1992). The influence of ethnicity and family structure on relapse in first-episode schizophrenia: A comparison of Asian, Afro-Caribbean, and white patients. *British Journal of Psychiatry, 161*, 783-790.

Bisbee, C. (1991). *Educating patients and families about mental illness: A practical guide*. Gaithersburg, MD: Aspen.

Blanch, A. K., & Parrish, J. (1991). *Report on round table on alternatives to involuntary treatment. September 14-15, 1990*. Rockville, MD: National Institute of Mental Health Community Support Program.

Bornstein, R. F., & O'Neill, R. M. (1992). Parental perceptions and psychopathology. *Journal of Nervous & Mental Disease, 180*, 475-483.

Boyle, M. (1990). *Schizophrenia, a scientific delusion?* London: Routledge.

Bracha, H. S., Torrey, E. F., Gottesman, I. I., Bigelow, L. B., & Cunniff, C. (1992). Second-trimester markers of fetal size in schizophrenia. *American Journal of Psychiatry, 149*, 1355-1361.

Breznitz, S. (1985). Chores as a buffer against risky interaction. *Schizophrenia Bulletin, 11*, 357-360.

Brodoff, A. S. (1988). First person account: Schizophrenia through a sister's eyes—the burden of invisible baggage. *Schizophrenia Bulletin, 14*, 113-116.

Brown, G. (1985). The discovery of expressed emotion: Induction or deduction? In J. Leff & C. Vaughn (Eds.), *Expressed emotion in families* (pp. 7-25). New York: Guilford.

Brown, G. W., Birley, J. L. T., & Wing, J. K. (1972). Influence of family life on the course of schizophrenic disorder: A replication. *British Journal of Psychiatry, 121,* 241-258.

Bulger, M. W., Wandersman, A., & Goldman, C. R. (1993). Burdens and gratifications of caregiving: Appraisal of parental care of adults with schizophrenia. *American Journal of Orthopsychiatry, 63,* 255-265.

Burland, J. (1992). *The journey of hope family education course.* Baton Rouge: Louisiana Alliance for the Mentally Ill.

Campbell, J. (Ed.). (1989). *The well-being project: Mental health clients speak for themselves* (California Department of Mental Health, In Pursuit of Wellness, Vol. 6). Sacramento: The California Network of Mental Health Clients.

Cardin, V. A., McGill, C. W., & Falloon, I. R. H. (1986). An economic analysis: Costs, benefits, and effectiveness. In I. R. H. Falloon (Ed.), *Family management of schizophrenia* (pp. 115-123). Baltimore: Johns Hopkins University Press.

Carpentier, N., Lesage, A., Goulet, J., Lalonde, P., & Renaud, M. (1992). Burden of care for families not living with young schizophrenic relatives. *Hospital & Community Psychiatry, 43,* 38-43.

Carter, B., & McGoldrick, M. (1989). *The changing family life cycle* (2nd ed.). Boston: Allyn & Bacon.

Carver, C. S., Scheier, M. F., & Weintraub, J. K. (1989). Assessing coping strategies: A theoretically-based approach. *Journal of Personality & Social Psychology, 56,* 267-283.

Catalano, R., & McConnell, W. (1993). *Do civil commitments reduce violence in the community? A time-series test (Working Paper #2-93).* Berkeley, CA: Institute for Mental Health Services Research.

Center for Mental Health Services. (1993). *Additions and resident patients at end of year, state and county mental hospitals, by age and diagnosis, by state, United States, 1990.* Washington, DC: U.S. Government Printing Office.

Chamberlin, J. (1978). *On our own: Patient controlled alternatives to the mental health system.* New York: Hawthorn Books.

Chamberlin, J. (1984). Speaking for ourselves: An overview of the ex-psychiatric inmates movement. *Psychosocial Rehabilitation Journal, 8*(2), 56-64.

Clark, R. E., & Drake, R. E. (1994). Expenditures of time and money of families of people with severe mental illness and substance abuse disorders. *Community Mental Health Journal, 30,* 145-163.

Cockerham, W. C. (1985). Sociology and psychiatry. In H. I. Kaplan & B. J. Sadock (Eds.), *Comprehensive textbook of psychiatry/IV* (4th ed., pp. 265-273). Baltimore: Williams & Wilkins.

Coffman, S. J., & Jacobson, N. S. (1990). Social learning-based marital therapy and cognitive therapy as a combined treatment for depression. In G. I. Keitner (Ed.), *Depression and families: Impact and treatment* (pp. 137-155). Washington, DC: American Psychiatric Press.

Cohen, A. (1992). Prognosis for schizophrenia in the third world: A reevaluation of cross-cultural research. *Culture, Medicine, & Psychiatry, 16,* 53-75.

Coleman, S. (1987). Milan in Bucks County: Palazzoli and the family game. *Family Therapy Newsletter, 11*(5), 42-47.

Cook, J. A. (1988). Who "mothers" the chronically mentally ill? *Family Relations, 37,* 42-49.

Cook, J. A., Hoffschmidt, A., Cohler, B. J., & Pickett, S. (1992). Marital satisfaction among parents of the severely mentally ill living in the community. *American Journal of Orthopsychiatry, 62,* 552-563.

Cook, J. A., Jonikas, J. A., & Razzano, L. (1993). *A randomized evaluation of consumer versus non-consumer training of state mental health service providers.* Unpublished paper. Chicago: Thresholds National Research and Training Center on Rehabilitation and Mental Illness.

Cook, J. A., Lefley, H. P., Pickett, S. A., & Cohler, B. J. (1994). Age and family burden among parents of offspring with severe mental illness. *American Journal of Orthopsychiatry, 64,* 435-447.

Cook, J. A., & Pickett, S. A. (1988). Burden and criticalness among parents living with their chronically mentally ill offspring. *Journal of Applied Social Sciences, 12,* 79-107.

Cowan v. Montana, 114 S. Ct. 1371 (1994).

Day, R., Nielsen, A., Korten, A., Ernberg, G., Dube, K. C., Gebhart, J., Jablensky, A., Leon C., Marsella, A., Olatawura, M., Sartorius, N., Stromgren, E., Takahashi, R., & Wynne, L. C. (1987). Stressful life events preceding the acute onset of schizophrenia: A cross-national study from the World Health Organization. *Culture, Medicine, and Psychiatry, 11,* 123-205.

Deegan, P. E. (1992). The independent living movement and people with psychiatric disabilities: Taking back control over our own lives. *Psychosocial Rehabilitation Journal, 15*(3), 3-19.

Deutsch, A. (1949). *The mentally ill in America: A history of their care and treatment from colonial times* (2nd ed.). New York: Columbia University Press.

Deveson, A. (1991). *Tell me I'm here.* New York: Penguin.

Dohrenwend, B. P., Dohrenwend, B. S., Gould, M. S., Link, B., Neugebauer, R., & Wunsch-Hitzig, R. (1980). *Mental illness in the United States.* New York: Praeger.

Drake, R. E., Racusin, R. J., & Murphy, T. A. (1990). Suicide among adolescents with mentally ill parents. *Hospital & Community Psychiatry, 41,* 921-922.

Drake, R. E., & Sederer, L. I. (1986). The adverse effects of intensive treatment of chronic schizophrenia. *Comprehensive Psychiatry, 27,* 313-326.

Dugger, C. W. (1994, August 28). Mentally ill given help on housing: Judge requires care for former patients. *New York Times,* p. 13.

Eaton, W. (1986). *The sociology of mental disorders* (2nd ed.). New York: Praeger.

El-Islam, M. F. (1982). Rehabilitation of schizophrenics by the extended family. *Acta Psychiatrica Scandinavica, 65,* 112-119.

Emerick, R. R. (1990). Self-help groups for former patients: Relations with mental health professionals. *Hospital & Community Psychiatry, 41,* 401-407.

Estroff, S. E. (1981). *Making it crazy.* Berkeley: University of California Press.

Estroff, S. E., Zimmer, C., Lachicotte, W. S., & Benoit, J. (1994). The influence of social networks and social support on violence by persons with serious mental illness. *Hospital & Community Psychiatry, 45,* 669-679.

Fabrega, H. (1982). Ethnomedicine and biomedicine. In A. J. Marsella & G. M. White (Eds.), *Cultural conceptions of mental health and therapy.* Dordrecht, Holland: Reidel.

Fadden, G., Bebbington, P., & Kuipers, L. (1987). Caring and its burdens: A study of the spouses of depressed patients. *British Journal of Psychiatry, 151,* 660-667.

Falloon, I. R. H., Boyd, J. L., & McGill, C. W. (1984). *Family management of schizophrenia.* Baltimore: Johns Hopkins.

Falloon, I. R. H., McGill, C. W., Boyd, J. L., & Pederson, J. (1987). Family management in the prevention of morbidity of schizophrenia: A social outcome of a two-year longitudinal study. *Psychological Medicine, 17,* 59-66.

Favazza, A. R. (1985). Anthropology and psychiatry. In H. I. Kaplan & B. J. Sadock (Eds.), *Comprehensive textbook of psychiatry/IV* (4th ed., pp. 247-265). Baltimore: Williams & Wilkins.

Figley, C. R., & McCubbin, H. I. (1983). *Stress and the family: Vol. 2. Coping with catastrophe.* New York: Brunner/Mazel.

Fisher, G. A., Benson, P. R., & Tessler, R. C. (1990). Family response to mental illness: Developments since deinstitutionalization. In J. R. Greenley (Ed.), *Research in community and mental health: Mental disorder in social context* (pp. 203-236). Greenwich, CT: JAI.

Fleck, S. (1985). The family and psychiatry. In H. I. Kaplan & B. J. Sadock (Eds.), *Comprehensive textbook of psychiatry/IV* (4th ed., pp. 273-294). Baltimore: Williams & Wilkins.

Flynn, L. M. (1993). Political impact of the family-consumer movement. *National Forum, 73*(1), 8-12.

Fowler, L. (1992). Family psychoeducation: Chronic psychiatrically ill Caribbean patients. *Journal of Psychosocial Nursing, 30,* 27-32.

Francell, C. G., Conn, V. S., & Gray, D. P. (1988). Families' perceptions of burden of care for chronic mentally ill relatives. *Hospital & Community Psychiatry, 39,* 1296-1300.

Frese, F. (1993). Twelve aspects of coping skills for people with serious and persistent mental illness. *Innovations & Research, 2*(3), 39-46.

Furnham, A., & Bower, P. (1992). A comparison of academic and lay theories of schizophrenia. *British Journal of Psychiatry, 161,* 201-210.

Gaines, A. D. (Ed.). (1992). *Ethnopsychiatry: The cultural construction of professional and folk psychiatries.* Albany: State University of New York Press.

Gamache, G. M. (1989). *Aging parents as caregivers of mentally ill adult children: An empirical test of the Lefley hypothesis.* Unpublished master's thesis, University of Massachusetts, Amherst.

Gantt, A. B., Goldstein, G., & Pinsky, S. (1989). Family understanding of psychiatric illness. *Community Mental Health Journal, 25,* 101-108.

Garmezy, N., & Rutter, M. (1983). *Stress, coping, and development in children.* New York: McGraw-Hill.

Gerace, L. M., Camilleri, D., & Ayres, L. (1993). Sibling perspectives on schizophrenia and the family. *Schizophrenia Bulletin, 19,* 637-647.

Gerhart, U. C. (1990). *Caring for the chronic mentally ill.* Itasca, IL: Peacock.

Giel, R., de Arango, M. V., Babikir, A. H., Bonifacio, M., Climent, C. E., Harding, T. W., Ibrahim, H. H., Ladrido-Ignacio, L., Murthy, R. S., & Wig, N. N. (1983). The burden of mental illness on the family: Results of observations in four developing countries. *Acta Psychiatrica Scandinavica, 68,* 186-201.

Goffman, E. (1961). *Asylums: Essays on the social situations of mental patients and other inmates.* Garden City, NY: Doubleday.

Goldman, H. H. (1982). Mental illness and family burden: A public health perspective. *Hospital & Community Psychiatry, 33,* 557-560.

Goldstein, M. J. (Ed.). (1981). *New developments in interventions with families of schizophrenics* (New Directions in Mental Health Services No. 12). San Francisco: Jossey-Bass.

Goldstein, M. J. (1985). Family factors that antedate the onset of schizophrenia and related disorders: The results of a fifteen-year prospective longitudinal study. *Acta Psychiatrica Scandinavica, 71*(Suppl. 319), 7-18.

Goldstein, M. J., Hand, I., & Hahlweg, K. (Eds.). (1986). *Treatment of schizophrenia: Family assessment and intervention.* Berlin: Springer-Verlag.

Goldstein, M. J., & Miklowitz, D. J. (1994). Family interventions for persons with bipolar disorder. In A. B. Hatfield (Ed.), *Family interventions in mental illness* (New Directions for Mental Health Services No. 62, pp. 23-35). San Francisco: Jossey-Bass.

Goldstein, M. Z. (1986). *Family involvement in the treatment of schizophrenia.* Washington, DC: American Psychiatric Press.

Gordon, R. E., Edmunson, E., & Bedell, J. (1982). Reducing rehospitalization of state mental patients: Peer management and support. In S. Jeger & A. Slotnick (Eds.), *Community mental health.* New York: Plenum.

Greenberg, J. S., Greenley, J. R., & Benedict, P. (1994). Contributions of persons with serious mental illness to their families. *Hospital & Community Psychiatry, 45,* 475-480.

Greenberg, J., Greenley, J. R., McKee, D., Brown, R., & Griffin-Francell, C. (1993). Mothers caring for an adult child with schizophrenia: The effects of subjective burden on maternal health. *Family Relations, 42,* 205-211.

Greenberg, J. S., Seltzer, M. M., & Greenley, J. R. (1993). Aging parents of adults with disabilities: The gratifications and frustrations of later-life caregiving. *The Gerontologist, 33,* 542-550.

Grella, C. E., & Grusky, O. (1989). Families of the seriously mentally ill and their satisfaction with services. *Hospital & Community Psychiatry, 40,* 831-835.

Griffith, E. E. H., & Gonzalez, C. A. (1994). Essentials of cultural psychiatry. In R. E. Hales, S. C. Yudofsky, & J. A. Talbott (Eds.), *The American psychiatric press textbook of psychiatry* (pp. 1379-1421). Washington, DC: American Psychiatric Press.

Grob, G. N. (1994). *The mad among us: A history of the care of America's mentally ill.* New York: Free Press.

Grosser, R. C., & Conley, E. K. (1995). Projections of housing disruptions among adults with mental illness who live with aging parents. *Psychiatric Services, 46,* 390-394.

Group for the Advancement of Psychiatry. (1986). *A family affair: Helping families cope with mental illness.* New York: Brunner/Mazel.

Guarnaccia, P. J., Parra, P., Deschamps, A., Milstein, G., & Argiles, N. (1992). Si dios quiere: Hispanic families' experiences of caring for a seriously mentally ill family member. *Culture, Medicine, and Psychiatry, 16*(2), 187-216.

Guarnaccia, P. J., Parra, P., Miller, H., Henderson, H., West, M., & Milstein, G. (in press). Ethnicity, social status, and families' experiences of caring for their mentally ill member. *Community Mental Health Journal.*

Gubman, G. D., & Tessler, R. C. (1987). The impact of mental illness on families: Concepts and priorities. *Journal of Family Issues, 8,* 226-245.

Gubman, G. D., Tessler, R. C., & Willis, G. (1987). Living with the mentally ill: Factors affecting household complaints. *Schizophrenia Bulletin, 13,* 727-736.

Hanson, J. G., & Rapp, C. A. (1992). Families' perception of community mental health programs for their relatives with a severe mental illness. *Community Mental Health Journal, 28,* 181-127.

Harding, C. M. (1988). Course types in schizophrenia: An analysis of European and American studies. *Schizophrenia Bulletin, 14,* 633-643.

Hare-Mustin, R. T. (1980). Family therapy may be dangerous to your health. *Professional Psychology, 11,* 935-938.

Hatfield, A. B. (1983). What families want of family therapists. In W. R. McFarlane (Ed.), *Family therapy in schizophrenia* (pp. 41-65). New York: Guilford.

Hatfield, A. B. (1987). Families as caregivers: A historical perspective. In A. B. Hatfield & H. P. Lefley (Eds.), *Families of the mentally ill: Coping and adaptation* (pp. 3-29). New York: Guilford.

Hatfield, A. B. (1990). *Family education in mental illness.* New York: Guilford.

Hatfield, A. B. (1992). Leaving home: Separation issues in psychiatric illnesses. *Psychosocial Rehabilitation Journal, 15*(4), 37-48.

Hatfield, A. B. (1993). A family perspective on supported housing. *Innovations & Research, 2*(3), 47-59.

Hatfield, A. B. (1994a). Family education: Theory and practice. In A. B. Hatfield (Ed.), *Family interventions in mental illness* (New Directions for Mental Health Services No. 62, pp. 3-11). San Francisco: Jossey-Bass.

Hatfield, A. B. (Ed.). (1994b). *Family interventions in mental illness* (New Directions for Mental Health Services No. 62). San Francisco: Jossey-Bass.

Hatfield, A. B. (1994c). The family's role in caregiving and service delivery. In H. P. Lefley & M. Wasow (Eds.), *Helping families cope with mental illness* (pp. 65-77). Newark, NJ: Harwood Academic.

Hatfield, A. B., & Lefley, H. P. (1987). *Families of the mentally ill: Coping and adaptation.* New York: Guilford.

Hatfield, A. B., & Lefley, H. P. (1993). Surviving mental illness: Stress, coping and adaptation. New York: Guilford.

Hatfield, A. B., Spaniol, L., & Zipple, A. M. (1987). Expressed emotion: A family perspective. *Schizophrenia Bulletin, 13,* 221-226.

Hegarty, J. D., Baldessarini, R. J., Tohen, M., Waternaux, C., & Oepen, G. (1994). One hundred years of schizophrenia: A meta-analysis of outcome literature. *American Journal of Psychiatry, 151,* 1409-1416.

Hirsch, S., Cramer, P., & Bowen, J. O. (1992). The triggering hypothesis and the role of life events in schizophrenia. *British Journal of Psychiatry, 161*(Suppl. 18), 84-87.

Hirsch, S. R., & Leff, J. P. (1975). *Abnormalities in parents of schizophrenics.* London: Oxford University Press.

Hogarty, G. E., Anderson, C. M., Reiss, D. J., Kornblith, S. J., Greenwald, D. P., Ulrich, R. F., Carter, M., & Environmental-Personal Indicators in the Course of Schizophrenia (EPICS) Research Group. (1991). Family psychoeducation, social skills training, and maintenance chemotherapy in the aftercare treatment of schizophrenia: II. Two-year effects of a controlled trial on relapse and adjustment. *Archives of General Psychiatry, 48,* 340-347.

Hoge, S. K., Lidz, C., Mulvey, E., Roth, L., Bennett, N., Siminoff, L., Arnold, R., & Monahan, J. (1993). Patient, family, and staff perceptions of coercion in mental hospital admission: An exploratory study. *Behavioral Sciences and the Law, 11,* 281-293.

Holden, D. F., & Lewine, R. R. J. (1982). How families evaluate mental health professionals, resources, effects of illness. *Schizophrenia Bulletin, 8,* 626-633.

Holder, D., & Anderson, C. M. (1990). Psychoeducational family intervention for depressed patients and their families. In G. I. Keitner (Ed.), *Depression and families: Impact and treatment* (pp. 157-184). Washington, DC: American Psychiatric Press.

Hooley, J. M. (1987). The nature and origins of expressed emotion. In K. Hahlweg & M. J. Goldstein (Eds.), *Understanding mental disorders: The contribution of family interaction research.* New York: Family Process Press.

Hooley, J. M. (1990). Expressed emotion and depression. In G. I. Keitner (Ed.), *Depression and families: Impact and treatment* (pp. 55-83). Washington, DC: American Psychiatric Press.

Horwitz, A. V. (1982). *The social control of mental illness.* New York: Academic Press.

Howells, J. G., & Guirguis, W. R. (1985). *The family and schizophrenia.* New York: International Universities Press.

Isaac, R. J., & Armat, V. C. (1990). *Madness in the streets: How psychiatry and the law abandoned the mentally ill.* New York: Free Press.

Jablensky, A., Sartorius, N., Ernberg, G., Anker, M., Korten, A., Cooper, J. E., Day, R., & Bertelsen, A. (1991). Schizophrenia: Manifestations, incidence, and course in different cultures (World Health Organization Ten Country Study). *Psychological Medicine Monograph Supplement 20.* Cambridge, UK: Cambridge University Press.

Jaffe, D. J. (1994, November 18). A better dangerousness commitment standard is needed. *Psychiatric News, 29,* p. 16.

Jamison, K. R. (1993). *Touched with fire: Manic-depressive illness and the artistic temperament.* New York: Free Press.

Jed, J. (1989). Social support for caretakers and psychiatric rehospitalization. *Hospital & Community Psychiatry, 49,* 1297-1299.

Jenike, M. A. (1993). Obsessive-compulsive disorder: Efficacy of specific treatments as assessed by controlled trials. *Psychopharmacology Bulletin, 29,* 487-499.

Jenkins, J. H., & Karno, M. (1992). The meaning of expressed emotion: Theoretical issues raised by cross-cultural research. *American Journal of Psychiatry, 149,* 9-21.

Johnson, D. L. (1994). Current issues in family research: Can the burden of mental illness be relieved? In H. P. Lefley & M. Wasow (Eds.), *Helping families cope with mental illness* (pp. 309-328). Newark, NJ: Harwood Academic.

Johnson, J. T. (1994). *Hidden victims, hidden healers: An eight-stage healing process for families and friends of the mentally ill* (2nd ed.). Edina, MN: PEMA.

Jones, K., & Poletti, A. (1985, Spring-Summer). The Italian transformation of the asylum: A commentary and review. *International Journal of Mental Health,* 210.

Jones, S. L., Roth, D., & Jones, P. K. (1995). Effect of demographic and behavioral variables on burden of caregivers of chronic mentally ill persons. *Psychiatric Services, 46,* 141-145.

Judge David L. Bazelon Center for Mental Health Law (1994, December). *Legislative alert on health care reform.* Washington, DC: Author.

Judge, K. (1994). Serving children, siblings, and spouses: Understanding the needs of other family members. In H. P. Lefley & M. Wasow (Eds.), *Helping families cope with mental illness* (pp. 161-194). Newark, NJ: Harwood Academic.

Kagan, J. (1994). *Galen's prophecy: Temperament in human nature.* New York: Basic Books.

Kaplan, H. I., & Sadock, B. J. (1991).Synopsis of psychiatry (6th ed.). Baltimore: Williams & Wilkins.

Katz, S. E. (1985). Psychiatric hospitalization. In H. I. Kaplan & B. J. Sadock (Eds.), *Comprehensive textbook of psychiatry/IV* (4th ed., pp. 1576-1582). Baltimore: Williams & Wilkins.

Kaufmann, C. L., Ward-Colasante, C., & Farmer, J. (1993). Development and evaluation of drop-in centers operated by mental health consumers. *Hospital & Community Psychiatry, 44,* 675-678.

Keefe, R. S. E., & Harvey, P. D. (1994). *Understanding schizophrenia: A guide to new research on causes and treatment.* New York: Free Press.

Keitner, G. I., Miller, I. W., Epstein, N. B., & Bishop, D. S. (1990). Family processes and the course of depressive illness. In G. I. Keitner (Ed.), *Depression and families: Impact and treatment* (pp. 1-29). Washington, DC: American Psychiatric Press.

Kellam, S., Ensminger, M., & Turner, R. J. (1977). Family structure and the mental health of children: Concurrent and longitudinal community-wide studies. *Archives of General Psychiatry, 34,* 1012-1022.

Kendler, K. S., Neale, M. C., Kessler, R. C., Heath, A. C., & Eaves, L. J. (1993). The lifetime history of major depression in women: Reliability of diagnosis and heritability. *Archives of General Psychiatry, 50,* 863-870.

Kersker, S. (1994a). A consumer perspective on family involvement. In H. P. Lefley & M. Wasow (Eds.), *Helping families cope with mental illness* (pp. 331- 341). Newark, NJ: Harwood Academic.

Kersker, S. (1994b, February). Just shipping "them" off to jails. *Florida Drop-In Center News and Notes, 2.*

Kessler, R. C. (1989). Sociology and psychiatry. In H. I. Kaplan & B. J. Sadock (Eds.), *Comprehensive textbook of psychiatry/V* (5th ed., pp. 299-307). Baltimore: Williams & Wilkins.

Kety, S. S. (1985). Comments on the NIMH-Israeli high risk study. *Schizophrenia Bulletin, 11,* 354-356.

Kleinman, A., & Good, B. (Eds.). (1985). *Culture and depression.* Berkeley, CA: University of California Press.

Koss, J. D. (1987). Expectations and outcomes for patients given mental health care or spiritist healing in Puerto Rico. *American Journal of Psychiatry, 144,* 56-61.

Kreisman, D. E., & Joy, V. D. (1974). Family response to the mental illness of a relative: A review of the literature. *Schizophrenia Bulletin, 10,* 34-57.

Kuipers, L., Leff, J., & Lam, D. (1992). *Family work for schizophrenia: A practical guide.* London: Gaskell Press.

Lam, D. H. (1991). Psychosocial family intervention in schizophrenia: A review of empirical studies. *Psychological Medicine, 21,* 423-441.

Lamb, H. R., Bachrach, L. L., & Kass, F. I. (Eds.). (1992). *Treating the homeless mentally ill.* Washington, DC: American Psychiatric Association.

Lanquetot, R. (1984). First person account: Confessions of the daughter of a schizophrenic. *Schizophrenia Bulletin, 10,* 467-471.

Laskin, P. L., & Moskowitz, A. (1991). *Wish upon a star: A story for children with a parent who is mentally ill.* New York: Magination Press.

Leete, E. (1993).The interpersonal environment—a consumer's personal recollection. In A. B. Hatfield & H. P. Lefley (Eds.), *Surviving mental illness: Stress, coping and adaptation* (pp. 114-128). New York: Guilford.

Leff, J. (1988). *Psychiatry around the globe* (2nd ed.). London: Gaskell.

Leff, J. P., Berkowitz, R., Shvitt, N., Strachan, A. S., Glass, I. A., & Vaughn, C. (1990). A trial of family therapy versus a relatives' group for schizophrenia. Two year follow-up. *British Journal of Psychiatry, 157,* 571-577.

Leff, J. P., Kuipers, L., Berkowitz, R., & Sturgeon, D. (1985). A controlled trial of social intervention in the families of schizophrenia patients: Two-year follow-up. *British Journal of Psychiatry, 146,* 594-600.

Leff, J., & Vaughn, C. (Eds.). (1985). *Expressed emotion in families.* New York: Guilford.

Lefley, H. P. (1976). Acculturation, child-rearing, and self-esteem in two North American Indian tribes. *Ethos, 4,* 385-401.

Lefley, H. P. (1982). Self-perception and primary prevention for American Indians. In S. Manson (Ed.), *New directions in prevention among American Indian and Alaska Native communities,* (pp. 65-89). Portland, OR: Oregon Health Sciences University.

Lefley, H. P. (1987a). Aging parents as caregivers of mentally ill adult children: An emerging social problem. *Hospital & Community Psychiatry, 38,* 1063-1070.

Lefley, H. P. (1987b). Impact of mental illness in families of mental health professionals. *Journal of Nervous & Mental Disease, 175,* 613-619.

Lefley, H. P. (1987c). The family's response to mental illness in a relative. In A. B. Hatfield (Ed.), *Families of the mentally ill: Meeting the challenges* (New Directions for Mental Health Services No. 34, pp. 3-21). San Francisco: Jossey-Bass.

Lefley, H. P. (1990a). Cultural issues in training psychiatric residents to work with families of the long-term mentally ill. In E. Sorel (Ed.), *Family, culture, and psychobiology,* (pp. 165-180). Toronto, Canada: Legas.

Lefley, H. P. (1990b). Culture and chronic mental illness. *Hospital & Community Psychiatry, 41,* 277-286.

Lefley, H. P. (1990c). Research directions for a new conceptualization of families. In H. P. Lefley & D. L. Johnson (Eds.), *Families as allies in treatment of the mentally ill* (pp. 127-162). Washington, DC: American Psychiatric Press.

Lefley, H. P. (1992a). Expressed emotion: Conceptual, clinical, and social policy issues. *Hospital & Community Psychiatry, 43,* 591-598.

Lefley, H. P. (1992b). The stigmatized family. In P. J. Fink & A. Tasman (Eds.), *Stigma and mental illness* (pp. 127-138). Washington, DC: American Psychiatric Press.

Lefley, H. P. (1993). Involuntary treatment: Concerns of consumers, families, and society. *Innovations & Research, 2*(1), 7-9.

Lefley, H. P. (1994a). Mental health treatment and service delivery in cross-cultural perspective. In L. L. Adler & U. P. Gielen (Eds.), *Cross-cultural topics in psychology* (pp. 179-199). Westport CT: Praeger.

Lefley, H. P. (1994b). Service needs of culturally diverse patients and families. In H. P. Lefley & M. Wasow (Eds.), *Helping families cope with mental illness* (pp. 223-242). Newark: Harwood Academic.

Lefley, H. P., & Johnson, D. L. (Eds.). (1990). *Families as allies in treatment of the mentally ill: New directions for mental health professionals.* Washington, DC: American Psychiatric Press.

Lefley, H. P., Nuehring, E. M., & Bestman, E. W. (1992). Homelessness and mental illness: A transcultural family perspective. In H. R. Lamb, L. L. Bachrach, & F. I. Kass (Eds.), *Treating the homeless mentally ill.* Washington, DC: American Psychiatric Association.

Lefley, H. P., Sandoval, M. C., & Charles, C. (in press). Traditional healing systems in a multicultural setting. In S. Okpaku (Ed.), *Clinical methods in transcultural psychiatry.* Washington, DC: American Psychiatric Press.

Lefley, H. P., & Wasow, M. (Eds.). (1994). *Helping families cope with mental illness.* Newark, NJ: Harwood Academic.

Leighton, A. H., Clausen, J. A., & Wilson, R. N. (1957). *Explorations in social psychiatry.* New York: Basic Books.

Lewis, D. A., Riger, S., Rosenberg, H., Wagenaar, H., Lurigio, A. J., & Reed, S. (1991). *Worlds of the mentally ill: How deinstitutionalization works in the city.* Carbondale, IL: Southern Illinois University Press.

Liberman, R. P. (1987). *Psychiatric rehabilitation of chronic mental patients.* Washington, DC: American Psychiatric Press.

Liberman, R., Cardin, V., McGill, C., Falloon, I., & Evans, C. (1987). Behavioral family management of schizophrenia: Clinical outcome and costs. *Psychiatric Annals, 17,* 610-619.

Lidz, T., Fleck, S., & Cornelison, A. R. (1965). *Schizophrenia and the family.* New York: International Universities.

Liem, J. H. (1980). Family studies of schizophrenia: An update and commentary. *Schizophrenia Bulletin, 6,* 429-455.

Lin, K.-M., & Kleinman, A. M. (1988). Psychopathology and clinical course of schizophrenia: A cross-cultural perspective. *Schizophrenia Bulletin, 14,* 555-567.

Link, B. G., Andrews, H., & Cullen, F. T. (1992). The violent and illegal behavior of mental patients reconsidered. *American Sociological Review, 57,* 275-292.

Link, B. G., & Cullen, F. T. (1990). The labeling theory of mental disorder: A review of the evidence. In J. R. Greenley (Ed.), *Research in community and mental health: Mental disorder in social context* (pp. 75-105). Greenwich, CT: JAI.

Lyons, J. S., Cook, J., Ruth, A., Karver, M., & Slagg, N. B. (1993). *Consumer service delivery in a mobile crisis assessment program.* Unpublished research report. Chicago: Thresholds National Research & Training Center.

Manderscheid, R. W., & Barrett, S. A. (Eds.). (1987). *Mental Health, United States, 1987* (DHHS Publication No. ADM 87-1518). Washington, DC: U.S. Government Printing Office.

Manderscheid, R. W., & Sonnenschein, M. A. (Eds.). (1992). *Mental Health, United States, 1992* (DHHS Publication No. SMA 92-1942). Washington, DC: U.S. Government Printing Office.

Mannion, E., Meisel, M., Solomon, P., & Draine, J. (1994). *A comparative analysis of families with mentally ill adult relatives: Support group members vs. non-members.* Unpublished paper. School of Social Work, University of Pennsylvania, Philadelphia.

Mari, de J., & Streiner, D. L. (1994). An overview of family interventions and relapse in schizophrenia: Meta-analysis of research findings. *Psychological Medicine, 24,* 565-578.

Marsh, D. T. (1992). *Families and mental illness: New directions in professional practice.* New York: Praeger.

Marsh, D. T. (1994). Services for families: New modes, models, and intervention strategies. In H. P. Lefley & M. Wasow (Eds.), *Helping families cope with mental illness* (pp. 39-62). Newark, NJ: Harwood Academic.

Marsh, D. T., Appleby, N., Dickens, R. M., Owens, M., & Young, N. (1993). Anguished voices: Impact of mental illness on siblings and children. *Innovations & Research, 2*(2), 25-34.

Marsh, D. T., Dickens, R. M., Koeske, R. D., Yackovich, N. S., Wilson, J. M., Leichliter, J. S., & McQuillis, V. (1994). Troubled journey: Siblings and children of people with mental illness. *Innovations & Research, 2*(2), 13-23.

Martyns-Yellowe, I. S. (1992). The burden of schizophrenia on the family: A study from Nigeria. *British Journal of Psychiatry, 161,* 779-782.

McCubbin, H. I., & Figley, C. R. (1983). *Stress and the family: Vol. 1. Coping with normative transitions.* New York: Brunner/Mazel.

McCubbin, M. A., & McCubbin, H. I. (1989). Theoretical orientations to family stress and coping. In C. R. Figley (Ed.), *Treating stress in families* (pp. 3-43). New York: Brunner/Mazel.

McElroy, E. M. (1987). The beat of a different drummer. In A. B. Hatfield & H. P. Lefley (Eds.), *Families of the mentally ill: Coping and adaptation* (pp. 225-243). New York: Guilford.

McElroy, E. M., & McElroy, P. D. (1994). Family concerns about confidentiality and the seriously mentally ill: Ethical implications. In H. P. Lefley & M. Wasow (Eds.), *Helping families cope with mental illness* (pp. 243-257). Newark, NJ: Harwood Academic.

McFarland, B. H., Faulkner, L. R., Bloom, J. D., Hallaux, R. J., & Bray, J. D. (1989). Investigators' and judges' opinions about civil commitment. *Bulletin of American Academy of Psychiatry & Law, 17*(1), 15-24.

McFarlane, W. (1994). Families, patients, and clinicians as partners: Clinical strategies and research outcomes in single and multiple-family psychoeducation. In H. P. Lefley & M. Wasow (Eds.), *Helping families cope with mental illness* (pp. 195-222). Newark, NJ: Harwood Academic.

McFarlane, W. R., & Beels, C. C. (1983). Family research in schizophrenia: A review and integration for clinicians. In W. R. McFarlane (Ed.), *Family therapy in schizophrenia* (pp. 311-323). New York: Guilford.

McFarlane, W. R., & Lukens, E. (1994). Systems theory revisited: Research on family expressed emotion and communication deviance. In H. P. Lefley & M. Wasow (Eds.), *Helping families cope with mental illness* (pp. 79-103). Newark, NJ: Harwood Academic.

McGill, C. W., & Patterson, C. J. (1990). Former patients as peer counselors on locked psychiatric inpatient units. *Hospital & Community Psychiatry, 41,* 1017-1019.

McGlashan, T. H. (1988). A selective review of recent North American long-term follow-up studies of schizophrenia. *Schizophrenia Bulletin, 14,* 515-542.

McGlashan, T. H. (1989). Schizophrenia: Psychodynamic theories. In H. I. Kaplan & B. J. Sadock (Eds.), *Comprehensive textbook of psychiatry/V* (5th ed., pp. 745-756). Baltimore: Williams & Wilkins.

McLean, A. (1990). Contradictions in the social production of clinical knowledge: The case of schizophrenia. *Social Science & Medicine, 30,* 969-985.

McLean, A. (1994, June 2-4). *Institutionalizing the ex-patient movement in the United States: Advantages and costs.* Paper presented at the conference on the "Understanding of Mental Illness and Dealing with the Mentally Ill in Western Cultures," University of Free Berlin, Berlin, Germany.

Mednick, S. A., Huttunen, M. O., & Machon, R. A. (1994). Prenatal influenza infections and adult schizophrenia. *Schizophrenia Bulletin, 20,* 263-267.

Mednick, S. A., & Schulsinger, F. (1968). Some premorbid characteristics related to breakdown in children with schizophrenic mothers. In D. Rosenthal & S. S. Kety (Eds.), *The transmission of schizophrenia* (pp. 267-291). New York: Pergamon.

Meisel, M., & Mannion, E. (1989). *Teaching manual for coping skills workshops* (Rev. ed.). Philadelphia: Mental Health Association of Southeastern Pennsylvania/T. E. C. Network.

Merikangas, K. R., Weissman, M. M., & Prusoff, B. A. (1990). Psychopathology in offspring of parents with affective disorders. In G. I. Keitner (Ed.), *Depression and families: Impact and treatment* (pp. 85-100). Washington, DC: American Psychiatric Press.

Miklowitz, D., Velligan, D., Goldstein, M., Nuechterlein, K. M., Ranlett, G., & Doane, J. (1991). Communication deviance in families of schizophrenic and manic patients. *Journal of Abnormal Psychology, 100,* 163-173.

Miller, F., Dworkin, J., Ward, M., & Barone, D. (1990). A preliminary study of unresolved grief in families of seriously mentally ill patients. *Hospital & Community Psychiatry, 41,* 1321-1325.

Miller, J. G. (1994). Cultural diversity in the morality of caring: Individually oriented versus duty-based interpersonal moral codes. *Cross-Cultural Research, 28*(1), 3-39.

Milstein, G., Guarnaccia, P., & Midlarsky, E. (1994). *Ethnic differences in the interpretation of mental illness: Perspectives of caregivers.* Brunswick, NJ: Rutgers University, Institute for Health, Health Care Policy, and Aging Research.

Mirsky, A. F., Silberman, E. K., Latz, A., & Nagler, S. (1985). Adult outcome of high-risk children: Differential effects of town and kibbutz-rearing. *Schizophrenia Bulletin, 11,* 150-154.

Monahan, J. (1977). Empirical analyses of civil commitment: Critique and context. *Law & Society, 11,* 619-628.

Moorman, M. (1992). *My sister's keeper.* New York: Norton.

Mowbray, C. T., Chamberlain, P., Jennings, M., & Reed, C. (1988). Consumer-run mental health services: Results from five demonstration projects. *Community Mental Health Journal, 24,* 151-156.

Mueser, K. T., & Gingerich, S. (1994). *Coping with schizophrenia: A guide for families.* Oakland, CA: New Harbinger.

Mueser, K. T., Glynn, S. M., & Liberman, R. P. (1994). Behavioral family management for serious psychiatric illness. In A. B. Hatfield (Ed.), *Family interventions in mental illness* (New Directions for Mental Health Services No. 62, pp. 37-50). San Francisco: Jossey-Bass.

Myers, J. K., & Roberts, B. H. (1959). *Family and class dynamics in mental illness.* New York: Wiley.

Nasar, S. (1994, November 13). The lost years of a Nobel laureate. *New York Times,* pp. 3-1, 3-8.

National Association of State Mental Health Program Directors. (1989, December 13). *NASMHPD Position Paper on Consumer Contributions to Mental Health Service Delivery Systems.* Washington, DC: Author.

National Association of State Mental Health Program Directors. (1993, March 22). *NASMHPD Studies Survey #92-720.*

National Institute of Mental Health (1990). Clinical training in serious mental illness (DHHS Publication No. ADM 90-1679). Washington, DC: Government Printing Office.

National Mental Health Consumers Association. (1992, December). *Mission Statement.*

Nicholson, J., & Blanch, A. (1994). Rehabilitation for parenting roles for people with serious mental illness. *Psychosocial Rehabilitation Journal, 18,* 109-119.

Nicholson, J., Geller, J. L., Fisher, W. H., & Dion, G. L. (1993). State policies and programs that address the needs of mentally ill mothers in the public sector. *Hospital & Community Psychiatry, 44,* 484-489.

Nikkel, R. E., Smith, G., & Edwards, D. (1992). A consumer-operated case-management project. *Hospital & Community Psychiatry, 43,* 577-579.

Noh, S., & Avison, W. R. (1988). Spouses of discharged patients: Factors associated with their experience of burden. *Journal of Marriage and the Family, 50,* 377-389.

Noh, S., & Turner, R. J. (1987). Living with psychiatric patients: Implications for the mental health of family members. *Social Science & Medicine, 25,* 263-272.

Norton, S., Wandersman, A., & Goldman, C. R. (1993). Perceived costs and benefits of membership in a self-help group: Comparisons of members and nonmembers of the Alliance for the Mentally Ill. *Community Mental Health Journal, 29,* 143-160.

234 FAMILY CAREGIVING IN MENTAL ILLNESS

Ohio Study Committee on Mental Health Services. (1993). *Final Report of the Study Committee on Mental Health Services.* Columbus, Ohio: Author.

Oldridge, M. L., & Hughes, I. C. T. (1992). Psychological well-being in families with a member suffering from schizophrenia. *British Journal of Psychiatry, 161,* 249-251.

Park, C. C., & Shapiro, L. N. (1976). *You are not alone: Understanding and dealing with mental illness.* Boston: Little, Brown.

Parker, G., & Hadzi-Pavlovic, D. (1990). Expressed emotion as a predictor of schizophrenic relapse: An analysis of aggregated data. *Psychological Medicine, 20,* 961-965.

Parsons, T., & Fox, R. C. (1952). Illness, therapy, and the modern urban American family. *Journal of Social Issues, 8,* 31-44.

Paul, G. L., & Lentz, R. J. (1977). *Psychosocial treatment of chronic mental patients.* Cambridge, MA: Harvard University Press.

Pearlin, L. I., & Schooler, C. (1978). The structure of coping. *Journal of Health and Science Behavior, 19,* 2-12.

Pepper, B., & Ryglewicz, H. (1987). Is there expressed emotion away from home? Interaction intensity ("II") in the treatment program. *Tie-Lines, 4*(1), 1-3.

Perring, C., Twigg, J., & Atkin, K. (1990). *Families caring for people diagnosed as mentally ill: The literature re-examined.* London: Her Majesty's Stationery Office, Social Policy Research Unit.

Peschel, E., Peschel, R., Howe, C. W., & Howe, J. W. (1992). *Neurobiological disorders in children and adolescents* (New Directions in Mental Health Services No. 54). San Francisco: Jossey-Bass.

Pickett, S. A., Vraniak, D. A., Cook, J. A., & Cohler, B. A. (1993). Strength in adversity: Blacks bear burden better than whites. *Professional Psychology: Research and Practice, 24,* 460-467.

Potasznik, H., & Nelson, G. (1984). Stress and social support: The burden experienced by the family of a mentally ill person. *American Journal of Community Psychology, 12,* 589-607.

Reynolds, D., and Farberow, N. L. (1981). *The family shadow: Sources of suicide and schizophrenia.* Berkeley, CA: University of California Press.

Rice, E. P., Ekdahl, M. C., & Miller, L. (1971). *Children of mentally ill parents.* New York: Behavioral Publications.

Richardson, D. (1990). Dangerousness and forgiveness. *Journal of the California Alliance for the Mentally Ill, 2*(1), 4-5.

Riesser, G., Minsky, S., & Schorske, B. (1991). *Intensive family support services: A cooperative evaluation* (Bureau of Research & Evaluation Report). Trenton: New Jersey Department of Human Services.

Riesser, G. G., & Schorske, B. J. (1994). Relationships between family caregivers and mental health professionals: The American experience. In H. P. Lefley & M. Wasow (Eds.), *Helping families cope with mental illness* (pp. 3-26). New York: Harwood Academic.

Rivera, C. (1988). Culturally sensitive aftercare services for chronically mentally ill Hispanics: The case of the psychoeducation treatment model. *Hispanic Research Center Research Bulletin, 11*(1), 1-9.

Robins, L. N., & Regier, D. A. (Eds.). (1991). *Psychiatric disorders in America: The epidemiologic catchment area study.* New York: Free Press.

Rogers, J. A., & Centifanti, J. B. (1991). Beyond "self-paternalism": Response to Rosenson and Kasten. *Schizophrenia Bulletin, 17,* 9-14.

Rogers, P. (1993, June 20). Cries and whispers from a cell. *Miami Herald,* pp. 1A, 16A-17A.

Rogers, S. (1994, May). A consumer's perspective (on involuntary interventions). *Proceedings of the Symposium on Involuntary Interventions: The Call for a National Legal and Medical Response.* Symposium conducted at Harris County Psychiatric Center, Houston, Texas.

Rolland, J. S. (1994). *Families, illness, and disability.* New York: Basic Books.

Romney, D. M. (1990). Thought disorder in the relatives of schizophrenics. *Journal of Nervous and Mental Disease, 178,* 481-486.

Rosenson, M. K., & Kasten, A. M. (1991). Another view of autonomy: Arranging for consent in advance. *Schizophrenia Bulletin, 17,* 1-7.

Rothman, D. J. (1971). *The discovery of the asylum.* Boston: Little, Brown.

Rothman, D. J. (1980). *Conscience and convenience: The asylum and alternatives in progressive America.* Boston: Little, Brown.

Sacuzzo, D. P., Callahan, L. A., and Madsen, J. (1988). Thought disorder and associative dysfunction in the first-degree relatives of adult schizophrenics. *Journal of Nervous and Mental Disease, 176,* 368-371.

Sandoval, M. (1979). Santeria as a mental health care system: An historical overview. *Social Science & Medicine, 13B,* 137-151.

Saylor, A. V. (1994). Nannie: A sister's story. *Innovations & Research, 3*(2), 34-37.

Schene, A. H., Tessler, R. C., & Gamache, G. M. (1994). Instruments measuring family or caregiver burden in severe mental illness. *Social Psychiatry and Psychiatric Epidemiology, 29,* 228-240.

Schene, A. H., Tessler, R. C., & Gamache, G. M. (in press). Caregiving in severe mental illness: Conceptualization and measurement. In H. C. Knudsen & G. Thornicroft (Eds.), *Mental health service evaluation.* New York: Cambridge University Press.

Scheper-Hughes, N. (1987). "Mental" in Southie. *Culture, Medicine, and Psychiatry, 11*(1), 53-78.

Schooler, N. R., & Keith, S. J. (1993). The clinical research base for the treatment of schizophrenia. *Psychopharmacology Bulletin, 29,* 431-446.

Schuman, M. (1983). The Bowen theory and the hospitalized patient. In R. F. Luber & C. M. Anderson (Eds.), *Family interventions with psychiatric patients* (pp. 29-47). New York: Human Sciences Press.

Scottish Schizophrenia Research Group. (1985). First episode schizophrenia: IV. Psychiatric and social impact on the family. *British Journal of Psychiatry, 150,* 340-344.

Seeman, M. V. (1988). The family and schizophrenia. *Humane Medicine, 4*(2), 96-100.

Segal, J. (Ed). (1975). *Research in the service of mental health. Report of the Research Task Force of the National Institute of Mental Health* (DHEW Publication No. ADM 75-236). Washington, DC: U.S. Government Printing Office.

Selvini, M. (1992). Schizophrenia as a family game: Posing a challenge to biological psychiatry. *Family Therapy Networker, 16*(3), 81-86.

Shacnow, J. (1987). Preventive intervention with children of hospitalized psychiatric patients. *American Journal of Orthopsychiatry, 57,* 66-77.

Shankar, R., & Menon, M. S. (1991). Interventions with families of people with schizophrenia: The issues facing a community rehabilitation center in India. *Psychosocial Rehabilitation Journal, 15,* 85-90.

Shaw, D. (1987). Families and schizophrenia: Repair and replacement in the treatment of families. *American Journal of Social Psychiatry, 7*(1), 27-31.

Sherman, P. S., & Porter, R. (1991). Mental health consumers as case management aides. *Hospital & Community Psychiatry, 42,* 494-498.

Shetler, H. (1986). *A history of the National Alliance for the Mentally Ill.* Arlington, VA: National Alliance for the Mentally Ill.

Silverman, M. M. (1989). Children of psychiatrically ill parents: A prevention perspective. *Hospital & Community Psychiatry, 40,* 1257-1265.

Skinner, E. A., Steinwachs, D. M., & Kasper, J. D. (1992). Family perspectives on the service needs of people with serious and persistent mental illness. *Innovations & Research, 1*(3), 23-30.

Sleek, S. (1995, January). Confidentiality may suffer with work-based programs. *APA Monitor, 26*(1), 33-34.

Slobogin, C. (1994). Involuntary community treatment of people who are violent and mentally ill. *Hospital & Community Psychiatry, 45,* 685-689.

Smith, J. V., & Birchwood, M. J. (1987). Specific and non-specific effects of educational intervention with families living with a schizophrenic relative. *British Journal of Psychiatry, 150,* 645-652.

Snowden, L. R., & Cheung, F. K. (1990). Use of inpatient service by members of ethnic minority groups. *American Psychologist, 45,* 347-355.

Solomon, P. (1994). Families' views of service delivery: An empirical assessment. In H. P. Lefley & M. Wasow (Eds.), *Helping families cope with mental illness* (pp. 259-274). Newark, NJ: Harwood Academic.

Solomon, P., & Draine, J. (1994a). *Examination of adaptive coping among individuals with a seriously mentally ill relative.* Unpublished paper. Hahnemann University, Department of Psychiatry and Mental Health Sciences, Philadelphia, Pennsylvania.

Solomon, P., & Draine, J. (1994b). Family perceptions of consumers as case managers. *Community Mental Health Journal, 30,* 165-176.

Solomon, P., & Marcenko, M. O. (1992a). Families of adults with severe mental illness: Their satisfaction with inpatient and outpatient treatment. *Psychosocial Rehabilitation Journal, 16,* 121-134.

Solomon, P., & Marcenko, M. (1992b). Family members' concerns regarding community placement of their mentally disabled relative: Comparisons one month after release and a year later. *Family Relations, 41,* 341-347.

Spaniol, L., & Zipple, A. M. (1994). Coping strategies for families of people who have a mental illness. In H. P. Lefley & M. Wasow (Eds.), *Helping families cope with mental illness* (pp. 131-145). Newark, NJ: Harwood Academic.

Stein, L. I., & Test, M. A. (1980). Alternative to mental hospital treatment: I. Conceptual model, treatment program, and clinical evaluation. *Archives of General Psychiatry, 37,* 392-397.

Stoneall, L. (1983). Dilemmas of support: Accordion relations between families and the deinstitutionalized mentally ill. *Journal of Family Issues, 4,* 659-676.

Strachan, A. (1992). Family interventions. In R. P. Liberman (Ed.), *Handbook of psychiatric rehabilitation.* New York: Macmillan.

Straznickas, K. A., McNiel, D. E., & Binder, R. L. (1993). Violence toward family caregivers by mentally ill relatives. *Hospital & Community Psychiatry, 44,* 385-387.

Stroul, B. (1989). Community support systems for persons with long-term mental illness: A conceptual framework. *Psychosocial Rehabilitation Journal, 12,* 9-26.

Struening, E., & Steuve, A. (1994, December). *Research findings on low income and minority families.* Paper presented at the National Institute of Mental Health Knowledge

Exchange Workshop for Research on Families of Persons with Severe and Persistent Mental Illness, Chantilly, Virginia.

Styron, W. (1990). *Darkness visible*. New York: Random House.

Swan, R. W., & Lavitt, M. R. (1986). *Patterns of adjustment to violence in families of the mentally ill*. New Orleans, LA: Tulane University, School of Social Work, Elizabeth Wisner Research Center.

Swan, R. W., & Lavitt, M. R. (1988). Patterns of adjustment to violence in families of the mentally ill. *Journal of Interpersonal Violence, 3*, 42-54.

Tardiff, K. (1984). Characteristics of assaultive patients in private hospitals. *American Journal of Psychiatry, 141*, 1232-1235.

Tarrier, N., Barrowclough, V., Porceddu, K., & Watts, B. (1988). The assessment of psycho-physiological reactivity to the expressed emotion of relatives of schizophrenic patients. *British Journal of Psychiatry, 153*, 618-624.

Tarrier, N., Barrowclough, V., Vaughn, C., Bamrah, J. S., Porceddu, K., Watts, S., & Freeman, H. L. (1989). Community management of schizophrenia: A two-year follow-up of a behavioral intervention with families. *British Journal of Psychiatry, 154*, 625-628.

Terkelsen, K. G. (1982). The straight approach to a knotty problem: Managing parental guilt about psychosis. In A. S. Gurman (Ed.), *Questions and answers in the practice of family therapy* (Vol. 2, pp. 179-183). New York: Brunner/Mazel.

Terkelsen, K. G. (1987). The evolution of family responses to mental illness through time. In A. B. Hatfield & H. P. Lefley (Eds.), *Families of the mentally ill: Coping and adaptation* (pp. 151-166). New York: Guilford.

Terkelsen, K. G. (1990). A historical perspective on family-provider relationships. In H. P. Lefley & D. L. Johnson (Eds.), *Families as allies in treatment of the mentally ill: New directions for mental health professionals* (pp. 3-21). Washington, DC: American Psychiatric Press.

Tessler, R. C., Fisher, G. A., & Gamache, G. M. (1990). *Dilemmas of kinship: Mental illness and the modern American family*. Amherst: University of Massachusetts, Amherst Social and Demographic Research Institute.

Tessler, R. C., Killian, L. M., & Gubman, G. D. (1987). Stages in family response to mental illness: An ideal type. *Psychosocial Rehabilitation Journal, 10*, 3-16.

Thurer, S. L. (1983). Deinstitutionalization and women: Where the buck stops. *Hospital & Community Psychiatry, 34*, 1162-1163.

Tienari, P. (1991). Interaction between genetic vulnerability and family environment: The Finnish adoptive family study of schizophrenia. *Acta Psychiatrica Scandinavica, 84*, 460-465.

Torrey, E. F. (1988a). Foreword. In J. T. Johnson (Ed.), *Hidden victims: An eight-stage healing process for families and friends of the mentally ill* (pp. xi- xiii). New York: Doubleday.

Torrey, E. F. (1988b). *Surviving schizophrenia* (Rev. ed.). New York: Harper & Row.

Torrey, E. F. (1994). Violent behavior by persons with serious mental illness. *Hospital & Community Psychiatry, 45*, 653-662.

Torrey, E. F., Wolfe, S. M., & Flynn, L. M. (1990). *Care of the seriously mentally ill: A rating of state programs* (3rd ed.). Arlington, VA: Public Citizens Health Research Group and the National Alliance for the Mentally Ill.

Torrey, E. F., Wolfe, S. M., & Flynn, L. M. (1992). *Criminalizing the seriously mentally ill: The abuse of jails as mental hospitals*. Arlington, VA: Public Citizens Health Research Group & the National Alliance for the Mentally Ill.

Trochim, W., Dumont, J., & Campbell, J. (1993). *Mapping mental health outcomes from the perspective of consumers/survivors.* Alexandria, VA: National Association of State Mental Health Program Directors.

Turner, B. A. (1993). First person account: Children of madness. *Schizophrenia Bulletin, 19,* 649-650.

Vine, P. (1982). *Families in pain.* New York: Pantheon.

Walsh, M. (1985). *Schizophrenia: Straight talk for families and friends.* New York: Warner.

Wasow, M. (1982). *Coping with schizophrenia: A survival manual for parents, relatives, and friends.* Palo Alto, CA: Science & Behavioral Books.

Weinberger, D. (1994, August). *Keynote Address.* Presentation at the conference on Schizophrenia, Vancouver, Canada.

Wesseley, S. C., Castle, D., Douglas, A. J., et al. (in press). The criminal careers of incident cases of schizophrenia. *Psychological Medicine.*

White, B. J., & Madara, E. J. (1992). *The self-help source book: Finding and forming mutual aid self-help groups* (4th ed.). Denville, NJ: American Self-Help Clearinghouse.

Willick, M. S. (1990). Psychoanalytic concepts of the etiology of severe mental illness. *Journal of the American Psychoanalytic Association, 38,* 1049-1081.

Winefield, H. R., & Harvey, E. J. (1993). Determinants of psychological distress in relatives of people with chronic schizophrenia. *Schizophrenia Bulletin, 19,* 619-635.

Winefield, H. R., & Harvey, E. J. (1994). Needs of family caregivers in chronic schizophrenia. *Schizophrenia Bulletin, 20,* 557-566.

Winick, B. J. (1992). On autonomy: Legal and psychological perspectives. *Villanova Law Review, 37,* 1705-1777.

World Health Organization. (1979). *Manual of the international classifications of diseases, injuries, and causes of death* (9th ed., revised, Clinical modification, ICD-9-CM). Geneva: Author.

Wynne, L. C. (1988, May-June). Changing views of schizophrenia and family interventions. *Family Therapy News,* pp. 3-4.

Wynne, L. C., McDaniel, S. H., & Weber, T. T. (1986). *Systems consultation: A new perspective for family therapy.* New York: Guilford.

Wynne, L. C., Singer, M. T., Bartko, J. J., & Toohey, M. L. (1977). Schizophrenics and their families: Research on parental communication. In J. M. Tanner (Ed.), *Developments in psychiatric research* (pp. 254-286). London: Hodder & Stoughton.

Xiang, M., Ran, M., & Li, S. (1994). A controlled evaluation of psychoeducational family intervention in a rural Chinese community. *British Journal of Psychiatry, 165,* 544-548.

Zinermon v. Burch, 494 U.S. 113,118 (1990).

Zinman, S., Harp, H., & Budd, S. (Eds.). (1987). *Reaching across: Mental health clients helping each other.* Riverside, CA: California Network of Mental Health Clients.

Index

About the Author

Harriet P. Lefley, Ph.D., is Professor of Psychiatry and Behavioral Sciences at the University of Miami School of Medicine, is a licensed psychologist, and for many years was the director of research and evaluation of the University of Miami-Jackson Memorial Community Mental Health Center (now New Horizons Community Mental Health Center). She has been principal investigator and director of many projects sponsored by the National Institute of Mental Health (NIMH), including the Interdisciplinary Collaborative Family Training Project conducted at three universities and the national Cross-Cultural Training Institute for Mental Health Professionals at the University of Miami. She was also director of two national forums on training mental health professionals to work with the seriously mentally ill and their families, cosponsored by NIMH and the National Alliance for the Mentally Ill (NAMI). She serves on many national boards, holds memberships in numerous national and international professional societies, and has editorial or reviewer roles on 18 scientific journals.

Her publications include six books and over 100 articles, monographs, and book chapters on community mental health, cultural issues in mental health service delivery, clinical training, and family support systems for persons with major mental illness. She was named a National Switzer Scholar in 1988. In 1992, she received the Steven V. Logan Award for Outstanding Psychologist from NAMI and a special achievement award from the American Psychological Association's Division of Psychologists in Public Service. In 1995, she received the McNeil Pharmaceutical Award from the American Association of Community Psychiatrists for outstanding contributions to the field of community mental health.